Preface

This publication contains the names of the members of the diplomatic staffs of all missions and their spouses. Members of the diplomatic staff are the members of the staff of the mission having diplomatic rank. These persons, with the exception of those identified by asterisks, enjoy full immunity under provisions of the Vienna Convention on Diplomatic Relations. Pertinent provisions of the Convention include the following:

Article 29

The person of a diplomatic agent shall be inviolable. He shall not be liable to any form of arrest or detention. The receiving State shall treat him with due respect and shall take all appropriate steps to prevent any attack on his person, freedom or dignity.

Article 31

A diplomatic agent shall enjoy immunity from the criminal jurisdiction of the receiving State. He shall also enjoy immunity from its civil and administrative jurisdiction, except in the case of:

(a) a real action relating to private immovable property situated in the territory of the receiving State, unless he holds it on behalf of the sending State for the purposes of the mission;

(b) an action relating to succession in which the diplomatic agent is involved as executor, administrator, heir or legatee as a private person and not on behalf of the sending State;

(c) an action relating to any professional or commercial activity exercised by the diplomatic agent in the receiving State outside of his official functions.

A diplomatic agent's family members are entitled to the same immunities unless they are United States nationals. ASTERISKS(*) IDENTIFY UNITED STATES NATIONALS

NOTE: The information contained herein was compiled as of February 22, 2013. The names of the diplomatic agents are not in protocol order of precedence.

This publication is a reference guide as status of diplomatic personnel working at foreign missions changes on a daily basis.

The **Diplomatic List** is available free of charge on the Department of State internet web site under: http://www.state.gov/s/cpr/rls/dpl/

The **Diplomatic List** is available to the public for a fee through the Superintendent of Documents, U.S. Government Printing Office, Washington, D.C. 20402 (telephone [202] 512-1800).

National Holidays

January 1 .... Haiti, Sudan, Slovakia
January 4 .... Burma
January 26 .... Australia, India

February 4 .... Sri Lanka
February 6 .... New Zealand
February 7 .... Grenada
February 15 .... Serbia
February 16 .... Lithuania
February 17 .... Kosovo
February 18 .... Gambia
February 22 .... Saint Lucia
February 23 .... Brunei, Guyana
February 24 .... Estonia
February 25 .... Kuwait
February 27 .... Dominican Republic

March 3 .... Bulgaria
March 6 .... Ghana
March 12 .... Mauritius
March 17 .... Ireland
March 20 .... Tunisia
March 21 .... Namibia
March 23 .... Pakistan
March 25 .... Greece
March 26 .... Bangladesh

April 4 .... Senegal
April 16 .... Denmark
April 17 .... Syria
April 18 .... Zimbabwe
April 19 .... Holy See
April 26 .... Tanzania
April 27 .... Sierra Leone, Togo
April 27 .... South Africa
April 30 .... Netherlands

May 1 .... Marshall Islands
May 3 .... Poland
May 8 .... Czech Republic
May 9 .... European Union
May 12 .... Israel
May 14 .... Paraguay
May 17 .... Norway
May 20 .... Cameroon
May 22 .... Yemen
May 24 .... Eritrea
May 25 .... Argentina, Jordan
May 26 .... Great Britain, Guyana
May 28 .... Azerbaijan, Ethiopia
May 30 .... Croatia

June 1 .... Samoa
June 2 .... Italy
June 4 .... Tonga

June 6 .... Sweden
June 10 .... Portugal
June 12 .... Philippines, Russia
June 17 .... Iceland
June 18 .... Seychelles
June 23 .... Luxembourg
June 25 .... Mozambique, Slovenia
June 26 .... Madagascar
June 27 .... Djibouti
June 30 .... D. R. of Congo

July 1 .... Burundi, Canada, Rwanda
July 3 .... Belarus
July 5 .. Cape Verde, Venezuela, Slovakia
July 6 .... Comoros, Malawi
July 7 .... Nepal, Solomon Islands
July 10 .... Bahamas
July 11 .... Mongolia
July 13 .... Montenegro
July 14 .... France
July 20 .... Colombia
July 21 .... Belgium
July 23 .... Egypt
July 26 .... Liberia
July 28 .... Peru
July 30 .... Morocco

August 1 .... Benin, Switzerland
August 2 .... Macedonia
August 6 .... Bolivia
August 6 .... Jamaica
August 7 .... Cote d' Ivoire
August 9 .... Singapore
August 10 .... Ecuador
August 11 .... Chad
August 15 .... R. of Congo, Korea,
Liechtenstein
August 17 .... Gabon, Indonesia
August 20 .... Hungary
August 24 .... Ukraine
August 25 .... Uruguay
August 27 .... Moldova
August 29 .... Slovakia
August 31 .... Kyrgyzstan, Malaysia,
Trinidad and Tobago

September 1 Libya, Slovakia, Uzbekistan
September 6 .... Swaziland
September 7 .... Brazil
September 8 .... Macedonia
September 15 ..... Costa Rica, El Salvador,
Guatemala, Honduras, Nicaragua
September 16 .... Mexico,
Papua New Guinea
September 18 .... Chile

September 19 .... Saint Kitts and Nevis
September 21 .... Belize, Malta
September 22 .... Mali
September 23 .... Saudi Arabia
September 24 .... Guinea-Bissau
September 30 .... Botswana

October 1 .... Cyprus, Nigeria, Palau,
People's Republic of China
October 2 .... Guinea
October 3 .... Germany
October 4 .... Lesotho
October 9 .... Uganda
October 11 .... Fiji
October 12 .... Spain, Equatorial Guinea
October 18 .... Azerbaijan
October 24 .... Zambia
October 26 .... Austria
October 27 .... Turkmenistan,
Saint Vincent and the Grenadines
October 28 ... Czech Republic, Turkmenistan
October 29 .... Turkey

November 1 .... Algeria,
Antigua and Barbuda
November 3 .... Panama, Dominica
November 11 .... Angola
November 17 .... Slovakia
November 18 .... Latvia, Oman
November 19 .... Monaco
November 22 .... Lebanon
November 25 .... Suriname
November 28 .... Mauritania, Albania
November 30 .... Barbados

December 1 .... Central African Republic,
Romania
December 2 .Laos, United Arab Emirates
December 5 .... Thailand
December 6 .... Finland
December 11 .... Burkina Faso
December 12 .... Kenya
December 16 .... Bahrain, Kazakhstan
December 18 .... Niger
December 18 .... Qatar
December 23 .... Japan

Order of Precedence and Date of Presentation of Credentials

DJIBOUTI
H.E. Roble Olhaye.. March 22, 1988
Dean of the Diplomatic Corps

———————

PALAU
H.E. Hersey Kyota... November 12, 1997

CONGO, D.R. OF
H.E. Faida Maramuke Mitifu................February 03, 2000

LIECHTENSTEIN
H.E. Claudia Fritsche.. December 07, 2000

TURKMENISTAN
H.E. Meret Bairamovich Orazov ....February 14, 2001

BENIN
H.E. Segbe Cyrille Oguin...March 13, 2001

CONGO, R. of
H.E. Serge Mombouli...July 31, 2001

KUWAIT
H.E. Sheikh Salem Abdullah Al Jaber Al-Sabah.October 10, 2001

SAMOA
H.E. Ali' ioaiga Feturi Elisaia........................... December 04, 2003

GUYANA
H.E. Bayney R. Karran .... December 04, 2003

SOLOMON ISLANDS
H.E. Collin D. Beck..March 31, 2004

ANTIGUA AND BARBUDA
H.E. Deborah Mae Lovell ....March 08, 2005

ARMENIA
H.E. Tatoul Markarian ....May 26, 2005

OMAN
H.E. Hunaina Sultan Ahmed Al Mughairy .... November 09, 2005

EQUATORIAL GUINEA
H.E. Purificacion Angue Ondo .... November 30, 2005

ZIMBABWE
H.E. Machivenyika Tobias Mapuranga .... November 30, 2005

NAURU
H.E. Marlene Inemwin Moses............................February 10, 2006

MONACO
H.E. Gilles Alexandre Noghes......................... November 14, 2006

SAUDI ARABIA

H.E. Adel A.M. Al-Jubeir.................................... February 21, 2007

MACEDONIA
H.E. Zoran Jolevski ....March 22, 2007

RWANDA
H.E. James Kimonyo... May 18, 2007

SAN MARINO
H.E. Paolo Rondelli .... July 16, 2007

IRELAND
H.E. Michael Collins .... August 14, 2007

CAPE VERDE
H.E. Maria de Fatima da Veiga .... August 16, 2007

SWEDEN
H.E. Sven Jonas Hafstroem .... August 29, 2007

NORWAY
H.E. Wegger Christian Strommen .... October 04, 2007

ROMANIA
H.E. Adrian Cosmin Vierita................................January 02, 2008

SIERRA LEONE
H.E. Bockari Kortu Stevens.................................... March 28, 2008

ST. VINCENT AND THE GRENADINES
H.E. La Celia Aritha Prince.. May 30, 2008

LEBANON
H.E. Antoine Chedid .... June 04, 2008

BELIZE
H.E. Nestor E. Mendez .... July 10, 2008

SRI LANKA
H.E. Jaliya Chitran Wickramasuriya.......................... July 18, 2008

BAHRAIN
H.E. Huda Ezra Ebrahim Nonoo .... July 24, 2008

UNITED ARAB EMIRATES
H.E. Yousif Mana Saeed Alotaiba............................. July 25, 2008

CAMEROON
H.E. Bienvenu Joseph C. Foe Atangana ....September 12, 2008

RUSSIA
H.E. Sergey Ivanovich Kislyak ....September 16, 2008

ALGERIA
H.E. Abdallah Baali...November 05, 2008

CAMBODIA
H.E. Hem Heng...January 29, 2009

H.E. Kim Christian Beazley .... February 17, 2010

BARBADOS
H.E. John Ernest Beale .... January 29, 2009

BELGIUM
H.E. Jan Jozef Matthysen .... February 17, 2009

SERBIA
H.E. Vladimir Petrovic.................................... April 14, 2009

FIJI
H.E. Winston Thompson .... April 20, 2009

SLOVENIA
H.E. Roman Kirn .... May 26, 2009

ISRAEL
H.E. Michael Scott Oren.............................. June 22, 2009

TOGO
H.E. Edawe Limbiya Kadangha Bariki .... July 14, 2009

GRENADA
H.E. Gillian M.S. Bristol .... July 17, 2009

CENTRAL AFRICAN REPUBLIC
H.E. Stanislas Moussa-Kembe. .... August 24, 2009

BANGLADESH
H.E. Akramul Qader .... September 01, 2009

BURUNDI
H.E. Angele Niyuhire .... September 18, 2009

BRUNEI
H.E. Dato Yusoff Abd Hamid .... October 02, 2009

TIMOR-LESTE
H.E. Constancio da Conceicao Pinto .... October 23, 2009

CANADA
H.E. Gary Albert Doer .... October 23, 2009

MOZAMBIQUE
H.E. Amelia Narciso Matos Sumbana............. November 02, 2009

ANDORRA
H.E. Narcis Casal de Fonsdeviela................... November 02, 2009

NEPAL
H.E. Shankar Prasad Sharma .... November 18, 2009

GHANA
H.E. Daniel Ohene Agyekum............................ December 07, 2009

BRAZIL
H.E. Mauro L. I. Vieira............................January 11, 2010

AUSTRALIA

TURKEY
H.E. Namik Tan...................................... February 18, 2010

TONGA
H.E. Sonatane Tua Taumoepeau Tupou .... February 22, 2010

UZBEKISTAN
H.E. Ilhomjon Tuychievich Nematov .... February 26, 2010

CHINA
H.E. Zhang Yesui .... March 16, 2010

NIGERIA
H.E. Adebowale Ibidapo Adefuye......................... March 26, 2010

GAMBIA
H.E. Alieu Momodou Ngum .... May 10, 2010

LAOS
H.E. Seng Soukhathivong .... June 04, 2010

HONDURAS
H.E. Jorge Ramon Hernandez Alcerro .... June 09, 2010

EL SALVADOR
H.E. Francisco R. Altschul Fuentes........................... June 16, 2010

NICARAGUA
H.E. Francisco Obadiah Campbell Hooker.............. June 23, 2010

UKRAINE
H.E. Olexander Motsyk .... June 24, 2010

DOMINICA
H.E. Hubert John Charles .... July 16, 2010

SWAZILAND
H.E. Abednego Mandla Ntshangase .... July 19, 2010

KENYA
H.E. Elkanah Odembo Absalom .... July 27, 2010

MAURITANIA
H.E. Mohamed Lemine El Haycen............................ July 28, 2010

SOUTH AFRICA
H.E. Ebrahim Rasool................................... August 04, 2010

BULGARIA
H.E. Elena Borislavova Poptodorova Petrova......August 04, 2010

NEW ZEALAND
H.E. Michael Kenneth Moore .... August 05, 2010

LITHUANIA
H.E. Zygimantas Pavilionis .... August 05, 2010

DENMARK
H.E. Peter Taksoe-Jensen .... September 01, 2010

NAMIBIA
H.E. Martin Andjaba .... September 03, 2010

MOLDOVA
H.E. Igor Munteanu .... September 07, 2010

COSTA RICA
H.E. Meta Shanon Figueres Boggs .... September 07, 2010

MALAWI
H.E. Stephen Dick Tennyson Matenje............. September 10, 2010

INDONESIA
H.E. Dino Patti Djalal .... September 14, 2010

JORDAN
H.E. Alia M. A. Hatough Bouran...................... September 14, 2010

SWITZERLAND
H.E. Manuel Sager.. November 01, 2010

MONTENEGRO
H.E. Srdan Darmanovic.................................... November 30, 2010

KYRGYZSTAN
H.E. Muktar Djumaliev .... December 03, 2010

ALBANIA
H.E. Gilbert Galanxhi.. January 05, 2011

ETHIOPIA
H.E. Girma Birru Geda .... January 06, 2011

SURINAME
H.E. Subhas Chandra Mungra...................... January 28, 2011

MAURITIUS
H.E. Somduth Soborun........ .... January 28, 2011

HUNGARY
H.E. Gyoergy Bela Szapary.... .... January 31, 2011

PORTUGAL
H.E. Nuno Filipe Alves Salvador e Brito. .... February 10, 2011

COTE D' IVOIRE
H.E. Daouda Diabate............................ February 11, 2011

TRINIDAD AND TOBAGO
H.E. Neil Nadesh Parsan...................... February 14, 2011

ST. KITTS AND NEVIS
H.E. Jacinth Lorna Henry Martin.............. February 14, 2011

BOTSWANA

H.E. Tebelelo Mazile Seretse................ .... February 16, 2011

AFGHANISTAN
H.E. Eklil Ahmad Hakimi................... .... February 16, 2011

PANAMA
H.E. Mario Ernesto Jaramillo Castillo........... February 17, 2011

FRANCE
H.E. Francois M. Delattre................ .... February 18, 2011

PHILIPPINES
H.E. Joes L. Cuisia, Jr..................................April 07, 2011

VIETNAM
H.E. Cuong Quoc Nguyen..........................May 02, 2011

CZECH REPUBLIC
H.E. Petr Gandalovic................................May 23, 2011

DOMINICAN REPUBLIC
H.E. Anibal de Jesus de Castro Rodriguez...........July 05, 2011

GERMANY
H.E. Niels Peter Georg Ammon.................August 09, 2011

PERU
H.E. Harold Winston Forsyth Mejia..............August 29, 2011

FINLAND
H.E. Ritva Inkeri Koukku Ronde.............September 01, 2011

ANGOLA
H.E. Alberto do Carmo Bento Ribeiro........September 01, 2011

GUINEA
H.E. Blaise Cherif...............................September 02, 2011

BURKINA FASO
H.E. Seydou Bouda...........................September 02, 2011

GABON
H.E. Michael Moussa Adamo.................September 02, 2011

ESTONIA
H.E. Marina Kaljurand.........................September 06, 2011

MARSHALL ISLANDS
H.E. Charles Rudolph Paul......................September 06, 2011

INDIA
H.E. Nirupama Rao............................September 07, 2011

LIBYA
H.E. Ali Suleiman Aujali......................September 08, 2011

ICELAND
H.E. Gudmundur Arni Stefansson.............October 12, 2011

LESOTHO
H.E. Eliachim Molapi Sebatane...............November 02, 2011

HOLY SEE
H.E. Carlo Maria Vigano......................November 16, 2011

AUSTRIA
H.E. HansPeterManz.........................December 02, 2011

ECUADOR
H.E. Saskia Nathalie Cely Suarez..............December 02, 2011

NIGER
H.E. MamanSamboSidikou.................December 02, 2011

AZERBAIJAN
H.E. Elin Suleymanov.........................December 05, 2011

MOROCCO
H.E. Mohammed Rachad Bouhlal..............December 22, 2011

IRAQ
H.E. Jabir Habeb Jabir Hemaidawi..............January 04, 2012

PAKISTAN
H.E.SherryRehman...........................January07,2012

MALI
H.E. Al Maamoun Baba Lamine Keita...........January 08, 2012

ITALY
H.E.ClaudioBisogniero.........................January13,2012

MICRONESIA
H.E. Asterio R. Takesy...........................January 13, 2012

UNITED KINGDOM
H.E. Peter John Westmacott.....................January 17, 2012

KOREA
H.E. Choi Youngjin.............................March09,2012

QATAR
H.E. Mohamed Abdulla M. Al-Rumaihi..........March 29, 2012

CHILE
H.E.FelipeBulnesSerrano.........................April05,2012

HAITI
H.E.PaulGettyAltidor..........................April17,2012

GUATEMALA
H.E. JoseFranciscoVillagranDeLeon............April 17, 2012

THAILAND
H.E. Chaiyong Satjipanon.........................April18,2012

CROATIA

H.E.JosipParo....................................April20,2012

KOSOVO
H.E.AkanIsmaili..................................April23,2012

LIBERIA
H.E. JeremiahCongbehSulunteh..................April25,2012

MALAYSIA
H.E. Othman BinHashim.........................April26,2012

SPAIN
H.E. Ramon Gil Casares Satrustegui.................June 05, 2012

CHAD
H.E. Maitine Djoumbe...........................July12,2012

SENEGAL
H.E. CheikhNiang.................................July13,2012

BOSNIA AND HERZEGOVINA
H.E.JadrankaNegodic............................July 19, 2012

MALTA
H.E.JosephCole..................................July 19, 2012

JAMAICA
H. E. Stephen Charles Vasciannie...................July 20, 2012

NETHERLANDS
H.E. RudolfSimonBekink.........................July20,2012

SOUTH SUDAN
H.E. AkecKhocAciewKhoc........................July24,2012

SINGAPORE
H.E. Asok Kumar .... July 24, 2012

BURMA
H.E. ThanSwe...................................July25,2012

TAJIKISTAN
H.E.NuriddinShamsov............................July26,2012

LATVIA
H.E. Andris Razans...................................... July 27, 2012

SEYCHELLES
H.E. Marie-Louise Cecile Potter..............September 06, 2012

COMOROS
H.E. Kaambi Roubani ....September 06, 2012

EGYPT
H.E. Mohamed Mostafa Mohamed Tawfik...September 07, 2012

URUGUAY
H.E. JuanCarlosPitaAlvariza...............September 11, 2012

LUXEMBOURG
H.E. Jean-Louis Wolzfeld .... September 11, 2012

ST. LUCIA
H.E. Sonia Merlyn Johnny .... September 12, 2012

COLOMBIA
H.E. Carlos Alfredo Urrutia Valenzuela .... September 13, 2012

SLOVAK RELPUBLIC
H.E. Peter Kmec... September 17, 2012

GREECE
H.E. Christos Panagopoulos .... September 17, 2012

POLAND
H.E. Ryszard Marian Schnepf.......................... September 28, 2012

JAPAN
H.E. KenichiroSasae............................November 19, 2012

ZAMBIA
H.E. PalanMulonda................................January 08, 2013

MONGOLIA
H.E.AltangerelBulgaa............................January08,2013

KAZAKHSTAN
H.E.KairatUmarov................................January09, 2013

PARAGUAY
H.E. Fernando Antonio Pfannl Caballero.........January 09, 2013

TUVALU
H.E. AuneseMakoi Simati.....................................January 11, 2013

MALDIVES
H.E. AhmedSareer................................January11,2013

MEXICO
H.E. Eduardo Tomas Medina Mora Icaza.........January 11,2013

ARGENTINA
H.E. MariaCeciliaNahon........................January19,2013

AFRICAN UNION MISSION
H.E. Amina Salum Ali ....April 13, 2007

EUROPEAN UNION
H.E. Joao P. Castanheira do Vale De Almeida........July 16, 2010

GUINEA BISSAU
Ambassador departed...................................... November 12, 2000

BELARUS
Mr. Oleg Kravchenko, Counselor
Chargé d' Affaires ad interim ....June 05, 2009

ERITREA
Mr. Berhane Gebrehwet Solomon, First Secretary
Chargé d' Affaires ad interim ....March 15, 2011

BOLIVIA
T.H. Freddy Bersatti Tudela, Minister-Counselor
Chargéd' Affairesadinterim........................April01,2011

MADAGSCAR
Ms. Velotiana Rakotoanosy Raobelina, Counselor
Chargé d' Affaires ad interim........................June 20, 2011

VENEZUELA
T.H. Angelo Agustin Rivero Santos, Minister-Counselor
Chargéd' Affairesadinterim........................July 07, 2011

SUDAN
T.H. Emad Mirghani Abdelhamid Altohamy, Minister
Chargé d' Affaires ad interim...........................July08, 2011

PAPUA NEW GUINEA
T.H. Elias Rahuromo Wohengu, Minister
Chargé d' Affaires ad interim........................May 07, 2012

SYRIA
T.H. Mounir Koudmani, Minister-Counselor
Chargéd' Affairesadinterim........................June 02, 2012

SAO TOME AND PRINCIPE
Ambassadordeparted...............................June30,2012

YEMEN
Mr.Adel Ali Ahmed Alsunaini, Counselor
Chargéd' Affairesadinterim........................July05,2012

TUNISIA
Mr. Tarek Amri, Counselor
Chargé d' Affairesadinterim.....................August 01, 2012

BAHAMAS
Mr. Freddie Cleveland Tucker, Counselor
Chargé d' Affaires ad interim...................September 01, 2012

UGANDA
T.H. Aldred Nnam, Minister
Chargé d' Affairesadinterim...................December 31, 2012

CYPRUS
Ms. Olympia Neocleous, Counselor
Chargé d' Affaires ad interim...................February 11, 2013

TANZANIA
T.H. Lily Letawo Munanka, Minister
Chargé d' Affaires ad interim...................February 19, 2013

GEORGIA
T.H. Mikheil Darchiashvili, Miniter-Counselor

Chargé d' Affaires ad interim........................March 1, 2013

ALBANIA
www.embassyofalbania.org

ANGOLA
www.angola.org

ARGENTINA
www.embajadaargentina-usa.org

AUSTRALIA
www.austemb.org

AUSTRIA
www.austria.org

AZERBAIJAN
www.azembassy.com
azerbaijan@azembassy.com

BANGLADESH
www.bangladoot.org

BAHRAIN
www.bahrainembassy.org

BELARUS
www.belarusembassy.org
usa@belarusembassy.org

BELGIUM
www.diplobel.us
Washington@diplobel fed.be

BENIN
www.beninembassyus.org

BRAZIL
www.brasilemb.org

BULGARIA
www.bulgaria-embassy.org
office@bulgaria-embassy.org

CAMBODIA
www.embassy.org/cambodia
cambodia@embassy.org

CANADA
www.canadianembassy.org
www.ambassadeducanada.org

CAPE VERDE
www.capeverdeusaembassy.org

COLOMBIA
www.colombiaemb.org

COSTA RICA
www.costarica-embassy.org
consulate@costarica-embassy.org

CROATIA
www.croatiaemb.org
webmaster@croatiaemb.org

CYPRUS
www.cyprusembassy net
cypembwash@earthlink.net

CZECH REPUBLIC
washington@embassy.mzv.cz

DENMARK
www.ambwashington.um.dk
wasamb@um.dk

DOMINICA
embdomdc@aol.com

DOMINICAN REPUBLIC
www.domrep.org

ECUADOR
www.ecuador.org/ecuador
mecuawaa@pop.erols.com

EGYPT
Embassy@egyptembdc.org

EL SALVADOR
www.elsalvador.org
correo@elsalvador.org

EQUATORIAL GUINEA
www.equatorialguinea.org
info@equatorialguinea.org

ESTONIA
www.estemb.org
info@estemb.org

FIJI
info@fijiembassydc.com

FINLAND
www.finland.org
info@finland.org

X

FRANCE
www.info-france-usa.org

GABON
www.gabonembassy.net
info@gabonembassy net

GEORGIA
www.georgiaemb.org
embgeorgiausa@yahoo.com

GERMANY
www.germany.info
german-embassy-us@germany.info

GREECE
www.greekembassy.org
greece@greekembassy.org

GUATEMALA
www.guatemala-embassy.org
info@guatemala-embassy.org

GUINEA
EmbaGuinea@aol.com

GUYANA
guyanaembassy@hotmail.com

HAITI
www.haiti.org/embassy
embassy@haiti.org

HONDURAS
embhondu@aol.com

HUNGARY
www.hungaryemb.org
huembwas@attmail.com

ICELAND
www.iceland.org.
icemb.wash@utn.stjr.is

INDIA
http://www.indianembassy.org
indembwash@indiagov.org

IRAN
www.daftar.org
Requests@daftar.org

IRELAND
www.irelandemb.org
embirlus@aol.com

ISRAEL
www.israelemb.org

ITALY
www.italyemb.nw.dc.us:80/Italy/

JAMAICA
contactus@jamaicaembassy.org

JAPAN
www.embjapan.org
www.embjapan.org/jicc html

JORDAN
www.jordanembassyus.org
hkjembassydc@aol.com

KAZAKHSTAN
www.kazakhembus.com
kazakh.embusa@verizon.net

KOREA
korea.emb.washington.dc.us

KOSOVO
http://ambasada-ks net/us/

LAOS
www.laoembassy.com

LATVIA
www.latvia-usa.org
embassy.usa@mfa.gov.lv

LEBANON
www.lebanonembassyus.org
info@lebanonembassyus.org

LESOTHO
lesothowashington@compuserve.com

LIBERIA
www.liberianembassy.com
Liberia-Embassy@msn.com

LIECHTENSTEIN
www.liechtenstein.li

LITHUANIA
www.ltembassyus.org

MACEDONIA
www.macedonianembassy.org
usoffice@macedonianembassy.org

MADAGASCAR
Malagasy@embassy.org

MALAWI
www.malawidc.org
malawi@passportregidtry.com
malawidc@aol.com

MALAYSIA
malwashdc@kln.gov.my

MALDIVES
www maldivesembassy.us
Info@maldivesembassy.us

MALI
infos@mali.embassy.us

MALTA
www.magnet.mt

MAURITIUS
mauritius.embassy@verizon.net

MOLDOVA
www.sua.mfa.md
Washington@mfa.md

MONACO
www.monaco-usa.org
embassy@monaco-usa.org

MONGOLIA
www.mongolnet.com
monemb@aol.com

MOROCCO
SifaraUSA@erols.com
AnnexUSA@erols.com

MOZAMBIQUE
www.embamoc-usa.org
embamoc@aol.com

NETHERLANDS
www.netherlands-embassy.org
nlgovwas@netherlands-embassy.org

NEW ZEALAND
http://www.emb.com/nzemb

NIGER
www.embassyofiger.org

NIGERIA
chanceryadmin@nigeriaembassyusa.org

NORWAY
www norway.org
emb.washington@mfa.no

PANAMA
www.embassyofpanama.org
info@embassyofpanama.org

PAPUA NEW GUINEA
Kundu Wash@AOL.com

PERU
www.peruvianembassy.us

PHILIPPINES
USWashpe@aol.com

QATAR
www.qatarembassy.net
infoqatarembassy.org

ROMANIA
www.roembus.org
office@roembus.org

RUSSIA
www.russianembassy.org
russ-amb@cerfnet.com

RWANDA
www.rwandemb.org/rwanda/
embrwawash@aol.com

SAUDI ARABIA
www.saudiembassy.net
info@saudiembassy.net

SERBIA
www.serbiaembusa.org
info@serbiaembusa.org

SEYCHELLES
seychelles@un.int

SINGAPORE
www.gov.sg/mfa/washington

SLOVAK
info@slovakembassy-us.org

SOUTH AFRICA
www.saembassy.org
info@saembassy.org

SPAIN
www.spainemb.org
embespus@mail mae.es

SRI LANKA
www.slembassyusa.org
slembassy@slembassyusa.org

SURINAME
embsur@erols.com

SYRIA
eosdc@yahoo.com

SWAZILAND
Swaziland@compuserve.com

SWEDEN
www.swedenabroad.com
ambassaden.washington@foreign.ministry.se

SWITZERLAND
www.swissemb.org

TAJIKISTAN
tajik.embassy@verizon.net

TANZANIA
<tanz-us@clark.net>

THAILAND
www.thaiembdc.org/

TIMOR-LESTE
embtlusa@comcast.net

TURKEY
www.turkey.org
embassy@turkey.org

TURKMENISTAN
www.dc.infi.net/~embassy

UGANDA
www.ugandaembassy.com
ambuganda@aol.com

UKRAINE
www.ukraineinfo.us
letters@ukremb.com

UNITED KINGDOM
UKintheUSA@fco.gov.uk
britishembassyenquiries@gmail.com

URUGUAY
www.embassy.org/uruguay
uruwashi@uruwashi.org

VENEZUELA
www.embavenez-us.org
despacho@embavenez-us.org

VIETNAM
www.vietnambassy-usa.org
vietnamembassy@msn.com

EUROPEAN UNION
www.eurunion.org
DELEGATION-USA-DL@eeas.europa.eu

AFGHANISTAN

EMBASSY OF AFGHANISTAN
Chancery: 2341 WYOMING AVENUE, NW 20008
(EMBASSY 202-483-6410)   (FAX 202-483-6488)

HIS EXCELLENCY EKLIL AHMAD HAKIMI
AMBASSADOR EXTRAORDINARY & PLENIPOTENTIARY

MR. ABDUL HAKIM ATARUD
MRS. MADINA ATARUD
COUNSELOR (POLITICAL)

MR. ZEMARY AZAMI
MRS. NAJIBA AZAMI
COUNSELOR (ECONOMIC AFFAIRS)

MR. MEERWAIS NAB
COUNSELOR (POLITICAL)

MR. MIRWAIS SAMADI
MRS. NABILA SAMADI
COUNSELOR (POLITICAL)

MR. MOHAMMAD ASHOR AZIMI
FIRST SECRETARY (POLITICAL)

MR. ABDUL QADIER NUR
FIRST SECRETARY (ECONOMIC & POLITICAL)

MR. AHMAD SHAH DAUD
MRS. NAJMALA AHMAD DAUD
SECOND SECRETARY (POLITICAL)

MR. MORTAZA HAQJO
MS. FAYEQA HAQJO
SECOND SECRETARY (POLITICAL)

MR. FARHAD ROIEN
MRS. MARWA ROIEN
SECOND SECRETARY

MS. GHAZAL HASSAN
THIRD SECRETARY (ADMINISTRATIVE)

MRS. SURAYA MAHEER AYOUBI
MR. KHALID IKRAMI
THIRD SECRETARY (PASSPORT OFFICER)

MRS. ANGIZA NASIREE
MR. EHSANULLAH NASIREE
THIRD SECRETARY (PASSPORT)

MR. SIKANDAR NOORI
MRS. JIAN CHEN
THIRD SECRETARY (TECHNICAL)

MR. AHMAD PEROSE SHOKORY
THIRD SECRETARY (PROTOCOL)

MR. SAYED HAMED MOHAMOOD ELMI
ATTACHE (CULTURAL)

MR. AHMAD FARID HAIDARI
MRS. MARIAM HAIDARI
ATTACHE (CULTURAL)

MR. SHAKIB NOORI
ATTACHE (COMMERCIAL)

CONSULAR SECTION
2233 WISCONSIN AVENUE, NW, SUITE 216 20007
(OFFICE 202-298-9125)   (FAX 202-298-9127)

AFRICAN UNION

DELEGATION OF THE AFRICAN UNION MISSION
Chancery: 2200 PENNSYLVANIA AVENUE, NW, FLOOR 4
20037
(EMBASSY 202-293-8006)   (FAX 202-429-7130)

HER EXCELLENCY AMINA SALUM ALI
MR. ALI MANSOUR VUAI
AMBASSADOR (HEAD OF DELEGATION)

MR. TAREK BEN YOUSSEF
MRS. YOSRA DEBBABI BEN YOUSSEF
COUNSELOR (POLITICAL)

MS. NAOMI BASETSANAGAPE L. RANTAO
FIRST SECRETARY (FINANCE & ADMINISTRATION)

MRS. MIRIAM MENDA DEBELA
ATTACHE (ADMINISTRATIVE)

ALBANIA

EMBASSY OF THE REPUBLIC OF ALBANIA
Chancery: 1312 18TH STREET, NW, FLOOR 4 20036
(EMBASSY 202-223-4942)   (FAX 202-628-7342)

HIS EXCELLENCY GILBERT GALANXHI
MRS. ETLEVA GALANXHI
AMBASSADOR EXTRAORDINARY & PLENIPOTENTIARY

MR. ANTON KOLIQI
MINISTER

MISS MIGENA NURI
COUNSELOR

MRS. DANIELA NESHO
FIRST SECRETARY

LIEUTENANT COMMANDER EVEREST HAXHI
MRS. JULIANA HAXHI
ASST. DEFENSE, MILITARY, NAVAL & AIR ATTACHE

ALGERIA

EMBASSY OF THE PEOPLE'S DEMOCRATIC REPUBLIC OF
ALGERIA
Chancery: 2118 KALORAMA ROAD, NW 20008
(EMBASSY 202-265-2800)   (FAX 202-667-2174)

HIS EXCELLENCY ABDALLAH BAALI
MRS. YASMINA BAALI
AMBASSADOR EXTRAORDINARY & PLENIPOTENTIARY

MR. MOHAMED YAZID BOUZID
MINISTER-COUNSELOR (DEPUTY CHIEF OF MISSION)

MR. MOHAMED SAID BENAZZOUZ
MRS. NEDJMA BENAZZOUZ
COUNSELOR (POLITICAL)

MR. MALEK DJAOUD
MRS. HAFIDA DJAOUD
COUNSELOR (ECONOMIC)

MR. AZZEDDINE SOUIDI
MRS. FATIHA SOUIDI
COUNSELOR (CONSULAR AFFAIRS)

* U.S. Citizen

MR. IHCENE ELNAOUQ
MRS. LIDIA ELNAOUQ
FIRST SECRETARY

MR. AMIR MAAMAR
MRS. AICHA MAAMAR
FIRST SECRETARY

MRS. HAFIDA DJAOUD
MR. MALEK DJAOUD
SECOND SECRETARY

MS. NASSIMA HOCINE
SECOND SECRETARY

MRS. LIDIA ELNAOUQ
MR. IHCENE ELNAOUQ
ATTACHE

MR. ABDELOUAHEB GHODBANE
MRS. OUARDA GHODBANE
ATTACHE (FINANCIAL)

MRS. ASMA GUEBILI
MR. MOHAMED GUEBILI
ATTACHE

MR. MOHAMED GUEBILI
MRS. ASMA GUEBILI
ATTACHE

MR. ABDELKADER HADDAD
MRS. DJAMILA HADDAD
ATTACHE (ADMINISTRATIVE & FINANCIAL)

MR. KARIM KRID
MRS. SELMA KRID
ATTACHE

MR. BELGACEM MEKOUI
MRS. KARIMA MEKOUI
ATTACHE (ADMINISTRATIVE)

MR. ABDELHAMID SEBTI
MRS. SALIMA SEBTI
ATTACHE (ADMINISTRATIVE)

COLONEL HAMID KALLA
MRS. BELAIDA KALLA
DEFENSE, MILITARY & NAVAL ATTACHE

LIEUTENANT COLONEL SAMY ANISSE LAMMARI
MRS. LAMIA FAWZIA LAMMARI
AIR ATTACHE

CONSULAR OFFICE
2137 WYOMING AVENUE, NW 20008

ECONOMIC AND ADMINISTRATIVE OFFICE
2133 WYOMING AVENUE, NW 20008

MILITARY OFFICE
2135 WYOMING AVENUE, NW 20008

ANDORRA

EMBASSY OF ANDORRA
Chancery: 2 UNITED NATIONS PLAZA, FLOOR 27TH
NEW YORK, NY 10017
(EMBASSY 212-750-8064)   (FAX 212-750-6630)

HIS EXCELLENCY NARCIS CASAL DE FONSDEVIELA
AMBASSADOR EXTRAORDINARY & PLENIPOTENTIARY

MR. ANDREU JORDI TOMAS
FIRST SECRETARY

ANGOLA

EMBASSY OF THE REPUBLIC OF ANGOLA
Chancery: 2100-2108 16TH STREET, NW 20009
(EMBASSY 202-785-1156)   (FAX 202-785-1258)

HIS EXCELLENCY ALBERTO DO CARMO BENTO RIBEIRO
MRS. MARIA ODETE F G BENTO RIBEIRO
AMBASSADOR EXTRAORDINARY & PLENIPOTENTIARY

MR. AMADEU DE JESUS ALVES L. NUNES
MRS. FLORBELA MARIA DA S.F. L. NUNES
MINISTER-COUNSELOR

MRS. SOFIA SILVERIO PEREIRA DA SILVA
MR. AGNELO DA CONCEICAO PEREIRA SILVA
MINISTER-COUNSELOR

MR. MARIO MIGUEL MANUEL
MRS. MADALENA AGOSTINHO JOSE
COUNSELOR (ECONOMIC)

MR. FREDERICO JOAQUIM GASPAR DA SILVA
COUNSELOR

MS. LAURINDA DA SILVA SANTOS ALMEIDA
FIRST SECRETARY (INFORMATION)

MR. CESAR MANUEL JOAO
FIRST SECRETARY

MR. INECLITO ANASTACIO DE ALMEID LIMA
FIRST SECRETARY

MR. MANUEL FRANCISCO LOURENCO
FIRST SECRETARY

MRS. MERCEDES DE FATIMA QUINTINO
FIRST SECRETARY

MRS. MARIA DE FATIMA M RODRIGU VELASCO
FIRST SECRETARY

MR. DAVID MANUEL DIOGO JUSTINO
SECOND SECRETARY

MISS LUZIELA DE JESUS GASPAR MARTINS
SECOND SECRETARY

MRS. DELFINA ABEL CORDEIRO NASCIMENTO
MR. MANUEL GOVERFFO NASCIMENTO JR.
SECOND SECRETARY

MR. OCANTE TIM TEO RESENDE RODRIGUES
MRS. LAURA CHANDA SIKOTA RODRIGUES
SECOND SECRETARY

MR. ISMAEL ALEIXO FILIPE
MRS. MARISA GALIANO NOVAIS FILIPE
THIRD SECRETARY

MRS. MARISA GALIANO NOVAIS FILIPE
MR. ISMAEL ALEIXO FILIPE
THIRD SECRETARY

MR. FLAVIO PEREIRA LOUREIRO
MRS. CLARA ANTONIO MATEUS
THIRD SECRETARY

* U.S. Citizen

MR. GIL DOS SANTOS CARDOSO
    MRS. ANA SOLANO MCOELHO DOS S CARDOSO
ATTACHE (FINANCIAL)

MS. SILVIA PRAZERES SIMOES DA CRUZ
ATTACHE

MR. ABEL ADAO JOAO
    MRS. PAULINA SEBASTIAO TEIXEIRA JOAO
ATTACHE (ADMINISTRATIVE)

MR. PEDRO BENEDITO NETO
ATTACHE (TECOMUNICATIONS)

MAJOR ADAO EDUARDO SILVA
    MRS. ADELIA FLORA PAULO SILVA
ASST. DEFENSE & MILITARY ATTACHE

COMMERCIAL REPRESENTATION
    1317 F STREET, NW, SUITE 450 20004
        (OFFICE 202-783-4740) (FAX 202-783-4743)

TRADE OFFICE
    1925 K STREET, NW, SUITE 225 20006
        (OFFICE 202-317-7604) (FAX 202-331-7605)

TRADE OFFICE
    1925 K STREET, NW, SUITE 225 20006

ANTIGUA AND BARBUDA

EMBASSY OF ANTIGUA AND BARBUDA
Chancery: 3216 NEW MEXICO AVENUE, NW 20016
(EMBASSY 202-362-5122) (FAX 202-362-5225)

HER EXCELLENCY DEBORAH MAE LOVELL
AMBASSADOR EXTRAORDINARY & PLENIPOTENTIARY &
CONSUL GENERAL

MISS ANN MARIE PATRICE LAYNE
    MR. RICHARD EUGENE MAC LAREN CAMPBELL
MINISTER-COUNSELOR

MISS JOY DEE SAMANTHA DAVIS
    MR. LAWRENCE FRANSWORTH LAKE
FIRST SECRETARY

MS. GRACELYN GILIAN P HENRY
FIRST SECRETARY & CONSUL

ARGENTINA

EMBASSY OF THE ARGENTINE REPUBLIC
Chancery: 1600 NEW HAMPSHIRE AVENUE, NW 20009
(EMBASSY 202-238-6400) (FAX 202-332-3171)

HER EXCELLENCY MARIA CECILIA NAHON
    MR. SERGIO ALFREDO GARCIA GOMEZ
AMBASSADOR EXTRAORDINARY & PLENIPOTENTIARY

MR. CARLOS FEDERICO MASCIAS
MINISTER (DEPUTY CHIEF OF MISSION)

MR. ROBERTO HECTOR DIEZ
    MRS. MIRIAM MABEL CASTANO DE DIEZ
MINISTER

MR. LUIS ALEJANDRO LEVIT
    MRS. LILIANA EDITH SCLOVIN DE LEVIT
MINISTER

* U.S. Citizen

MR. HERNAN GASPAR LORENZINO
    MRS. BRIGIDA N. BASTIDA DE LORENZINO
MINISTER (FINANCIAL)

MR. JOSE DOMINGO MOLINA
    MRS. MARY ALICE TROAST*
MINISTER (AGRICULTURAL)

MR. CONRADO SOLARI YRIGOYEN
    MS. ANA MARCELA PASTORINO
MINISTER

MR. RUBEN EDUARDO MIGUEL TEMPONE
MINISTER

MR. GUSTAVO ARTURO TORRES
    MRS. MARCELA ROHAN DE TORRES
MINISTER

MRS. MARIA J. MARTINEZ GRAMUGLIA
    MR. DIEGO MARTIN HOFMAN
COUNSELOR

MR. JOSE LUIS VILA
    MRS. MONICA NIELSEN
COUNSELOR

MRS. MELINA ERKEKDJIAN
    MR. SEBASTIAN LEONARDO FELSCHER
FIRST SECRETARY

MR. CHRISTIAN FEDERICO HOTTON
    MRS. MARIA CECILIA RUBICINI DE HOTTON
FIRST SECRETARY

MS. SILVINA KHATCHERIAN
FIRST SECRETARY

MR. FRANCISCO LOPEZ ACHAVAL
    MRS. MARIA CELESTE ARRIZABALAGA
FIRST SECRETARY

MRS. SILVINA LAURA AGUIRRE
    MR. JUAN ENRIQUE BIANCHI
SECOND SECRETARY

MRS. MARIA CECILIA LOS ARCOS
    MR. MATIAS LABALE
SECOND SECRETARY

MR. GUILLERMO VALENTIN RODOLICO
    MRS. FERNANDA MARIEL AGUILERA
SECOND SECRETARY

MR. FEDERICO BLATON
    MRS. PAOLA ADRIANA BENAS
ATTACHE (ADMINISTRATIVE)

MRS. SABRINA SOLEDAD FARAONE
    MR. NORBERTO SANTIAGO MASSONI
ATTACHE

MR. HUMBERTO RUBEN MONZON
    MRS. PATRICIA ANDREA TAUS
ATTACHE (ADMINISTRATIVE)

COLONEL JORGE MARIO VEGA
    MS. CLAUDIA ROSAURA SILVA
DEFENSE & MILITARY ATTACHE

LIEUTENANT COLONEL PABLO GABRIEL LOPEZ BUENO
    MRS. VIVIANA LAURA JUAREZ
ASST. MILITARY ATTACHE

LIEUTENANT COLONEL RUBEN ANGEL MORADO
    MRS. MONICA BEATRIZ FIORE
ASST. AIR ATTACHE

COLONEL GUILLERMO HECTOR SANTILLI
MRS. GRACIELA ELENA BERARD
ASST. AIR ATTACHE

AIR ATTACHE OFFICE
2405 I STREET, NW, FLOOR 4TH-7TH 20037
(OFFICE 202-452-8500)

CONSULAR, CULTURAL, ACCOUNTING OFFICES
1811 Q STREET, NW 20009
(OFFICE 202-238-6460)

FINANCIAL ATTACHE OFFICE
1800 K STREET, NW, SUITE 924 20036
(OFFICE 202-466-3031)

LOGISTIC NAVAL COMMISSION
630 INDIANA AVENUE, NW 20004
(OFFICE 202-238-6467)

MILITARY ATTACHE OFFICE
1810 CONNECTICUT AVENUE, NW 20009
(OFFICE 202-667-4900)

NAVAL ATTACHE OFFICE
630 INDIANA AVENUE, NW 20004
(OFFICE 202-626-2100)

ARMENIA

EMBASSY OF THE REPUBLIC OF ARMENIA
Chancery: 2225 R STREET, NW 20008
(EMBASSY 202-319-1976)   (FAX 202-319-2982)

HIS EXCELLENCY TATOUL MARKARIAN
MRS. ANAHIT AGHUMIAN
AMBASSADOR EXTRAORDINARY & PLENIPOTENTIARY

MR. HARUTYUN KOJOYAN
MRS. YELENA YELIYAN
COUNSELOR

MR. ANDRANIK HOVHANNISYAN
MRS. MARINA HOVHANNISYAN
FIRST SECRETARY

MR. KAREN ISRAYELYAN
MRS. ANNA GRIGORYAN
FIRST SECRETARY

MS. LILIT SHAKARYAN
SECOND SECRETARY

MS. ANNA NAGHDALYAN
ATTACHE

LIEUTENANT COLONEL MESROP NAZARYAN
MRS. ROZA TOVMASYAN
DEFENSE, MILITARY, NAVAL & AIR ATTACHE

AUSTRALIA

EMBASSY OF AUSTRALIA
Chancery: 1601 MASSACHUSETTS AVENUE, NW 20036
(EMBASSY 202-797-3000)   (FAX 202-797-3331)

HIS EXCELLENCY KIM CHRISTIAN BEAZLEY
MS. SUSANNA JULIA ANNUS
AMBASSADOR EXTRAORDINARY & PLENIPOTENTIARY

MR. GRAHAM HUGH FLETCHER
MRS. LORRAINE KAY FLETCHER
MINISTER (DEPUTY CHIEF OF MISSION)

MR. JEFFREY WILLIAM MOYLE
MRS. JULIE ANNE MOYLE
MINISTER

MR. ANDREW WILLIAM CHANDLER
MINISTER-COUNSELOR

DR. DAVID HARRY DUTTON
MRS. MEGAN SIMONE GRANT
MINISTER-COUNSELOR

MR. ALASDAIR LUNDIE GORDON
MRS. FIONA CAROLINE DEVERY
MINISTER-COUNSELOR

MRS. JANETTE HAUGHTON
MR. COLIN WILLIAM HAUGHTON
MINISTER-COUNSELOR

MR. HUGH JOHN OWEN JEFFREY
MINISTER-COUNSELOR

DR. TORGNY WILHELM EMANUEL JOSEFSSON
MRS. ALISON LOUISE JOSEFSSON
MINISTER-COUNSELOR

MR. MICHAEL STUART KELSEY
MRS. MELANIE JANE KELSEY
MINISTER-COUNSELOR

MR. MAURO KOLOBARIC
MS. SILVANA KOLOBARIC
MINISTER-COUNSELOR & CONSUL GENERAL

MR. NIGEL DENYS WALTER MORRIS
MRS. KATHRYN FAY MORRIS
MINISTER-COUNSELOR (DEFENSE MATERIAL)

MR. SIMON GEORGE NEWNHAM
MRS. LORRAINE DUKE NEWNHAM
MINISTER-COUNSELOR (TRADE)

MR. CHRISTOPHER ALAN PARKER
MRS. JANE LOUISE PARKER
MINISTER-COUNSELOR (AGRICULTURE)

MS. KELLY LEE RALSTON
MINISTER-COUNSELOR (COMMERCIAL)

MS. AMANDA LOUISE SAYEGH
MINISTER-COUNSELOR

MR. MICHAEL JOHN SCHWAGER
MRS. MERREDY GAE BROWN
MINISTER-COUNSELOR

MR. CHRISTOPHER RAE TINNING
MS. LORELLE CATHERINE BAKKER
MINISTER-COUNSELOR

MR. CAMERON ROBERT ARCHER
MRS. EMMA LOUISE WHITE
COUNSELOR

MR. MARK STEWART DARBY
MS. CATHERINE GRACE CADDY
COUNSELOR

* U.S. Citizen

MR. BRIAN STEWART FLETCHER
    MRS. KYM JUNG WAH WADE
COUNSELOR

MR. DAVID LEMPRIERE HAMMOND
    MRS. WENDY CHERYL HAMMOND
COUNSELOR

MS. KRISTINA SUZANNE HICKEY
COUNSELOR

MR. DAVID IAN JESSUP
    MRS. ELLEN JANE JESSUP
COUNSELOR

MR. MICHAEL JAMES LANKOWSKI
COUNSELOR

MR. BEN MILTON
COUNSELOR

MS. JONNINE SUSAN NEGUS
COUNSELOR

MRS. JULIE ANN PETTREY
    MR. NICOLAS ANDREW PICKARD
COUNSELOR

MRS. ALISON JANE ROSE
    MR. PERCY LEE ROSE
COUNSELOR

MS. HELEN ANN SEIDEL
    MR. KEAN MUN WONG
COUNSELOR

MR. ARZAN MINOO TARAPORE
COUNSELOR

MR. JOHN HAMILTON WATTS
    MS. LIZA CHONG WATTS
COUNSELOR

MR. JOHN WILLIAM WELLARD
    MS. JOSEPHINE MAIE PONSFORD
COUNSELOR

MR. MATTHEW DAVID WILLIAMS
COUNSELOR

MRS. VICKY ELIZABETH BRIANT
FIRST SECRETARY

MR. BEN CAS
    MRS. OLIVIA CLAIRE BALDWIN CHAMBERS
FIRST SECRETARY

MR. SPIROS DROSSOS
    MS. MARIANTHI MAKARIOS
FIRST SECRETARY

MR. MICHAEL BENJAMIN KACHEL
    MS. SALLY-ANNE HENFRY
FIRST SECRETARY

MS. MIRANDA JAYNE LAUMAN
    MR. TAO GOSPER
FIRST SECRETARY (IMMIGRATION)

MR. JONATHAN CAMPBELL LEARMONTH
    MRS. BRIGETTE KATE LEARMONTH
FIRST SECRETARY

MR. NATHAN JOHN LEONARD
    MRS. MEREDITH HELEN LEONARD
FIRST SECRETARY

MS. KATE ELINOR ZOE LONGHURST
FIRST SECRETARY

MS. SUZANNE LEE MARNER
    MR. IAN LESLIE MARNER
FIRST SECRETARY

MRS. NINA MARTIN
    MR. BRETT MARTIN
FIRST SECRETARY

MR. TERRENCE DAVID MASTERSEN
    MRS. KELLIE LOUISE MASTERSEN
FIRST SECRETARY

MR. ANTHONY MICHAEL MCCLEMENT
    MRS. GINA AMY MCCLEMENT
FIRST SECRETARY

MS. KENDRA AMY MORONY
FIRST SECRETARY

MR. ADRIAN MORTON
FIRST SECRETARY (POLICE LIAISON)

MS. SALLY MEGAN NAPPER
FIRST SECRETARY

MR. JAMES WILLIAM NATION
    MRS. STACEY JANELLE NATION
FIRST SECRETARY

MR. ALEXANDER RUPERT NORTON
    MRS. BRIGITTA MARIA NORTON
FIRST SECRETARY (TECHNICAL)

MR. JOHN WILLIAM PYE
    MS. JENNIFER HARDY MCINTYRE
FIRST SECRETARY

MR. JASON RICHARD SHRAPNEL
    MRS. LEANNE MARY SHRAPNEL
FIRST SECRETARY

MR. TOBY GEORGE HENRY STORM
    MS. SHEY LEAH DIMON
FIRST SECRETARY

MR. MAX BENJAMIN AHERN WILLIS
FIRST SECRETARY

MR. MATTHEW DAVID CONNOLLY
SECOND SECRETARY & CONSUL

MS. ROBYN ANNE COOK
SECOND SECRETARY

MR. GREG TAYLOR ILLINGWORTH
    MS. LOUISE EMMA FOSTER
SECOND SECRETARY

MR. ANDREW GRAHAM POOLEY
    MS. NICOLLE ANNE DARGUSCH
SECOND SECRETARY

MS. SAMANTHA SAUNDERS
SECOND SECRETARY

MR. JOHN ANTHONY STANLEY
SECOND SECRETARY

MS. LEAH PAO LING YEAK
SECOND SECRETARY

MS. RACHAEL GRACE WEST
THIRD SECRETARY

* U.S. Citizen

MR. DANIEL FANKHAUSER
 MRS. KELLY JANE FANKHAUSER
 ATTACHE

DR. ANTHONY ROBERT SCHELLHASE
 MRS. DIANA MA SEN LIM
 ATTACHE (DEFENSE SCIENCE)

MAJOR GENERAL TIMOTHY JOSEPH MCOWAN
 MRS. DOMINICA MARGARET MCOWAN
 DEFENSE ATTACHE

COMMANDER PETER ROBERT DOWTON
 ASST. DEFENSE ATTACHE

CAPTAIN NICHOLAS JAMES YOUSEMAN
 MRS. MARY ELLEN YOUSEMAN
 ASST. DEFENSE ATTACHE

AIR COMMODORE JAMES MICHAEL BROWN
 MRS. KATHERINE ELIZABETH BROWN
 ASST. DEFENSE & AIR ATTACHE

BRIGADIER BARRY NEIL MCMANUS
 ASST. DEFENSE & MILITARY ATTACHE

LIEUTENANT COLONEL ROBERT JAMES CRAWFORD
 MRS. MICHELLE FRANCES CRAWFORD
 ASST. MILITARY ATTACHE

COMMANDER DAVID ANTHONY WRIGHT
 MRS. RACHEL DIANNE WRIGHT
 ASST. NAVAL ATTACHE

WING COMMANDER WAYNE ROBERT BRADLEY
 MRS. KIM MARIE BRADLEY
 ASST. NAVAL & AIR ATTACHE

COMMODORE STEPHEN RAYMOND WILLIAM MCDOWALL
 MRS. JANELLE MARGARET MCDOWALL
 NAVAL ATTACHE & ASST. DEFENSE ATTACHE

COMMODORE STEPHEN PETER WOODALL
 MRS. AMANDA LEE WOODALL
 NAVAL ATTACHE & ASST. DEFENSE ATTACHE

AUSTRIA

EMBASSY OF AUSTRIA
Chancery: 3524 INTERNATIONAL COURT, NW 20008-3035
(EMBASSY 202-895-6700) (FAX 202-895-6773)

HIS EXCELLENCY HANS PETER MANZ
 AMBASSADOR EXTRAORDINARY & PLENIPOTENTIARY

DR. SIGURD PACHER
 MRS. NICOLE PACHER
 MINISTER (DEPUTY CHIEF OF MISSION)

MR. GREGOR CSOERSZ
 COUNSELOR

MRS. ALICE EVA MARIA IRVIN
 MR. JOHN ALAN IRVIN*
 COUNSELOR (PRESS & INFORMATION)

MR. HANS CHRISTOPH KORDIK
 MRS. MANUELA LAIR KORDIK
 COUNSELOR (AGRICULTURAL & ENVIRONMENTAL AFFAIRS)

MR. WALTER NEUMAYER
 MRS. HERTA NEUMAYER
 COUNSELOR

MR. ANDREAS PAWLITSCHEK
 MRS. BRIGITTE PAWLITSCHEK
 COUNSELOR

MR. CHRISTIAN GRINSCHGL
 MRS. JENNIFER KATHRYN GRINSCHGL*
 FIRST SECRETARY

MR. THOMAS STOLZL
 FIRST SECRETARY

MR. KLAUS HOFSTADLER
 MRS. TATIANE SILVA HOFSTADLER
 ATTACHE (COMMERCIAL)

MS. EVA MARIA LIEBMANN
 ATTACHE (FINANCIAL OFFICER)

MR. PHILIPP MARXGUT
 MRS. ANGELIKA BERGER
 ATTACHE (SCIENCE)

MS. SUSANNE BARTON
 ASST. ATTACHE (ASST. TO ECONOMIC COUNSELOR)

MRS. GABRIELE DE ROUEN
 MR. RICO GERARD DE ROUEN*
 ASST. ATTACHE

MR. MANFRED KAISER
 MRS. ADRIENNE PALL KAISER
 ASST. ATTACHE (ADMINISTRATIVE)

MS. CHRISTINE MANSFIELD
 ASST. ATTACHE

BRIGADIER GENERAL HARALD GOELLINGER
 MRS. ELISABETH GOELLINGER
 DEFENSE, MILITARY, NAVAL & AIR ATTACHE

COLONEL GERHARD SCHWEIGER
 MRS. ANGELIKA SCHWEIGER
 ASST. DEFENSE & DEFENSE COOPERATION ATTACHE

AUSTRIAN PRESS AND INFORMATION OFFICE
3524 INTERNATIONAL COURT, NW 20008
(OFFICE 202-895-6775)

COMMERCIAL ATTACHE OFFICE
818 18TH STREET, NW, SUITE 500 20006

COMMERCIAL ATTACHE OFFICE
818 18TH STREET, NW, SUITE 500 20006--3523
(OFFICE 202-537-5047) (FAX 202-537-5048)

CONSULAR SECTION
3524 INTERNATIONAL COURT, NW 20008
(OFFICE 202-895-6767)

DEFENSE, MILITARY, NAVAL AND AIR ATTACHE OFFICE
3524 INTERNATIONAL COURT, NW 20008
(OFFICE 202-686-0095)

AZERBAIJAN

EMBASSY OF THE REPUBLIC OF AZERBAIJAN
Chancery: 2741 34TH STREET, NW 20008
(EMBASSY 202-337-3500) (FAX 202-337-5911)

HIS EXCELLENCY ELIN SULEYMANOV
 MRS. LALA ABDURAHIMOVA
 AMBASSADOR EXTRAORDINARY & PLENIPOTENTIARY

* U.S. Citizen

MS. NARGIZ AKIF GIZI GURBANOVA
COUNSELOR

MR. MAMMAD AFIG OGLU TALIBOV
MRS. KAMALA ELDANIZ GIZI TALIBOVA
COUNSELOR

MR. FAKHRADDIN NAJAF OGLU ISMAYILOV
MRS. AYTAN ISMIKHAN GIZI ISMAYILOVA
FIRST SECRETARY

MR. RASHAD NAJAF
MRS. SARA NAJAF
FIRST SECRETARY

MR. ROVSHAN SADIGBAYLI
MS. NARGIZ AKIF GIZI GURBANOVA
FIRST SECRETARY

MS. GUNAY RAHIMOVA
SECOND SECRETARY

MR. EMIN SHAIG OGLU IBRAHIMOV
MRS. SEVINJ NURADDIN GIZI IBRAHIMOVA
THIRD SECRETARY

MRS. VUSALA FIKRAT GIZI MURADALIYEVA
MR. EMIL SAFAROV
THIRD SECRETARY

MS. SABINA SADIGLI
THIRD SECRETARY

MR. EMIL SAFAROV
MRS. VUSALA FIKRAT GIZI MURADALIYEVA
THIRD SECRETARY

MS. KONUL SULEYMANLI
THIRD SECRETARY

MR. NATIG NAMIG OGLU BAKHISHOV
MRS. AYSEL ILGAR GIZI BAKHISHOVA
ATTACHE

LIEUTENANT COLONEL AGHAVERDI MAHMUD OGLU GULIYEV
MRS. SHIRINBAJI INGILAB GIZI GULIYEVA
DEFENSE, MILITARY, NAVAL & AIR ATTACHE

LIEUTENANT COMMANDER SHAFI ILYAS OGLU SULTANOV
MRS. SUSAN IDRIS GIZI SULTANOVA
ASST. DEFENSE, MILITARY, NAVAL & AIR ATTACHE

BAHAMAS

EMBASSY OF THE COMMONWEALTH OF THE BAHAMAS
Chancery: 2220 MASSACHUSETTS AVENUE, NW 20008
(EMBASSY 202-319-2660)   (FAX 202-319-2668)

MR. FREDDIE CLEVELAND TUCKER
COUNSELOR (CHARGE D'AFFAIRES AD INTERIM)

MS. KERRY FERN MEGAN BONAMY
FIRST SECRETARY & CONSUL

MS. KIMBERLEY ELIZABETH LAM
SECOND SECRETARY & VICE CONSUL

MS. BRIDGET MCKAY
SECOND SECRETARY & VICE CONSUL

DR. NICOLA ALICE VICTORIA VIRGILL
MR. JOHN ANDREW ROLLE
ATTACHE (ECONOMIC)

BAHRAIN

EMBASSY OF THE KINGDOM OF BAHRAIN
Chancery: 3502 INTERNATIONAL DRIVE, NW 20008
(EMBASSY 202-342-0741)   (FAX 202-362-2192)

HER EXCELLENCY HUDA EZRA EBRAHIM NONOO
MR. SALMAN MENASHI IDAFAR
AMBASSADOR EXTRAORDINARY & PLENIPOTENTIARY

MR. KHALED YUSUF AHMED ALJALAHMA
MRS. NOUF ALI HASSAN ALI ALKHAJA
COUNSELOR (DEPUTY CHIEF OF MISSION)

MR. YASSER HABIB ALI JASIM ABDULLA
MS. ASMA NASER HUSAIN ALMOSAWI
SECOND SECRETARY

MR. EBRAHIM ABDULLA E. I. ALSHAALAN
THIRD SECRETARY

MR. SALMAN ALJALAHMA
ATTACHE (MEDIA)

MS. AYSHA MURAD ALI NASEEB
MR. KHALED MOHAMMED NOOR I. FAQEEHI
ATTACHE (CULTURAL)

MR. MUBARAK ABDULLA MUBARAK BUTI
ASST. ATTACHE (CULTURAL)

LIEUTENANT COLONEL SHAIKH ABDULLA MOHAMED ALKHALIFA
SHEIKHA LATIFA MOHAMED ALKHALIFA
DEFENSE, MILITARY, NAVAL & AIR ATTACHE

LIEUTENANT COLONEL MOHAMED ALI EBRAHIM AHMED
MRS. HANAN ABDULNOOR MOHAMED HASAN
ASST. DEFENSE, MILITARY, NAVAL & AIR ATTACHE

BANGLADESH

EMBASSY OF THE PEOPLE'S REPUBLIC OF BANGLADESH
Chancery: 3510 INTERNATIONAL DRIVE, NW 20008
(EMBASSY 202-244-0183)   (FAX 202-244-5366)

HIS EXCELLENCY AKRAMUL QADER
MRS. RIFAT SULTANA AKRAM
AMBASSADOR EXTRAORDINARY & PLENIPOTENTIARY

MR. MUHAMMAD ABDUL MUHITH
MRS. RUBY PARVEEN
MINISTER (DEPUTY CHIEF OF MISSION)

MR. MD SHAMSUL HAQUE
MRS. ROSELINE TALUKDER
MINISTER (CONSULAR)

MR. MOHAMMAD WAHID HOSSAIN
MRS. BUSHRA FARAH WAHID
MINISTER (ECONOMICS)

MR. SWAPAN KUMAR SAHA
MRS. BINA RANI SAHA
MINISTER (PRESS)

MR. MUHAMMAD NAZMUL HOQUE
MRS. RASHEDA RAWNAK KHAN
COUNSELOR

* U.S. Citizen

MR. M SHAFIQUL ISLAM
MRS. MEZBAH NAHAR MASTURA
COUNSELOR (COMMERCIAL)

MR. MJH JABED
MRS. SONIA SHARMIN JABED
COUNSELOR

MRS. MOSAMMAT SHAHANARA MONICA
MR. MD FIROZ AKHTAR
FIRST SECRETARY

MR. NIRUPAM DEV NATH
MRS. SHAMPA ROY
FIRST SECRETARY

BRIGADIER GENERAL MOHAMMAD ABDUL MOEEN
MRS. NUSRAT MOEEN
DEFENSE, MILITARY, NAVAL & AIR ATTACHE

BARBADOS

EMBASSY OF BARBADOS
Chancery: 2144 WYOMING AVENUE, NW 20008
(EMBASSY 202-939-9200)   (FAX 202-332-7467)

HIS EXCELLENCY JOHN ERNEST BEALE
MRS. LEILA MOL BEALE
AMBASSADOR EXTRAORDINARY & PLENIPOTENTIARY

MS. NICOLLA SIMONE RUDDER
MINISTER-COUNSELOR (DEPUTY CHIEF OF MISSION)

MS. JANE ELIZABETH BRATHWAITE
COUNSELOR

DR. RICARDO TREVOR LEROY KELLMAN
MRS. SHEONA ALETHEA KELLMAN
FIRST SECRETARY

MS. PAMELA MARGARET D. CRAWFORD
ATTACHE

MISS MICHELLE GLENCORA JUANITA GIBBONS
ATTACHE

COMMANDER ERRINGTON RICARDO SHURLAND
DEFENSE ATTACHE

BELARUS

EMBASSY OF THE REPUBLIC OF BELARUS
Chancery: 1619 NEW HAMPSHIRE AVENUE, NW 20009
(EMBASSY 202-986-1604)   (FAX 202-986-1805)

MR. OLEG KRAVCHENKO
MRS. MARINA KRAVCHENKO
COUNSELOR (CHARGE D'AFFAIRES AD INTERIM)

MR. IHAR KLIMASHEVICH
MRS. ELENA VOLCHENKOVA
COUNSELOR

MR. ANDREI KALACHOU
SECOND SECRETARY

BELGIUM

EMBASSY OF BELGIUM
Chancery: 3330 GARFIELD STREET, NW 20008
(EMBASSY 202-333-6900)   (FAX 202-333-3079)

HIS EXCELLENCY JAN JOZEF MATTHYSEN
MRS. AGNES JULIA AERTS
AMBASSADOR EXTRAORDINARY & PLENIPOTENTIARY & CONSUL GENERAL

MR. BRUNO G.L.G. JANS
MINISTER-COUNSELOR (DEPUTY CHIEF OF MISSION)

MR. PAUL YVONNE GUY LAMBERT
MRS. ELIZANGELA ALVES DA COSTA ALMEIDA
MINISTER-COUNSELOR

MR. WILLIAM JEAN MAURICE DE BAETS
MRS. MARIA JESUS DEVOLX LOPEZ
COUNSELOR (POLITICAL)

MRS. ANNE FRANCE MARCELINE M. JAMART
COUNSELOR & CONSUL

MR. MARC RIFFLET
MRS. KABULA BARTSCH KABULA MUGURUSI
COUNSELOR (INTERNATIONAL COOPERATION)

MR. PATRICK STEVENS
MRS. VERONIQUE VERCAMMEN
COUNSELOR (POLICE)

MR. NICO ROGER VAN DIJCK
MRS. KRISTINA FIDELIEVNA BAYINGANA
COUNSELOR (POLITICAL AFFAIRS)

MR. PETER NORBERT JOOST VAN ACKER
MRS. ASTRID AIDA BELLIOT
FIRST SECRETARY (INTERNATIONAL DEVELOPMENT)

MR. BERNARD C. J. M. GEENEN
MRS. NATHALIE GEENEN DELFORGE
ATTACHE (COMMERCIAL)

MR. JORIS PAUL TOTTE
MRS. MARJANNE GILBERTE SEVENANT
ATTACHE (PRESS & PUBLIC AFFAIRS)

MR. FREDDY MARIE JEAN G. VANBAELEN
MRS. MYRIAM GHISLAINE MARIE RAMAEKERS
ATTACHE (INFORMATION TECHNOLOGY)

BRIGADIER GENERAL MIKE PAUL DELOBEL
MRS. AMNOUY DELOBEL
DEFENSE, MILITARY, NAVAL & AIR ATTACHE

MAJOR PATRICK DE SMEDT
MRS. REGINA DRIEGHE
ASST. DEFENSE, MILITARY, NAVAL & AIR ATTACHE

LIEUTENANT COLONEL LUC KAREL SIMOEN
MRS. BIRGIT VAN HOVE
DEFENSE COOPERATION ATTACHE

MAJOR PHILIPPE EDWIG ROBERT DEVOS
ASST. DEFENSE COOPERATION ATTACHE

BELIZE

EMBASSY OF BELIZE
Chancery: 2535 MASSACHUSETTS AVENUE, NW 20008
(EMBASSY 202-332-9636)   (FAX 202-332-6888)

HIS EXCELLENCY NESTOR ENRIQUE MENDEZ
MRS. ELVIRA R. MENDEZ
AMBASSADOR EXTRAORDINARY & PLENIPOTENTIARY

MS. KENDALL JOSEPHINE BELISLE
FIRST SECRETARY

MR. DANILO ORLANDO CHUC
FIRST SECRETARY

MS. LAUREN LAVERNE QUIROS
SECOND SECRETARY & CONSUL

BENIN

EMBASSY OF THE REPUBLIC OF BENIN
Chancery: 2124 KALORAMA ROAD, NW 20008
(EMBASSY 202-232-6656)   (FAX 202-265-1996)

HIS EXCELLENCY SEGBE CYRILLE OGUIN
MRS. HORTENSE DOSSA OGUIN
AMBASSADOR EXTRAORDINARY & PLENIPOTENTIARY

MR. HECTOR SEDOZAN RUFFIN F. POSSET
MRS. VIVIANE E. J. DOSSOU GBETE POSSET
MINISTER-COUNSELOR (POLITICAL AFFAIRS)

MR. PASCAL YVES ASSOGBA
MRS. ISABELLE O. HOUNGUE ASSOGBA
COUNSELOR (POLITICAL AFFAIRS)

MR. ABEL AGBEBLEO
MRS. SENAHIN NONKO C. CAKPO AGBEBLEO
FIRST SECRETARY (ADMINISTRATIVE & FINANCIAL)

MR. DENIS DESIRE HOUNSOU
ATTACHE (CONSULAR)

MRS. HISANATOU LAI PIO
ATTACHE

COLONEL TOUHOTA PASCAL TAWES
MRS. SENASENAHOUN CATHER SOMADON TAWES
DEFENSE, MILITARY, NAVAL & AIR ATTACHE

COLONEL VINCENT DEDO
MRS. EUNISE DINA OLYMPIO DEDO
ASST. DEFENSE, MILITARY & AIR ATTACHE

OFFICE OF THE DEFENSE ATTACHE
1101 17TH STREET, SUITE 607 20036

BOLIVIA

EMBASSY OF BOLIVIA
Chancery: 3014 MASSACHUSETTS AVENUE, NW 20008
(EMBASSY 202-483-4410)   (FAX 202-328-3712)

GENERAL FREDDY BERSATTI TUDELA
MRS. ROSAYDA ZUBIETA DE BERSATTI
MINISTER-COUNSELOR (CHARGE D'AFFAIRES AD INTERIM)

MR. MARCELO ANDRES MARTINEZ CESPEDES
MRS. MELINA ESMERALDA MONTES EGUINO
COUNSELOR & CONSUL

MR. LUIS ERNESTO GUSTAVO ALIPAZ LOETZ
FIRST SECRETARY

MR. ALEJANDRO R. BILBAO LA VIEJA RUIZ
FIRST SECRETARY

MR. RENE EFRAIN VERDUGUEZ LINARES
MRS. INGRID PATRICIA LUIZAGA PRUDENCIO
FIRST SECRETARY & VICE CONSUL

COLONEL JUAN SEJAS MARTINEZ
ATTACHE (POLICE)

CHANCERY ANNEX
4420 CONNECTICUT AVENUE, SUITE 250 20037
(OFFICE 202-232-4828)

CONSULATE OF BOLIVIA
1819 H STREET, NW, SUITE 240 20006
(OFFICE 202-232-4827)   (FAX 202-232-8017)

MILITARY, NAVAL AND AIR ATTACHE OFFICE
3014 MASSACHUSETTS AVENUE, NW 20008
(OFFICE 202-232-4309)   (FAX 202-232-4071)

BOSNIA AND HERZEGOVINA

EMBASSY OF BOSNIA AND HERZEGOVINA
Chancery: 2109 E STREET, NW 20037
(EMBASSY 202-337-1500)   (FAX 202-337-1502)

HER EXCELLENCY JADRANKA NEGODIC
AMBASSADOR EXTRAORDINARY & PLENIPOTENTIARY

MR. ADNAN HADROVIC
MRS. JADRANA HADROVIC*
MINISTER-COUNSELOR (DEPUTY CHIEF OF MISSION)

MR. EDIN SEHIC
MRS. DIANA SEHIC
MINISTER-COUNSELOR

MR. MARINKO AVRAMOVIC
MRS. LJILJA AVRAMOVIC
COUNSELOR

MR. HARIS BAZDAREVIC
MRS. AIDA BAZDAREVIC
COUNSELOR

MR. ALEKSANDAR DAMJANAC
COUNSELOR

MRS. ANKICA KOVACEVIC
MR. IBRAHIM SKENDER
COUNSELOR

MR. BERISLAV VUJEVA
MRS. DARIJA VUJEVA
FIRST SECRETARY

MRS. DRAGA VASILJEVIC
MR. PETAR ILIC
SECOND SECRETARY

MR. RIAD HABUL
ATTACHE

* U.S. Citizen

LIEUTENANT COLONEL BOZO SKOPLJAKOVIC
MRS. ZELJKA SKOPLJAKOVIC
DEFENSE, MILITARY, NAVAL & AIR ATTACHE

BOTSWANA

EMBASSY OF THE REPUBLIC OF BOTSWANA
Chancery: 1531-1533 NEW HAMPSHIRE AVENUE, NW 20036
(EMBASSY 202-244-4990)   (FAX 202-244-4164)

HER EXCELLENCY TEBELELO SERETSE
AMBASSADOR EXTRAORDINARY & PLENIPOTENTIARY

MS. EMOLEMO MORAKE
MINISTER-COUNSELOR

MR. INNOCENT SIRUMBU MATENGU
COUNSELOR

MS. DIMAKATSO RADIMAPO
FIRST SECRETARY (RESEARCH & INFORMATION)

MR. MASEGO SOLOMON DITIRO NKGOMOTSANG
SECOND SECRETARY

MISS MARINAH TSHEPE
SECOND SECRETARY (ADMINISTRATION)

MR. BARONGWA MASTER BAIPIDI
MRS. TSHWARAGANO BAIPIDI
ATTACHE (EDUCATION)

MS. NEO MARUPING
ATTACHE (EDUCATION)

MS. MAGHTY MOHURUTSHE
ATTACHE (ADMINISTRATIVE)

COLONEL CONRAD OTSILE ISAACS
MRS. ALICE BEATRICE ISAACS
DEFENSE, MILITARY & AIR ATTACHE

BRAZIL

BRAZILIAN EMBASSY
Chancery: 3006 MASSACHUSETTS AVENUE, NW 20008
(EMBASSY 202-238-2700)   (FAX 202-238-2827)

HIS EXCELLENCY MAURO LUIZ IECKER VIEIRA
AMBASSADOR EXTRAORDINARY & PLENIPOTENTIARY

MR. ERNESTO HENRIQUE FRAGA ARAUJO
MRS. MARIA EDUARDA DE SEIXAS CORREA
MINISTER-COUNSELOR (DEPUTY CHIEF OF MISSION)

MR. BENONI BELLI
MRS. CLAUDIA CRISTINA TOMAZI PEIXOTO
MINISTER

MR. LUIZ AUGUSTO S B DE ARAUJO CASTRO
MINISTER & CONSUL GENERAL

MS. GISELA MARIA FIGUEIREDO PADOVAN
MINISTER-COUNSELOR

MR. PAULO ROBERTO SOARES PACHECO
MINISTER-COUNSELOR

MR. FELIPE COSTI SANTAROSA
MRS. FERNANDA GUERRA SANTAROSA
COUNSELOR

MR. PEDRO MARCOS DE CASTRO SALDANHA
MRS. FABIOLA INEZ GUEDES D. SALDANHA
COUNSELOR

MRS. MARIA EDUARDA DE SEIXAS CORREA
MR. ERNESTO HENRIQUE FRAGA ARAUJO
COUNSELOR

MR. RICARDO DE SOUZA MONTEIRO
MRS. GABRIELA CUNHA CARDOSO MONTEIRO
COUNSELOR

MR. PHILIP FOX DRUMMOND GOUGH
MRS. MYRIAN CAROLINE HEIDER GOUGH
COUNSELOR

MR. JOAO PAULO ORTEGA TERRA
MRS. FERNANDA DE ALBUQUERQUE M. BURLE
COUNSELOR

MR. AULO TARRISSE DA FONTOURA
MRS. ARIA TEREZA BAPTISTA DE OLIVEIRA
COUNSELOR

MR. ANDRE VERAS GUIMARAES
MRS. MARIA DE LOURDES SIMAS FERNANDES
COUNSELOR

MR. GUILLERMO BARBOSA
FIRST SECRETARY

MR. BERNARDO BRASIL
FIRST SECRETARY

MR. ANTONIO COTTAS DE JESUS FREITAS
FIRST SECRETARY

MISS SYDMA AGUIAR DAMASCENO
FIRST SECRETARY

MS. CAROLINA DE CRESCE EL DEBS
FIRST SECRETARY

MR. RODRIGO OLIVEIRA GOVEDISE
MRS. LUISA ANGELA ZUFFO
FIRST SECRETARY

MR. ANDRE MACIEL SIAINES DE CASTRO
MRS. SILVINA JULIA TOMASINI
FIRST SECRETARY (CULTURAL)

MR. RAFAEL PORTO SANTIAGO SILVA
MRS. MAR ORTEGA MENEZES SANTIAGO SILVA
FIRST SECRETARY

MRS. CHRISTIANE SILVA AQUINO BONOMO
MR. DIEGO ZANCAN BONOMO
FIRST SECRETARY

MR. CARLOS HENRIQUE ANGRISANI SANTANA
MRS. TAUANA MONTEIRO GUEDES DOS SANTOS
SECOND SECRETARY

MR. FLAVIO CAMPESTRIN BETTARELLO
SECOND SECRETARY

MR. FABIO CEREDA CORDEIRO
MRS. PATRICIA DE SOUZA LEAL
SECOND SECRETARY

MR. FILIPE CORREA NASSER SILVA
MRS. BRUNNA GAROTTI IVO
SECOND SECRETARY

MR. RAPHAEL TOSTI DE ALMEIDA VIEIRA
MRS. CYNTHIA EMILIA M R ALMEIDA VIEIRA
SECOND SECRETARY

* U.S. Citizen

MR. LUIZ FELLIPE FLORES SCHMIDT
MRS. MARIANA LEAL SCHMIDT
SECOND SECRETARY

MR. EDUARDO FRIGHETTO
SECOND SECRETARY

MR. EDUARDO MARAGNA GUIMARAES LESSA
MRS. CAROLINA MONTEIRO VILALVA
SECOND SECRETARY

MR. CIRO MARQUES RUSSO
SECOND SECRETARY

MR. RAPHAEL OLIVEIRA DO NASCIMENTO
MRS. ANA H DE ATHAYDE BOHRER CUMMINGS
SECOND SECRETARY

MR. DIOGO ROSAS GUGISCH
MRS. TATIANA RUEDA FAUCZ
SECOND SECRETARY

MS. LUCIANA SERRAO SAMPAIO
SECOND SECRETARY

MR. BRUNO SOARES LEITE
SECOND SECRETARY

MRS. JULIA ABREU BRAGA
ATTACHE & VICE CONSUL

MR. JOSE ARIEL BERGEMANN DE AGUIAR
MRS. MARISA MACHADO B. AGUIAR
ATTACHE

MRS. MARISA MACHADO B. AGUIAR
MR. JOSE ARIEL BERGEMANN DE AGUIAR
ATTACHE

MR. JOSE VICENTE BRAGA
MRS. ROSENGELADAS DORES NEVES BRAGA
ATTACHE

MR. CYRO ESPIRITO CARDOSO NETO
MRS. KARIN ISABEL CARDOSO
ATTACHE

MR. PAULO CESAR PAGI CHAVES
MISS ANA LUCIA PALMEIRA PEREIRA
ATTACHE

MR. LUIZ GONZAGA, JR COELHO
MRS. RACHEL MARIA MONTEZZO COELHO
ATTACHE

MRS. DIVA MARIA JACOME DE GOES BEZERRA
MR. CARLOS ALBERTO DE MORAES
ATTACHE

MS. ANDREIA MARIA DE LIMA
ATTACHE

MR. FLORIANO DE OLIVEIRA JUNIOR
MRS. NELLY ELISA REGIS DE OLIVEIRA
ATTACHE & VICE CONSUL

MAJOR PAULO CEZAR FISCHER DA SILVA
MRS. DANIELE BUENOFISCHER DA SILVA
ATTACHE

MR. HORRYS FRIACA SILVA
MRS. CLAUDIA TERCILIA ZUCHERATO
ATTACHE

MR. PEHKX JONES GOMES DA SILVEIRA
MRS. DAYSE SOARES PEREIRA DA SILVEIRA
ATTACHE

* U.S. Citizen

MR. WAGNER DA SILVA KOSCHECK
MRS. ANA ROSA DAUMAS PACHECO KOSCHECK
ATTACHE

MR. LEONARDO PEREZ LIMA
ATTACHE

MRS. LUZIA PANDOLFI
ATTACHE

MS. LIVIA PAULA GIRADE PAVARINO
ATTACHE

MR. JORGE ANTONIO DEHER RACHID
MRS. ANDREA CHRISTINA PARANHOS FALEIRO
ATTACHE (TAX & CUSTOMS)

MR. ROGERIO AUGUSTO VIANA GALLORO
MRS. MARIA JOSE TRENTO GALLORO
ATTACHE

MAJOR GENERAL ROGERIO LUIZ VERISSIMO CRUZ
MRS. ELIETE LISBOA DANTAS VERISSIMO
DEFENSE & AIR ATTACHE

MAJOR GENERAL WALTER SOUZA BRAGA NETTO
MRS. KATHYA MARIA P. BRAGA NETTO
MILITARY ATTACHE

REAR ADMIRAL CELSO LUIZ NAZARETH
MRS. FATIMA CRISTINA AFFONSO NAZARETH
NAVAL ATTACHE

COLONEL MAXNEIF CABRAL MENDES DE CASTRO
MRS. CRISTIA CARVALHO MENDES DE CASTRO
ASST. DEFENSE & AIR ATTACHE

COLONEL FLAVIO RAIMUNDO FERES
MRS. VITANIA M DE PAIVA BARRETO FERES
ASST. DEFENSE & AIR ATTACHE

COLONEL JOAO CHALELLA JUNIOR
MRS. MARIA INES ROSSETTI CHALELLA
ASST. MILITARY ATTACHE

COLONEL ROBERT FRANCO DE OLIVEIRA
MRS. M. RODRIGUES DOS REIS DE OLIVEIRA
ASST. MILITARY ATTACHE

CAPTAIN ENEAS TADEU FERNANDES ERVILHA
MRS. SANTOS VELASCO FERNANDES ERVILHA
ASST. NAVAL ATTACHE

CAPTAIN MARCOS INOI DE OLIVEIRA
MRS. S VIEGAS RUIZ INOI DE OLIVEIRA
ASST. NAVAL ATTACHE

BRAZILIAN AERONAUTICAL COMMISSION
1701 22ND STREET, NW 20008
(OFFICE 202-483-4031)

BRAZILIAN ARMY COMMISSION
4632 WISCONSIN AVENUE, NW 20016
(OFFICE 202-244-5010)

BRAZILIAN NAVAL COMMISSION
5126&5130 MACARTHUR BOULEVARD, NW 20016--3344
(OFFICE 202-244-3950)

CONSULAR SECTION
1030 15TH STREET, NW 20005

BRUNEI

EMBASSY OF THE STATE OF BRUNEI DARUSSALAM
Chancery: 3520 INTERNATIONAL COURT, NW 20008
(EMBASSY 202-237-1838)   (FAX 202-885-0560)

HIS EXCELLENCY DATO YUSOFF ABD HAMID
DATIN DATIN MAHANI ABU ZAR
AMBASSADOR EXTRAORDINARY & PLENIPOTENTIARY

MR. ABD HARIS TUAH
MRS. DK HANIMAH PG METUSSIN
MINISTER-COUNSELOR (DEPUTY CHIEF OF MISSION)

MS. NADIAH PIUT
SECOND SECRETARY

MR. ARAHMAN LAMIT
THIRD SECRETARY

MR. ABD WAHAB JUMAAT
MRS. SITI AMINAH IBRAHIM
ATTACHE (COMMUNICATIONS)

MR. MOHD FIRDAUS MOHD ZIN
MRS. SITI BAZILAH ALI YAKOP
ATTACHE (COMMUNICATION)

MR. SOFRY OTHMAN
MRS. ROSE AZYYATI ABDULLAH
ATTACHE (EDUCATION)

COLONEL MOHD SHARIF IBRAHIM
MRS. NORAIDAH IBRAHIM
DEFENSE, MILITARY, NAVAL & AIR ATTACHE

BULGARIA

EMBASSY OF THE REPUBLIC OF BULGARIA
Chancery: 1621 22ND STREET, NW 20008
(EMBASSY 202-387-0174)   (FAX 202-234-7973)

HER EXCELLENCY ELENA B. POPTODOROVA PETROVA
MR. GEORGI CVETANOV PETROV
AMBASSADOR EXTRAORDINARY & PLENIPOTENTIARY

MR. IVAN VENTZESLAVOV ANCHEV
MRS. LILI DELCHEVA ANCHEVA
COUNSELOR

MR. DEYAN ANGELOV KATRATCHEV
MRS. EKATERINA A DANDAROVA KATRATCHEVA
COUNSELOR

MR. IVO MARTINOV KONSTANTINOV
COUNSELOR (ECONOMIC)

MR. GEORGI VELIKOV PANAYOTOV
MRS. DANIELA VELINOVA SIRAKOVA
COUNSELOR

MRS. LYUBOMIRA DIMITROVA GEORGIEVA
SECOND SECRETARY

MR. PETAR GUEORGUIEV KRAYTCHEV
MRS. DIANA IVANOVA KRAYTCHEVA
SECOND SECRETARY (POLITICAL)

MR. CHRISTO CHRISTOV LAZAROV
MRS. GERGANA NIKOLAEVA LAZAROVA
SECOND SECRETARY & CONSUL

MR. IVAYLO DIMITROV STANEV
MRS. JORDANKA DIMITROVA STANEVA
ATTACHE

BRIGADIER GENERAL STEFAN DINCHEV YANEV
MS. PENKA KRASTEVA YANEVA
DEFENSE ATTACHE

ARMED FORCES ATTACHE OFFICE
1621 22ND STREET, NW 20008
(OFFICE 202-332-6616)

COMMERCIAL COUNSELOR OFFICE
1621 22ND STREET, NW 20008
(OFFICE 202-332-6609)

CONSULAR OFFICE
1621 22ND STREET, NW 20008
(OFFICE 202-387-7969)

BURKINA FASO

EMBASSY OF BURKINA FASO
Chancery: 2340 MASSACHUSETTS AVENUE, NW 20008
(EMBASSY 202-332-5577)   (FAX 202-667-1882)

HIS EXCELLENCY SEYDOU BOUDA
AMBASSADOR EXTRAORDINARY & PLENIPOTENTIARY

MR. PASCAL BATJOBO
MRS. OLIVIA OUELY BATJOBO PALE
MINISTER-COUNSELOR

MRS. MAIMOUNATA COMPAORE
MR. HAROUNA COMPAORE
COUNSELOR

MR. LASSINA BITIE
MRS. SETOU BITIE SOUGUE
SECOND SECRETARY

MRS. ADELE BOUDA ZOUGMORE
HIS EXCELLENCY SEYDOU BOUDA
ATTACHE

MR. ISSAKA DEME
MRS. MAMOUNA DEME OUEDRAOGO
ATTACHE (FINANCE)

MRS. MARIAM KABORE OUEDRAOGO
MR. KARIM KABORE
ATTACHE (CULTURAL)

MR. KARIM KABORE
MRS. MARIAM KABORE OUEDRAOGO
ATTACHE (SOCIAL AFFAIRS)

MRS. SOAGUI JOSIANE THIOMBIANO LOMPO
ATTACHE

MR. PIERRE WAONGO
MRS. MONIQUE WAONGO KOURAOGO
ATTACHE (PRESS)

* U.S. Citizen

BURMA

EMBASSY OF THE UNION OF BURMA
Chancery: 2300 S STREET, NW 20008
(EMBASSY 202-332-3344)   (FAX 202-332-4351)

HIS EXCELLENCY THAN SWE
MRS. KHIN WIN YEE
AMBASSADOR EXTRAORDINARY & PLENIPOTENTIARY

MR. YE LWIN
MRS. THI THI MAR
MINISTER-COUNSELOR

MR. KYAW TIN SHEIN
MRS. THEINGI AYE
COUNSELOR

MS. AYE AYE SOE
COUNSELOR

MISS PHOO PWINT KO KO
SECOND SECRETARY

MR. HLAING MYINT AUNG
MRS. SU MON HTWE
ATTACHE

MR. MYO LYNN AUNG
ATTACHE

MR. NAY KO AUNG
MRS. KHIN KHAT KHAT KHAING
ATTACHE

MRS. KHIN HTAY
MR. LIN HTUN
ATTACHE

MR. NE LINN
ATTACHE

MISS SAN SAN MAW
ATTACHE

MR. MIN CHAN MYAE
ATTACHE

MR. TIN WIN SOE
MRS. ZIN MAR MYO
ATTACHE

MR. YAN NAING SOE SOE
MRS. HMWAY HMWAY AUNG
ATTACHE

COLONEL MYINT THEIN
MRS. MAY MAY TIN
DEFENSE, MILITARY, NAVAL & AIR ATTACHE

DEFENSE, MILITARY, NAVAL & AIR ATTACHE OFFICE
2300 CALIFORNIA STREET, NW 20008
(OFFICE 202-332-1938)

BURUNDI

EMBASSY OF THE REPUBLIC OF BURUNDI
Chancery: 2233 WISCONSIN AVENUE, NW, SUITE 408 20007
(EMBASSY 202-342-2574)   (FAX 202-342-2578)

HER EXCELLENCY ANGELE NIYUHIRE
MR. SIMEON KIRABISHA
AMBASSADOR EXTRAORDINARY & PLENIPOTENTIARY

MR. JOEL NKURABAGAYA
MRS. MARIE JOSEE NTIHABOSE
COUNSELOR

CAMBODIA

ROYAL EMBASSY OF CAMBODIA
Chancery: 4530 16TH STREET, NW 20011
(EMBASSY 202-726-7742)   (FAX 202-726-8381)

HIS EXCELLENCY HENG HEM
MRS. SAVINE EK
AMBASSADOR EXTRAORDINARY & PLENIPOTENTIARY

MR. RITHIPOL TITH
COUNSELOR (COMMERCIAL)

MR. VUTH THEAM
MRS. MANOREN THA
SECOND SECRETARY

MR. DARAVUTH CHAN
MRS. NAVY UN
THIRD SECRETARY

MR. CHANNOCH VONG
MRS. CHANTHA LEANG
THIRD SECRETARY

MRS. NEARY SOKHA MEN
ATTACHE (ACCOUNTS)

MR. NAVUTH KOEUT
MRS. THAVY HENG
DEFENSE & MILITARY ATTACHE

CAPTAIN SAKSOVUTHY, III SAY
ASST. DEFENSE & MILITARY ATTACHE

DEFENSE ATTACHE'S OFFICE
4530 16TH STREET, NW 20011
(OFFICE 202-726-7742)   (FAX 202-726-8381)

CAMEROON

EMBASSY OF THE REPUBLIC OF CAMEROON
Chancery: 3400 INTERNATIONAL DRIVE, NW, SUITE 5L 5M
20008
(EMBASSY 202-265-8790)   (FAX 202-387-3826)

HIS EXCELLENCY BIENVENU JOSEPH C. FOE ATANGANA
MRS. VERONIQUE FOE BILOA
AMBASSADOR EXTRAORDINARY & PLENIPOTENTIARY

MS. NAOMIE BEGALA MIKEL
COUNSELOR

MR. FRANCOIS NGOUBENE
MRS. MARIE THERESE NGOUBENE NKEN
COUNSELOR (FINANCIAL)

MR. RICHARD NYAMBOLI NGWA
MRS. PATIENCE NGWECHO NYAMBOLI YANCHO
COUNSELOR (COMMUNICATION)

MR. GERVAIS EDMOND BINDZI EDZIMBI
    MRS. MADELEINE VIRGINIE BINDZI ABOUI
FIRST SECRETARY

MR. OUMAROU CHINMOUN
    MRS. MARIE J CHINMOUN MANGA NYAMVONGO
FIRST SECRETARY

MR. MODESTE MICHEL ESSONO
    MRS. PULCHERIE ESSONO CHEMBOU
FIRST SECRETARY

MRS. AICHA REGINE BOUDJIHO
    SECOND SECRETARY (CONSULAR & PROTOCOL)

MR. PETER MBONGO MOTOMA
    MRS. MBONGO MOTOMA LUCIA LIMUNGA ISOKO
SECOND SECRETARY

MR. CHARLES DI MINTYENE
    MRS. BRIGITTE NICOLE DI MINTYENE
ATTACHE (CULTURAL)

COLONEL ELIE BANBARA
    MRS. REBECA BANBARA REPELI
DEFENSE & MILITARY ATTACHE

MAJOR ANDRE HUBERT ONANA MFEGE
    MRS. KARINE ESTHER ONANA MFEGE
AIR ATTACHE

CANADA

EMBASSY OF CANADA
Chancery: 501 PENNSYLVANIA AVENUE, NW 20001
(EMBASSY 202-682-1740)   (FAX 202-682-7726)

HIS EXCELLENCY GARY ALBERT DOER
AMBASSADOR EXTRAORDINARY & PLENIPOTENTIARY

MS. DEBORAH ANN LYONS
    MINISTER (DEPUTY CHIEF OF MISSION)

MS. DEANNA LYNN HORTON
    MINISTER

MS. ANYA ILLANA LISOWSKI
    MR. LONNIE DALE FLEISCHHACKER
MINISTER

MS. SHEILA BERNADINE RIORDON
    MINISTER

MR. MARIO BOT
    MRS. THU HUONG THI NGUYEN
MINISTER-COUNSELOR & CONSUL GENERAL

MRS. DIANE BURROWS
    MR. GREGORY M. BELL
MINISTER-COUNSELOR

MR. MICHAEL LLOYD EYESTONE
    MRS. MONIKA JUSTYNA SURMA EYESTONE
MINISTER-COUNSELOR

MR. RONALD GARSON
    MINISTER-COUNSELOR

MRS. CHRISTINE DAWN TANNOUS HANSON
    MR. VICTOR JERRY TANNOUS
MINISTER-COUNSELOR

MR. MARTIN OLAV MOEN
    MRS. SOOKYUNG IM
MINISTER-COUNSELOR

MRS. LISETTE ALLISON RAMCHARAN
    MR. SEAN TREVOR SUNDERLAND
MINISTER-COUNSELOR

MRS. ERYN SPROULE
    MR. MICHAEL CHELSEA THIEL
MINISTER-COUNSELOR

MS. LAURIE ANDERSON
    COUNSELOR (ADMINISTRATION) & CONSUL

MS. JENNIE CHEN
    MR. JOSEPH MICHAEL MCALLISTER
COUNSELOR

MR. PAUL JOSEPH CONNORS
    COUNSELOR

MRS. HEATHER NANCY DE SANTIS
    MR. DOUGLAS JEAN LAURIAULT
COUNSELOR

MS. PASCALE DUGRE SASSEVILLE
    COUNSELOR

MR. MICHAEL ELLIOTT
    MRS. SUZANNE CAROLINE ELLIOTT
COUNSELOR

MS. CATHERINE GODIN
    MR. JOHANN HENDRIK VAN HEERDEN
COUNSELOR

MR. DANIEL JOHN GROCHOWALSKI
    COUNSELOR

MR. TIMOTHY ANDREW HAHLWEG
    MRS. JODINE MICHELLE HAHLWEG
COUNSELOR

MR. WILLIAM JAMES HAWKE
    COUNSELOR (IMMIGRATION)

MRS. LISA SUZANNE JANES
    MR. WILLIAM STEVEN JANES*
COUNSELOR

MR. VASKEN KHABAYAN
    MRS. SABRINA DADRIAN KASSABIAN
COUNSELOR

MR. CHRISTOPHER LEE LEGGETT
    MRS. JULIE ANNE LEGGETT*
COUNSELOR

MR. DONALD ROBERT MACKAY
    COUNSELOR

MR. WILLIAM ARTHUR MACKEY
    MRS. KAREN BERGSTROM MACKEY
COUNSELOR

MR. JEROME PISCHELLA
    COUNSELOR

MR. CHRISTOPHER MICHAEL LEPA PLUNKETT
    COUNSELOR

MR. FRANK STRICKLAND RUDDOCK
    MRS. JANET LOUISE RUDDOCK
COUNSELOR

MR. SEAN TREVOR SUNDERLAND
    COUNSELOR

* U.S. Citizen

MR. THOMAS JOHN TRUEMAN
    MRS. KATHERINE TRUEMAN
COUNSELOR

MS. SALLY WADE
COUNSELOR (ADMINISTRATIVE)

MR. RICHARD MAREK WILLIAMS
    MS. MARGARET KATHLEEN BRANDON
COUNSELOR

MR. DARRIN STEVEN BAGGS
    MRS. MICHELE BAGGS
FIRST SECRETARY

MRS. MARTINE BELANGER
    MR. CHRISTIAN FRANCOIS CECIL
FIRST SECRETARY

MR. MICHAEL WILLIAM BLACKMORE
    MRS. SUSIE MIN JUNG LEE
FIRST SECRETARY

MS. SANDRA DARLENE BRANKER
    MR. FRANK BRANKER
FIRST SECRETARY

MR. JUSTIN OLIVER CHAN
    MRS. DINA DEVI CHAN
FIRST SECRETARY

MS. MEGAN JANE CLIFFORD
FIRST SECRETARY

MRS. NANCY MARIE CLOUTIER
    MR. EDWARD W. CLOUTIER
FIRST SECRETARY

MS. GENEVIEVE DOMPIERRE
FIRST SECRETARY

MRS. SUZANNE CAROLINE ELLIOTT
    MR. MICHAEL ELLIOTT
FIRST SECRETARY

DR. JOHN FRIM
    MRS. MONICA MARIA FRIM
FIRST SECRETARY (DEFENSE)

MR. GREGORY GALLIGAN
FIRST SECRETARY

MS. LENA GEE
FIRST SECRETARY

MRS. SUE ANNA GERVAIS
    MR. KELLY LEANDRE HEMBRUFF
FIRST SECRETARY

MR. LUKAS GUDINSKAS
FIRST SECRETARY

MR. HOWARD RAPHAEL ISAAC
FIRST SECRETARY

MR. CHRISTOPHER J. C. LINDGREN
    MRS. KORRINA O. LINDGREN
FIRST SECRETARY

MS. H. ANNE KATHERINE MATTSON
    MR. BENJAMIN JUSTIN GAUSS*
FIRST SECRETARY

DR. KEITH KIRK NIALL
FIRST SECRETARY

MS. JEANETTE ELITA PATELL
FIRST SECRETARY

MR. CHRISTIAN JEAN JACQUES A. RANGER
FIRST SECRETARY

MRS. SHANNON MARIE SONA SONI
    MR. IAN GORDON MARSHALL
FIRST SECRETARY

MS. PEGATHA JEAN TAYLOR
FIRST SECRETARY

MR. PIERRE THIVIERGE
    MRS. LYNDA BOURASSA
FIRST SECRETARY

MR. SEBASTIAN TIRADO
    MRS. SARA AMINI
FIRST SECRETARY

MR. MARC NAZAR TOWAIJ
    MS. KIRSTEN MADEL
FIRST SECRETARY

MS. SUZANNE ALICIA WILKINSON
FIRST SECRETARY

MS. SABA ZARGHAMI
FIRST SECRETARY

MR. SEAN THOMAS CLARK
    MRS. JULIE LINE CLARK
SECOND SECRETARY

MISS ALIA DEDHAR
SECOND SECRETARY

MS. LOUISA MARIE BENEDIKTE DELAPREE
SECOND SECRETARY

MISS SARAH QUIGLEY
SECOND SECRETARY

MS. ALEXANDRA ALYSSA VACHON WHITE
    MR. DORIAN KELLY PANCHYSON
SECOND SECRETARY

MR. DANIEL JOHN ZAHARYCHUK
    MS. GENEVIEVE MARIE A. N. LAURENCE
SECOND SECRETARY

CORPORAL CAROLINE ALLISON
ATTACHE (ADMINISTRATIVE)

CORPORAL KEVIN LEANDER ARSENAULT
ATTACHE (ADMINISTRATIVE)

MS. NATALIE AYERS
    MR. DEREK AYERS
ATTACHE

MRS. PATRICIA DANIELA BARROTTI
    MR. JOSEPH OSCAR PETERS
ATTACHE

MR. JEAN PHILIPPE BEDARD
    MS. CATHERINE ROXANNE DUBUC
ATTACHE (ADMINISTRATIVE)

LIEUTENANT RANDALL MILTON BINNIE
ATTACHE (HEALTH & TRAINING)

MS. AMELIE BLOUIN
ATTACHE

MRS. CHERYL GAYE BRUNTON DUBBS
ATTACHE

* U.S. Citizen

MR. DAVID ANDREW CAMPBELL
 MRS. BETTINA CAMPBELL
 ATTACHE

MS. CLAUDIANE CHARLESTON
 ATTACHE

MS. CHARMAINE MARGARET COX
 ATTACHE

LIEUTENANT COLONEL NORBERT JOSEPH LUDGER CYR
 MS. JEANNE AUDREY CURRIE
 ATTACHE (MEDIA & MILITARY AFFAIRS)

MASTER CORPORAL SHIRLEY LUCIA DE SOUZA
 ATTACHE (ADMINISTRATIVE)

MR. BLAIR CARLETON FOSTER
 MRS. STACY LEE FOSTER
 ATTACHE

MRS. STACY LEE FOSTER
 MR. BLAIR CARLETON FOSTER
 ATTACHE

CORPORAL YVAN LEO PAUL GUERIN
 MRS. GENEVIEVE BORDEIANU
 ATTACHE

MRS. JOUMANA HANNA
 MR. JOSEPH CHAMOUN
 ATTACHE

MS. ANITA GRACE HESSLING
 ATTACHE

CORPORAL ALLAN HUTCHISON
 ATTACHE

MS. KRISTIN MARLENE JAREMA
 ATTACHE

LIEUTENANT COLONEL YANNICK NICOLAS LEMIEUX
 MS. ERICA LYNN FRANK*
 ATTACHE

MR. DANIEL EARL MONGRAW
 MRS. NATASHA MARIE FRANCIS MONGRAW
 ATTACHE

MR. JOHN EDWARD MULHOLLAND
 MRS. NICOLE JEANNE MULHOLLAND
 ATTACHE

MR. KEVIN ROBERT PARADISE
 MS. AMY RACHAEL COMPAGNAT
 ATTACHE

MR. RICHARD ALLAN RHODES
 MS. CHARLOTTE ANNE RHODES
 ATTACHE (FINANCIAL)

MR. ANDRE ROBILLARD
 MS. SUZANNE ROBILLARD
 ATTACHE

MS. SUZANNE ROBILLARD
 MR. ANDRE ROBILLARD
 ATTACHE

MASTER WARRANT OFFICER WAYNE THOMAS RUTTER
 ATTACHE (ADMINISTRATIVE)

MRS. PAMELA YVONNE SAUNDERS
 MR. COLIN GEOFFREY SUTER
 ATTACHE

MR. DAVID THOMAS SORENSEN
 MRS. KHAWLA SORENSEN
 ATTACHE

MS. PAMELA MARIE VOKEY
 ATTACHE

MR. ROBERT JOSEPH WEATHERBY
 MRS. DONNA FERN WEATHERBY
 ATTACHE

LIEUTENANT COMMANDER JAMES GORDON BARNES
 CAPTAIN KIRSTEN RAE BARNES
 ASST. ATTACHE (HEALTH & TRAINING)

CORPORAL CHANTAL BOLDUC
 ASST. ATTACHE

LIEUTENANT COMMANDER JOHN PAUL GERARD COLLIER
 MRS. LORA ANN COLLIER
 ASST. ATTACHE (ENGINEERING)

MRS. LORA ANN COLLIER
 ASST. ATTACHE (PUBLIC AFFAIRS)

MR. LONNIE DALE FLEISCHHACKER
 MS. ANYA ILLANA LISOWSKI
 ASST. ATTACHE

MAJOR LUC FRENETTE
 MRS. JUDY MARIE FRENETTE
 ASST. ATTACHE (TRAINING & DOCTRINE)

MAJOR TAMMY MICHELLE HISCOCK
 CHIEF WARRANT OFFICER DAVID HARVEY HISCOCK
 ASST. ATTACHE (ADMIN.)

WARRANT OFFICER DAVID MICHAEL HITT
 ASST. ATTACHE

COMMANDER CHARLES MARIE MATTE
 MRS. GLORIA GABRIELA MICHEL AVALOS
 ASST. ATTACHE

SERGEANT JOSEPH REJEAN MICHEL
 ASST. ATTACHE

LIEUTENANT COLONEL KEITH EDWARD OSMOND
 MRS. MICHELLE TANYA OSMOND
 ASST. ATTACHE

MAJOR DANIEL ROBICHAUD
 MRS. NATHALIE ROBICHAUD
 ASST. ATTACHE

CORPORAL JOSEPH GUY FRANCOIS ROBICHAUD
 MS. SAMANTHA LYNN BILLARD
 ASST. ATTACHE

MAJOR STEPHANE ROUX
 MRS. CAROLINE BUJOLD
 ASST. ATTACHE (HEALTH)

CORPORAL ROWAN SMITH
 ASST. ATTACHE (HEALTH SERVICES)

SEAMAN KAREN GAYLE TAYLOR
 ASST. ATTACHE

LIEUTENANT GENERAL GUY THIBAULT
 MRS. BEVERLEY ANNE THIBAULT
 ASST. ATTACHE

SERGEANT JEAN MARC VERREAULT
 ASST. ATTACHE

* U.S. Citizen

MAJOR CHARITY WEEDEN
    MR. BRIAN CURT WEEDEN*
    ASST. ATTACHE (DEFENSE)

COMMANDER DAVID WILCOX
    MRS. DEBORAH ANN WILCOX
    ASST. ATTACHE (HEALTH)

MR. DAVID PETER WILLMORE
    ASST. ATTACHE

MAJOR GENERAL NICOLAS ERIK MATERN
    MRS. SONIA THIBAULT
    DEFENSE ATTACHE

COLONEL DAVID ALAN RUNDLE
    MRS. ANN IRENE DOBBINS
    MILITARY ATTACHE & ASST. DEFENSE ATTACHE

COLONEL HUGH ARCHIE FERGUSON
    MRS. VALLENA MARIE FERGUSON
    ASST. DEFENSE ATTACHE

COLONEL SCOTT ANTHONY HOWDEN
    MRS. SHARON JOAN HOWDEN
    ASST. DEFENSE & AIR ATTACHE

LIEUTENANT COLONEL PATRICK HARRY MCADAM
    MRS. MARY SUZETTE MCADAM
    ASST. MILITARY ATTACHE

COMMANDER DAVID TRUDEAU
    MS. LAURIE ANN ROSE
    ASST. NAVAL ATTACHE

CAPTAIN RICHARD PIERRE GRAVEL
    NAVAL ATTACHE & ASST. DEFENSE ATTACHE

LIEUTENANT COLONEL STEVE CHOUINARD
    MRS. CHRISTINE CARON
    ASST. AIR ATTACHE

COLONEL ALLAN RICHARD THOMPSON
    MRS. SUSAN BONNIE THOMPSON
    DEFENSE COOPERATION ATTACHE

MAJOR MICHAEL ALLEN ROSS
    MRS. LORI TREMBLAY
    ASST. DEFENSE COOPERATION ATTACHE

CAPE VERDE

EMBASSY OF THE REPUBLIC OF CAPE VERDE
Chancery: 3415 MASSACHUSETTS AVENUE, NW 20007
(EMBASSY 202-965-6820)   (FAX 202-965-1207)

HER EXCELLENCY MARIA DE FATIMA DA VEIGA
    AMBASSADOR EXTRAORDINARY & PLENIPOTENTIARY

MR. DANIEL LEOPOLDINA SOARES OLIVEIRA
    MRS. ISABEL SOARES OLIVEIRA
    MINISTER-COUNSELOR (DEPUTY CHIEF OF MISSION)

MS. MARIA MENDONCA SEMEDO
    FIRST SECRETARY

MRS. ISABEL SOARES OLIVEIRA
    MR. DANIEL LEOPOLDINA SOARES OLIVEIRA
    THIRD SECRETARY

CENTRAL AFRICAN REPUBLIC

EMBASSY OF THE CENTRAL AFRICAN REPUBLIC
Chancery: 2704 ONTARIO ROAD 20009
(EMBASSY 202-483-7800)   (FAX 202-332-9893)

HIS EXCELLENCY STANISLAS MOUSSA KEMBE
    AMBASSADOR EXTRAORDINARY & PLENIPOTENTIARY

MR. JEAN BAPTISTE DALOBA
    MRS. CAROLINE DALOBA NEE OUAMOUNDJOU
    COUNSELOR

MR. JEAN PAUL KAIKOUMI
    COUNSELOR

MR. HONORE MBAYE
    MRS. CLARISSE P. MBAYE ADOUM FATIGUET
    COUNSELOR (ECONOMIC)

MRS. MICHELE MARIE CLAUDE BENZOT
    MR. EUGENE DYKOIN GNOMBOU
    SECOND SECRETARY (FINANCE AND ADMINISTRATION)

MR. JONATHAN KPADEA SENKIAN
    MRS. GRACE ANNIE KPADEA
    ATTACHE (SECURITY)

MRS. SYLVIE YASSINGOU
    ATTACHE (CULTURAL)

CHAD

EMBASSY OF THE REPUBLIC OF CHAD
Chancery: 2401 MASSACHUSETTS AVENUE, NW 20008
(EMBASSY 202-462-4009)   (FAX 202-265-1937)

HIS EXCELLENCY DJOUMBE MAITINE
    MRS. DARKARIM NAOMI DJOUMBE
    AMBASSADOR EXTRAORDINARY & PLENIPOTENTIARY

MR. HAMID TAKANE YOUSSOUF
    MRS. IKRAM MAHAMAT SALEH
    COUNSELOR (DEPUTY CHIEF OF MISSION)

MR. N. BASHIR NURANE
    MRS. NEFISSA NURAN
    COUNSELOR

MR. TCHOULI GOMBO
    MRS. LIDA ELISABETH M. GOMBO TCHOULI
    FIRST SECRETARY

MR. MAHMOUD ADJI ABBASSE EL HADJ
    MRS. MAHAMAT ACHAKIR KALTOUMA
    ATTACHE

MR. HASSANE OUSMAN
    ATTACHE

MR. NAIMBAYE YELKE DASNAN
    MRS. BONODJI DJIMASNGAR DASNAN
    DEFENSE & MILITARY ATTACHE

* U.S. Citizen

CHILE

EMBASSY OF THE REPUBLIC OF CHILE
Chancery: 1732 MASSACHUSETTS AVENUE, NW 20036
(EMBASSY 202-785-1746)   (FAX 202-887-5579)

HIS EXCELLENCY FELIPE BULNES SERRANO
MRS. MONICA PELLEGRINI
AMBASSADOR EXTRAORDINARY & PLENIPOTENTIARY

MR. ROBERTO EDUARDO MATUS HARRIS
MRS. MYRIAM LUZ GOMEZ INOSTROZA
COUNSELOR (DEPUTY CHIEF OF MISSION)

COLONEL VICTOR JOAQUIN ACOSTA CONTRERAS
MRS. MARIA SOLEDAD JARA CAMPOS
COUNSELOR (TECHNICAL AFFAIRS)

MR. JULIO ANTONIO BRAVO YUBINI
MRS. ISABEL MARGARITA PUIG VALENZUELA
COUNSELOR

MR. CHRISTIAN U. HODGES NUGENT DOCMAC
MRS. MARIA ESTER VILLAR PELAEZ
COUNSELOR & CONSUL

MR. FELIPE COUSINO DONOSO
MRS. MARIA F. RODRIGUEZ FIGUEROA
FIRST SECRETARY

MR. JAIME EDUARDO FERRAZ ARAVENA
MRS. ELISA DEL CARMEN GARCIA JORQUERA
FIRST SECRETARY

MR. JAIME ALEXIS MUNOZ SANDOVAL
MRS. MARIA BERNARDITA RIOSECO ORTEGA
FIRST SECRETARY

MS. ANNEMARIE DUNKER STECHER
SECOND SECRETARY & CONSUL

MR. ARTURO GALEB H. GIADALA SUKNI
MRS. MARIA MOSTAFA ZAVAN
SECOND SECRETARY & CONSUL

MS. LORENA GABRIELA PALOMO PARADA
MR. RICARDO JAIME RODRIGUEZ GARRIDO
SECOND SECRETARY

MR. NICOLAS CHRISTIAN BAR ARMSTRONG
MS. MARIA JOSE C. LARRAIN EGUSQUIZA
ATTACHE (CULTURAL)

MRS. MARIA HILDA BOLVARAN MORALES
MR. PEDRO E. PINCUS*
ATTACHE (CIVIL)

MR. JOAQUIN TAGLE EDWARDS
MRS. MARIA ISABEL PRIETO ALCADE
ATTACHE (AGRICULTURAL)

CAPTAIN MARCELO GOMEZ GARCIA
MRS. PAOLA MONICA M MARCHESSE BUSCO
NAVAL ATTACHE

COLONEL LEONARDO GINO ROMANINI GUTIERREZ
MRS. VERONICA ANDREA JOFRE TABERNER
AIR ATTACHE

COLONEL MIGUEL JUAN ALFONSO BELLET
MRS. MARIA LUISA ARECHETA OJEDA
ASST. MILITARY ATTACHE

AIR ATTACHE OFFICE
1100 17TH STREET, NW, SUITE 900 20036
(OFFICE 202-872-1334)

EMBASSY OF CHILE
1736 MASSACHUSETTS AVENUE 20036

MILITARY ATTACHE OFFICE
2171-2174 WISCONSIN AVENUE, NW, SUITE 2-3 20007
(OFFICE 202-785-2083)

NAVAL ATTACHE OFFICE
1875 CONNECTICUT AVENUE, NW, SUITE 700 20009
(OFFICE 202-667-7790)

CHINA

EMBASSY OF CHINA
Chancery: 3505 INTERNATIONAL PLACE, NW 20008
(EMBASSY 202-495-2000)   (FAX 202-495-2138)

HIS EXCELLENCY YESUI ZHANG
MRS. NAIQING CHEN
AMBASSADOR EXTRAORDINARY & PLENIPOTENTIARY

MR. HONGBO DENG
MRS. LING SHI
MINISTER (DEPUTY CHIEF OF MISSION)

MR. NING HE
MRS. XIAOYAN LIU
MINISTER

MR. KANG LU
MINISTER

MRS. NAIQING CHEN
MINISTER-COUNSELOR

MR. MAOTIAN FANG
MRS. XIAOLING LIU
MINISTER-COUNSELOR

MR. XIAOJUN HENG
MRS. LING ZHU
MINISTER-COUNSELOR

MR. CHAOCHEN LI
MRS. KEKE SHANG
MINISTER-COUNSELOR

MR. DONGWEN LI
MRS. BAILING CHANG
MINISTER-COUNSELOR

MRS. CHENZI LIU
MINISTER-COUNSELOR

MR. WEIMIN LIU
MINISTER-COUNSELOR

MRS. YANXIA WANG
MR. HUAIYU WANG
MINISTER-COUNSELOR

MR. SHAOGANG ZHANG
MRS. XIAOYUE WANG
MINISTER-COUNSELOR

MR. BINGXI ZHEN
MINISTER-COUNSELOR

MR. JIANING CAI
    MRS. ZHENGYING GUAN
    COUNSELOR

MR. FULI CHEN
    MRS. MINGHONG XU
    COUNSELOR

MR. XIONG FENG CHEN
    MRS. YING CAI
    COUNSELOR

MR. WEI CUI
    COUNSELOR

MR. SHUANG GENG
    COUNSELOR

MR. JIN YONG HE
    MRS. JIN SONG LONG
    COUNSELOR

MRS. LANJING HE
    COUNSELOR

MR. BINCHEN HU
    COUNSELOR

MRS. WENLI HU
    COUNSELOR

MRS. YILI JIANG
    COUNSELOR

MR. BIN LI
    COUNSELOR

MR. GANG LI
    MRS. MING HE
    COUNSELOR

MR. JIAN LIU
    COUNSELOR

MR. WEIGUO LIU
    MRS. HONGYAN DU
    COUNSELOR

MR. YANTAO LIU
    MS. YAHUI HOU
    COUNSELOR

MR. GUOLIANG MA
    MRS. QIXIANG CUI
    COUNSELOR

MS. XIAO PING NIU
    COUNSELOR

MRS. LING SHI
    MR. HONGBO DENG
    COUNSELOR

MR. PING SONG
    MRS. LIN LI
    COUNSELOR

MR. JING SU
    MRS. CHUN WANG
    COUNSELOR

MR. JIN SUN
    MS. WEN FENG TAN
    COUNSELOR

MR. GUANGHUI TANG
    MRS. YAN ZHAO
    COUNSELOR

* U.S. Citizen

MR. GUOPING WANG
    COUNSELOR

MR. QI WANG
    MRS. XIAO JING WANG
    COUNSELOR

MRS. WEIYI XIAN
    MR. XIANG CHEN
    COUNSELOR

MRS. XUEYUAN XU
    MR. CHENGLIANG WANG
    COUNSELOR

MR. RUIJIN YANG
    MRS. XIAOLING KUANG
    COUNSELOR

MR. LIYOU ZHA
    MRS. HUIQUN ZHENG
    COUNSELOR

MR. JIANWEN ZHANG
    MRS. QIUHUAN SUN
    COUNSELOR

MR. MIN ZHANG
    MRS. YUQING LIU
    COUNSELOR

MR. YI ZHANG
    COUNSELOR

MR. JING XING ZHOU
    COUNSELOR

MR. RONGGUO ZHOU
    MRS. JINXIU ZHANG
    COUNSELOR

MRS. DAN DAN BAI
    MR. TONG WANG
    FIRST SECRETARY

MR. YONGSHENG CAI
    MRS. XI LU
    FIRST SECRETARY

MR. WEIMIN CHANG
    MRS. QINGYAN WANG
    FIRST SECRETARY

MR. XIANG CHEN
    MRS. WEIYI XIAN
    FIRST SECRETARY

MR. ZHI XIN CHEN
    MRS. YU FANG GUO
    FIRST SECRETARY

MRS. SHUQIN DU
    FIRST SECRETARY

MR. DINGJIAN DUAN
    MRS. WENJING LI
    FIRST SECRETARY

MR. KE FENG
    MRS. LIN WANG
    FIRST SECRETARY

MR. JUNYI GAO
    FIRST SECRETARY

MR. SHENGWU GUO
    MS. YAN WANG
    FIRST SECRETARY

MR. JIE HAO
    MRS. DAN ZHANG
    FIRST SECRETARY

MRS. WENLI HAO
    FIRST SECRETARY

MR. GANG HUANG
    MRS. XIAOMEI SHENG
    FIRST SECRETARY

MR. JINGRUI HUANG
    MRS. SHUQIN TAN
    FIRST SECRETARY

MRS. JUNYING HUANG
    MR. BINGWANG SUN
    FIRST SECRETARY

MR. XUEHU HUANG
    MRS. HUIJIE ZHANG
    FIRST SECRETARY

MR. FANGNING JIAN
    MRS. JING YAO
    FIRST SECRETARY

MS. HAIYING JIANG
    FIRST SECRETARY

MISS BING LI
    MR. XIYING ZHOU
    FIRST SECRETARY

MR. CHAOYANG LI
    MRS. YILIN SUN
    FIRST SECRETARY

MRS. SANGHUA LI
    FIRST SECRETARY

MR. WEI LI
    MRS. HONGYUAN WANG
    FIRST SECRETARY

MR. XIAOJUN LI
    MRS. MEI HE
    FIRST SECRETARY

MS. HANG LIN
    FIRST SECRETARY

MR. RUIHUA LIN
    MRS. QUANHONG NIE
    FIRST SECRETARY

MR. YI LIU
    MRS. JIE ZHAO
    FIRST SECRETARY

MRS. YANLIU LU
    FIRST SECRETARY

MR. YAODONG MA
    MRS. HAIPING WANG
    FIRST SECRETARY

MR. BING MAO
    MRS. CHUNPING PIAO
    FIRST SECRETARY

MR. FANG MENG
    MRS. FANG WANG
    FIRST SECRETARY

MR. LI QIAN
    MRS. FEI LU
    FIRST SECRETARY

MRS. XIAOYAN QIAN
    MR. YONG WANG
    FIRST SECRETARY

MRS. HAI JING QIN
    FIRST SECRETARY

MR. ANG SHEN
    MRS. ZHIYI YIN
    FIRST SECRETARY

MRS. JUN SHEN
    FIRST SECRETARY

MR. LEI SHI
    MRS. WEI LIANG
    FIRST SECRETARY

MR. YUAN QIANG SHI
    FIRST SECRETARY

MRS. YAN XIN TIAN
    MR. LIGONG CHEN
    FIRST SECRETARY

MR. GENHUA WANG
    MRS. MINGJIE PENG
    FIRST SECRETARY

MR. JIA CUN WANG
    FIRST SECRETARY

MR. LIANG WANG
    MRS. YIYIN GU
    FIRST SECRETARY

MR. QING WANG
    MRS. SHAOHUA GU
    FIRST SECRETARY

MR. XIN WANG
    MRS. QU CHEN
    FIRST SECRETARY

MS. YAN WANG
    FIRST SECRETARY

MR. YONG WANG
    MRS. YURONG CHAI
    FIRST SECRETARY

MR. DONG WEI
    MRS. MING QIU
    FIRST SECRETARY

MS. JINHUA XIN
    FIRST SECRETARY

MR. JINMING XU
    MRS. WEI CHEN
    FIRST SECRETARY

MR. DONGYE YAO
    FIRST SECRETARY

MR. DUNHAI YU
    MRS. XIAOXU CAI
    FIRST SECRETARY

MR. GENG YU
    MRS. GUANGLIN LAI
    FIRST SECRETARY

* U.S. Citizen

MR. XUEQIAN ZHANG
FIRST SECRETARY

MR. CHENGGANG ZHAO
MRS. ZAOFANG FU
FIRST SECRETARY

MR. XIANJIN ZHAO
MRS. HAOJIE XU
FIRST SECRETARY

MR. XIUCHUN ZHAO
MRS. CI WANG
FIRST SECRETARY

MR. BAOQUAN ZHOU
MRS. YAN WANG
FIRST SECRETARY

MRS. QIAN ZHOU
MR. JING XING ZHOU
FIRST SECRETARY

MR. SHENGHE ZHOU
MS. YAXIN WANG
FIRST SECRETARY

MR. JIAN PING CHEN
MRS. BO DENG
SECOND SECRETARY

MRS. TAO E
MR. QING ZHENG
SECOND SECRETARY

MR. JIANG HE
MRS. MENGMENG WU
SECOND SECRETARY

MR. YINGJIE HE
MRS. YAN LIU
SECOND SECRETARY

MR. BIN HU
MRS. YUNYUN LU
SECOND SECRETARY

MS. CHENG LI
MR. ZHENXIN PENG
SECOND SECRETARY

MR. QINGMEI LI
SECOND SECRETARY

MRS. RUIHONG LI
SECOND SECRETARY

MISS CUIHANG LIU
SECOND SECRETARY

MR. DONG LIU
MRS. YAMEI WANG
SECOND SECRETARY

MR. JIANG LIU
MRS. LIXIA ZHANG
SECOND SECRETARY

MR. XIANG LIU
MRS. RIPING LI
SECOND SECRETARY

MRS. YUQING LIU
MR. MIN ZHANG
SECOND SECRETARY

MRS. FEI LU
SECOND SECRETARY

* U.S. Citizen

MRS. XIN LUO
SECOND SECRETARY

MR. WEI MENG
MS. YUQING ZHANG
SECOND SECRETARY

MR. HUA QIN
SECOND SECRETARY

MR. BO QU
MRS. QINGHUA ZHANG
SECOND SECRETARY

MRS. RONG REN
SECOND SECRETARY

MR. JINSONG SI
SECOND SECRETARY

MR. JINSHUN TAO
MRS. JINGYU JIE
SECOND SECRETARY

MR. SONG TAO
MRS. YUYU DAI
SECOND SECRETARY

MR. YE WAN
MS. JIAYING MENG
SECOND SECRETARY

MR. ZHIGUANG WAN
MS. YING LU
SECOND SECRETARY

MRS. LIN WANG
SECOND SECRETARY

MRS. XIAO JING WANG
MR. QI WANG
SECOND SECRETARY

MRS. YAMEI WANG
MR. DONG LIU
SECOND SECRETARY

MS. CHAO YING WU
SECOND SECRETARY

MS. XIAOFANG YU
SECOND SECRETARY

MS. JIN ZHANG
SECOND SECRETARY

MRS. JINGPING ZHANG
SECOND SECRETARY

MR. MAO MING ZHANG
MRS. JIE YANG
SECOND SECRETARY

MR. YUWEI ZHANG
MS. LUXIA YI
SECOND SECRETARY

MR. ZHIQIANG ZHAO
SECOND SECRETARY

MRS. HUI ZHOU
SECOND SECRETARY

MR. LI ZHOU
MRS. YING CHEN
SECOND SECRETARY

MR. TAO CHEN
    MRS. LI WU
THIRD SECRETARY

MRS. ZAOFANG FU
THIRD SECRETARY

MR. YUAN GAO
    MRS. YUAN GAO
THIRD SECRETARY

MR. YI HAN
    MRS. JING WANG
THIRD SECRETARY

MR. SHUAI LI
THIRD SECRETARY

MS. NI LIU
THIRD SECRETARY

MRS. YUNYUN LU
    MR. BIN HU
THIRD SECRETARY

MR. QING LUO
THIRD SECRETARY

MR. XIAOHUI MA
    MRS. YING ZHANG
THIRD SECRETARY

MR. YUE MA
    MRS. XINXIN LI
THIRD SECRETARY

MS. TIAN QIAN
THIRD SECRETARY

MR. LIN QIU
    MS. XIAOXIAO LI
THIRD SECRETARY

MR. JIAN SHANG
THIRD SECRETARY

MR. ZHENZHONG WEI
    MRS. LIN LIN
THIRD SECRETARY

MR. PENG ZHANG
    MS. LI YAO
THIRD SECRETARY

MR. PENG ZHANG
    MRS. LI LI
THIRD SECRETARY

MRS. WEI ZHANG
THIRD SECRETARY

MR. YANYU ZHANG
    MRS. JING ZHAO
THIRD SECRETARY

MR. TIANZHUO ZHENG
    MRS. SIYING GE
THIRD SECRETARY

MR. PING ZHONG
    MS. YAN LIU
THIRD SECRETARY

MR. CHONG ZHOU
    MRS. XIAOFEN GENG
THIRD SECRETARY

MR. ZHENG DAI
    MRS. LI WANG
ATTACHE

MR. XIAOJUN GUO
ATTACHE

MR. FEI HAN
    MRS. XIAOLING CHEN
ATTACHE

MISS YU HAO
ATTACHE

MR. CHANGJIN HU
ATTACHE

MR. XUAN JIN
    MRS. RUIPING LI
ATTACHE

MR. GUOZHU YANG
ATTACHE

MR. YINAN ZHANG
    MRS. JIAWEI LIU
ATTACHE

MR. ZHUOJUN ZHENG
ATTACHE

MS. YANHUI ZHU
ATTACHE

MR. SHUANG DU
ATTACHE (CIVIL)

MRS. XIN QI
ATTACHE (CIVIL)

CAPTAIN XUE GUANG BIAN
    MRS. XIAOYUAN SONG
ASST. ATTACHE

MAJOR JIANQIANG HUANG
    MS. XI DING
ASST. ATTACHE

MR. QINGSHE WANG
    MRS. LI FAN
ASST. ATTACHE

MR. DENGFANG WEI
ASST. ATTACHE

MAJOR YUN YANG
    MS. XU PANG
ASST. ATTACHE

MAJOR GENERAL NANFENG XU
    MRS. JINGCHUAN SHEN
DEFENSE ATTACHE

COLONEL MAJOR HONG SHANG
    MS. YING LI
MILITARY ATTACHE

CAPTAIN YAPING SHEN
    MRS. HONG QU
NAVAL ATTACHE

BRIGADIER GENERAL ZHI JIANG ZHAO
    MRS. QUN GU
AIR ATTACHE

COLONEL JIANZHONG LI
    MRS. HUI LI
ASST. DEFENSE ATTACHE

* U.S. Citizen

COLONEL QIAN WU
MRS. DAN QU
ASST. DEFENSE ATTACHE

COLONEL HUIJING DONG
MRS. LI TIAN
ASST. MILITARY ATTACHE

COLONEL ZHENGMING JIANG
MRS. AIHONG MENG
ASST. MILITARY ATTACHE

MR. YONGXUAN LIU
ASST. MILITARY ATTACHE

MR. NING MA
MS. PEILIN ZHANG
ASST. MILITARY ATTACHE

BRIGADIER GENERAL JUN WANG
MRS. LI LIANG
ASST. MILITARY ATTACHE

MR. BEIQI HUANG
MRS. JUNRONG CAO
ASST. NAVAL ATTACHE

COLONEL SHI MIN CHEN
MRS. PING WU
ASST. AIR ATTACHE

AIR ATTACHE OFFICE
2300 CONNECTICUT AVENUE, NW 20008
(OFFICE 202-238-2542)

CONGRESSIONAL LIAISON OFFICE
2300 CONNECTICUT AVENUE, NW 20008
(OFFICE 202-328-2554)

CONSULAR AFFAIRS
2300 CONNECTICUT AVENUE, NW 20008
(OFFICE 202-328-2518)

CULTURAL AFFAIRS OFFICE
2300 CONNECTICUT AVENUE, NW 20008
(OFFICE 202-328-2597)

DEFENSE ATTACHE OFFICE
2139 WISCONSIN AVENUE, NW 20007
(OFFICE 202-295-2500)   (FAX 202-338-1690)

ECONOMIC & COMMERCIAL COUNSELOR'S OFFICE
2133 WISCONSIN AVENUE, NW 20007
(OFFICE 202-625-3380)   (FAX 202-337-5864)

ECONOMIC & COMMERCIAL COUNSELOR'S OFFICE
2133 WISCONSIN AVENUE, NW 20007

ECONOMIC AFFAIRS OFFICE
2300 CONNECTICUT AVENUE, NW 20008
(OFFICE 202-745-6505)   (FAX 202-234-8629)

EDUCATION OFFICE
2700-12 PORTER STREET, NW 20008
(OFFICE 202-885-0715)

EDUCATIONAL AFFAIRS OFFICE
2300 CONNECTICUT AVENUE, NW 20008
(OFFICE 202-328-2535)

MILITARY ATTACHE OFFICE
2300 CONNECTICUT AVENUE, NW 20008
(OFFICE 202-328-2553)

NAVAL ATTACHE OFFICE
2300 CONNECTICUT AVENUE, NW 20008
(OFFICE 202-328-2541)

POLITICAL AFFAIRS OFFICE
2300 CONNECTICUT AVENUE, NW 20008
(OFFICE 202-328-2507)

PRESS AFFAIRS OFFICE
2300 CONNECTICUT AVENUE, NW 20008
(OFFICE 202-328-2546)

PRESS AFFAIRS OFFICE
2300 CONNECTICUT AVENUE, NW 20008

SCIENCE AND TECHNOLOGY OFFICE
2300 CONNECTICUT AVENUE, NW 20008
(OFFICE 202-328-2630)

VISA SECTION OFFICE
2201 WISCONSIN AVENUE, NW, FLOOR 1ST 20008
(OFFICE 202-338-6688)

COLOMBIA

EMBASSY OF COLOMBIA
Chancery: 2118 LEROY PLACE, NW 20008
(EMBASSY 202-387-8338)   (FAX 202-232-8643)

HIS EXCELLENCY CARLOS ALFREDO URRUTIA VALENZUELA
MRS. LEONOR RESTREPO DE URRUTIA
AMBASSADOR EXTRAORDINARY & PLENIPOTENTIARY

MR. ALFONSO CUELLAR ARAUJO
MRS. ANGELA MARIA RIANO SANDINO
MINISTER (DEPUTY CHIEF OF MISSION)

MRS. PATRICIA CORTES ORTIZ
MR. JAIME CAMARGO SUAREZ
MINISTER-COUNSELOR

MR. VICENTE ECHANDIA ROLDAN
MRS. NATALIA PINZON GOMEZ
MINISTER-COUNSELOR

MRS. MARIA DEL P. FERNANDEZ RETAMOSO
MR. JOSE LUIS TORRES TRESPALACIOS
MINISTER-COUNSELOR

MR. EDGAR RODRIGO ROJAS GARAVITO
MRS. CLAUDIA E. HERNANDEZ HERNANDEZ
MINISTER-COUNSELOR

MISS CAROLINA ACOSTA RAMOS
COUNSELOR (COMMERCIAL)

MRS. CLAUDIA TERESA CANDELA BELLO
MR. JUAN CARLOS ORREGO OCAMPO
COUNSELOR (COMMERCIAL)

MR. ANDRES EDUARDO DE LA CADENA ORTIZ
MRS. KAREN ELENA MENDOZA MANJARRES
COUNSELOR (COMMERCIAL)

MISS MONICA DE NARVAEZ CANO
COUNSELOR (COMMERCIAL)

MR. DANIEL CAMILO PEDRAZA ABRIL
FIRST SECRETARY

MS. NATALIA PENA HERNANDEZ
SECOND SECRETARY

* U.S. Citizen

MISS ANGELICA MARIA RICO SANCHEZ
SECOND SECRETARY & VICE CONSUL

MRS. MARIA LUCIA AMADOR MEZA
THIRD SECRETARY

MRS. CLAUDIA PATRICIA CUEVAS ORTIZ
MR. EDUARDO MUNAR SANCHEZ
THIRD SECRETARY

MR. KLAUS ADOLFO KOCH SALDARRIAGA
MRS. ANA MARIA SALAMANCA VALDERRAMA
THIRD SECRETARY

MR. IVAN ALEJANDRO TRUJILLO ACOSTA
MRS. YULI MARCELA GUIO CAMARGO
THIRD SECRETARY

COLONEL GONZALO RICARDO LONDONO PORTELA
MRS. DALGIS CARMELA ROJAS BARRAGAN
ATTACHE (POLICE)

MR. GUSTAVO ALBERTO MORENO MALDONADO
MS. LINA MARIA MARIN DIAZ
ATTACHE (POLICE)

COLONEL SAMUEL ALBERTO RIOS SEPULVEDA
MRS. MARTHA NEYLA PARRA ULLOA
MILITARY ATTACHE

COLONEL MAURICIO ARCINIEGAS NARANJO
MRS. MONICA BEATRIZ VELASQUEZ CORREA
AIR ATTACHE

COLONEL RICHAR FABIO A. PRIETO VARGAS
MRS. NORMA PATRICIA OROZCO GARCIA
ASST. MILITARY ATTACHE

COMMERCIAL ATTACHE OFFICE
1901 L STREET, NW, SUITE 700 20036

CONSULAR OFFICE
1901 L STREET, NW, SUITE 700 20008
(OFFICE 202-887-9000)

CONSULAR OFFICE
1901 L STREET, NW, SUITE 700 20036
(OFFICE 202-887-9000)   (FAX 202-223-0526)

COMOROS

EMBASSY OF THE UNION OF COMOROS
Chancery: 866 UNITED NATIONS PLAZA, SUITE 418
NEW YORK, NY 10017
(EMBASSY 212-750-1637)   (FAX 212-750-1657)

HIS EXCELLENCY ROUBANI KAAMBI
MRS. BACAR MOHAMED MARIAMA
AMBASSADOR EXTRAORDINARY & PLENIPOTENTIARY

CONGO, DEMOCRATIC REPUBLIC

EMBASSY OF THE DEMOCRATIC REPUBLIC OF THE
CONGO
Chancery: 1726 M STREET, NW, SUITE 601 20036
(EMBASSY 202-234-7690)   (FAX 202-234-2609)

HER EXCELLENCY FAIDA MARAMUKE MITIFU
MR. MAURICE KASAZI SHALISHALI*
AMBASSADOR EXTRAORDINARY & PLENIPOTENTIARY

MR. TAMBO A KABILA MUKENDI
MS. PATRICIA ANDREA BURCHELL*
MINISTER-COUNSELOR

MR. CHIRIJI CELESTIN CHIZA CHIVA
COUNSELOR

MR. THOMAS SIOSI MBIMBA
MRS. ROMAINE LAZWE MBIMBA
COUNSELOR

MR. SERGE TSHAMALA
COUNSELOR

MR. YVES BASHONGA RUCHINAGIZA
MRS. LATIFA SHABANI BASHONGA
SECOND SECRETARY

MS. ODILE YEMBA NYOTA
SECOND SECRETARY

CONGO, REPUBLIC OF THE

EMBASSY OF THE REPUBLIC OF THE CONGO
Chancery: 1720 16TH STREET, NW 20009
(EMBASSY 202-726-5500)   (FAX 202-726-1860)

HIS EXCELLENCY SERGE MOMBOULI
MRS. STELLA CORINE MOMBOULI
AMBASSADOR EXTRAORDINARY & PLENIPOTENTIARY

MR. SYLVAIN BAYALAMA
MRS. CELINE BAYALAMA MILANDOU NSONDE
MINISTER-COUNSELOR

MRS. JACQUELINE MALANDA BAKOUETELA
COUNSELOR

MR. STEPHANE BERNARD MAMATY
MRS. REINE ERNELLA S MAMATY NEE BOTULI
COUNSELOR

MR. MELAND RICHARD NDJOUANDJOUAKA
MRS. EVLYDH F. NDJOUANDJOUAKA MOUTSILA
ATTACHE (ADMINISTRATIVE)

COLONEL PIERRE PARFAIT MANDZANDZA
MRS. GERMAINE MANDZANDZA BOMOLA
DEFENSE ATTACHE

DEFENSE ATTACHE OFFICE
4891 COLORADO AVENUE, NW 20011
(OFFICE 202-726-5500)   (FAX 202-726-1860)

DEFENSE ATTACHE OFFICE
4891 COLORADO AVENUE, NW 20011

COSTA RICA

EMBASSY OF COSTA RICA
Chancery: 2114 S STREET, NW 20008
(EMBASSY 202-234-2945)   (FAX 202-265-4795)

HER EXCELLENCY META SHANON FIGUERES BOGGS
MR. SANTIAGO FELIPE REAL DE AZUA
AMBASSADOR EXTRAORDINARY & PLENIPOTENTIARY

MS. LAURA DACHNER
MR. EDDY ADRIAN FRIEDMAN*
MINISTER-COUNSELOR (DEPUTY CHIEF OF MISSION)

* U.S. Citizen

MRS. ANA MARIA ODUBER ELLIOT
MR. ROY VANCE RICHARDSON CALVO*
MINISTER-COUNSELOR

MRS. PAOLA PATRICIA PORRAS PASTRAN
MR. FREDDY JOSE GARCIA OVIEDO
MINISTER-COUNSELOR (POLITICAL)

MS. ELIZABETH RODRIGUEZ OBUCH
MINISTER-COUNSELOR

MR. JUAN BAUTISTA SALAS ARAYA
MRS. ANA CATALINA GONZALEZ RIVERA
MINISTER-COUNSELOR & CONSUL GENERAL

MR. JOSE CARLOS QUIRCE RODRIGUEZ
ATTACHE (COMMERCIAL)

CHANCERY ANNEX - MISCELLANEOUS CONSULAR OFFICE
2112 S STREET, NW 20008

CONSULAR OFFICE
2112 S STREET, NW 20008
(OFFICE 202-328-6628)

TRADE AND CAFTA OFFICE
1701 K STREET, NW, SUITE 725 20036

TRADE AND CAFTA OFFICE
1701 K STREET, NW, SUITE 725 20036

COTE D`IVOIRE

EMBASSY OF THE REPUBLIC OF COTE D'IVOIRE
Chancery: 2424 MASSACHUSETTS AVENUE, NW 20008
(EMBASSY 202-797-0300)   (FAX 202-462-9444)

HIS EXCELLENCY DAOUDA DIABATE
MRS. CECILE DIABATE NEE COFFI
AMBASSADOR EXTRAORDINARY & PLENIPOTENTIARY

MR. KOUAME CHRISTOPHE KOUAKOU
MRS. EMMA THERESE AHOUO KOUAKOU ABY
COUNSELOR (DEPUTY CHIEF OF MISSION)

MR. GILCHRIST GUILLAUME DALIGOU YAHVE
MRS. MARIE FRANCE KOUOTO DALIGOU YAHVE
COUNSELOR

MRS. MAIMOUNA COULIBALY DOUKOURE
MR. OUSMANE DOUKOURE
COUNSELOR

MR. KOFFI LEON KONAN
COUNSELOR

MS. KOUABLAN MARIE MEA
COUNSELOR

MR. KOUEHI GILDAS ERIC SEYO
MRS. ATSE JANYCE BECHER SEYO
COUNSELOR

MR. YVES TADET
MRS. ANNE DORICE ZOUE TADET
COUNSELOR

MR. ADRIN DANIEL KOFFI
MRS. NIAMKEY MONIQUE EZOUA KOFFI
ATTACHE (FINANCIAL)

GENERAL KODJO MARC AKA
MRS. LOGBOH MADELEINE DON AKA
DEFENSE, MILITARY, NAVAL & AIR ATTACHE

CHANCERY ANNEX
2412 MASSACHUSETTS AVENUE, NW 20008

CROATIA

EMBASSY OF THE REPUBLIC OF CROATIA
Chancery: 2343 MASSACHUSETTS AVENUE, NW 20008
(EMBASSY 202-588-5899)   (FAX 202-588-8936)

HIS EXCELLENCY JOSIP PARO
MRS. JASENKA PARO
AMBASSADOR EXTRAORDINARY & PLENIPOTENTIARY

MR. MARIO SKUNCA
FIRST SECRETARY (DEPUTY CHIEF OF MISSION)

MRS. JELENA VRES
MINISTER-COUNSELOR

MRS. BRANKA PAZIN
MR. MIHOVIL PAZIN
FIRST SECRETARY & CONSUL

MR. NIKICA KOPACEVIC
SECOND SECRETARY

MR. DINO MIHANOVIC
MS. NIKOLINA JOZANC
SECOND SECRETARY

MS. MARTINA TENKO
THIRD SECRETARY

BRIGADIER GENERAL VLADO SINDLER
MRS. LJILJANA SINDLER
DEFENSE, MILITARY, NAVAL & AIR ATTACHE

MAJOR ROBERT KATIC
MRS. MASENJKA KATIC
ASST. DEFENSE, MILITARY, NAVAL & AIR ATTACHE

CYPRUS

EMBASSY OF THE REPUBLIC OF CYPRUS
Chancery: 2211 R STREET, NW 20008
(EMBASSY 202-462-5772)   (FAX 202-483-6710)

MS. OLYMPIA NEOCLEOUS
COUNSELOR (CHARGE D'AFFAIRES AD INTERIM)

MR. NICHOLAOS T. MANOLIS
MRS. REBECCA DEMETRIADOU MANOLI
COUNSELOR (POLITICAL)

MR. NEOPHYTOS CONSTANTINOU
SECOND SECRETARY & CONSUL

CZECH REPUBLIC

EMBASSY OF THE CZECH REPUBLIC
Chancery: 3900 SPRING OF FREEDOM STREET, NW 20008
(EMBASSY 202-274-9100)   (FAX 202-966-8540)

* U.S. Citizen

HIS EXCELLENCY PETR GANDALOVIC
MRS. PAVLINA GANDALOVICOVA
AMBASSADOR EXTRAORDINARY & PLENIPOTENTIARY

MR. JAROSLAV ZAJICEK
MRS. RADKA ZAJICKOVA
MINISTER-COUNSELOR (DEPUTY CHIEF OF MISSION)

MR. JAN PADOUREK
MRS. SIMONA PADOURKOVA
COUNSELOR

MR. JOSEF DVORACEK
MRS. ROMANA DVORACKOVA
FIRST SECRETARY

MR. VACLAV KOLAJA
MRS. DANA KOLAJOVA
FIRST SECRETARY

MR. DAVID FROUS
MRS. NADEZDA FROUSOVA
SECOND SECRETARY

MS. BARBARA KARPETOVA
SECOND SECRETARY

MRS. ALICE NAVRATILOVA
SECOND SECRETARY (CONSULAR)

MR. ROBERT REHAK
MRS. PETRA REHAKOVA
SECOND SECRETARY

MS. MARKETA BALKOVA
THIRD SECRETARY

MS. BARBORA ESNEROVA
MR. DAVID TESARCIK
THIRD SECRETARY

MS. LUCIE HINDLSOVA
THIRD SECRETARY

MR. PETR MICHALEK
THIRD SECRETARY

MR. MARTIN PIZINGER
MS. LENKA PIZINGER
THIRD SECRETARY

MR. FRANTISEK VINTR
MRS. BERNADETA VINTROVA
THIRD SECRETARY

MR. MIROSLAV MRAKOTA
MRS. JANA MRAKOTOVA
ATTACHE

MR. MARTIN PLUHAR
ATTACHE

BRIGADIER GENERAL PREMYSL SKACHA
MRS. DANA SKACHOVA
DEFENSE, MILITARY & AIR ATTACHE

COLONEL JOSEF KOPECKY
MRS. JITKA KOPECKA
ASST. DEFENSE ATTACHE

COMMERCIAL OFFICE
1109-1111 MADISON AVENUE
NEW YORK, NY 10028
(OFFICE 212-717-5064)

COMMERCIAL SECTION
3900 SPRING OF FREEDOM STREET, NW 20008
(OFFICE 202-274-9104)   (FAX 202-244-2147)

DEFENSE ATTACHE OFFICE
3900 SPRING OF FREEDOM STREET, NW 20008

VISA OFFICE
3900 SPRING OF FREEDOM STREET, NW 20008
(OFFICE 202-274-9123)

DENMARK

ROYAL DANISH EMBASSY
Chancery: 3200 WHITEHAVEN STREET, NW 20008
(EMBASSY 202-234-4300)   (FAX 202-328-1470)

HIS EXCELLENCY PETER TAKSOE JENSEN
AMBASSADOR EXTRAORDINARY & PLENIPOTENTIARY

AMBASSADOR SUSANNE WAGNER HOFFMANN SHINE
MR. TONY SHINE
MINISTER (DEPUTY CHIEF OF MISSION)

MR. CASPER LUND BORCH
MRS. CAMILLA LUND BORCH
MINISTER-COUNSELOR

MR. THOMAS DJURHUUS
MRS. LISA MARY DJURHUUS
MINISTER-COUNSELOR

MRS. IDA HEIMANN LARSEN
MR. CLAUS HEIMANN LARSEN
MINISTER-COUNSELOR

MR. HENRIK STEEN STEENSEN
MINISTER-COUNSELOR

MRS. LINA GANDLOESE HANSEN
MR. STEN GANDLOESE HANSEN
COUNSELOR

MR. JOAKIM STEEN MIKKELSEN
COUNSELOR (HEALTH CARE)

MR. LARS VON SPRECKELSEN SYBERG
MRS. SARAH VON SPRECKELSEN SYBERG
COUNSELOR

MR. ANDERS OESTERVANG
MRS. DIANE MAYA ZOUEIN
FIRST SECRETARY

MRS. CAMILLA BENEDIKTE RIEMER PENN
MR. SEBASTIAN PENN
ATTACHE

BRIGADIER GENERAL JOERGEN JACOBSEN
MRS. SYS HVIID JACOBSEN
DEFENSE & AIR ATTACHE & ASST. MILITARY & NAVAL ATTACHE

LIEUTENANT COLONEL JAN GRAUGAARD KRISTENSEN
MRS. STINE IBSEN
ASST. DEFENSE, MILITARY, NAVAL & AIR ATTACHE

LIEUTENANT COLONEL PER LYSE RASMUSSEN
MRS. PENELOPE WELLER RASMUSSEN
ASST. DEFENSE, MILITARY, NAVAL & AIR ATTACHE

* U.S. Citizen

DEFENSE, MILTARY, NAVAL AND AIR ATTACHE OFFICE
3200 WHITEHAVEN STREET, NW 20008
(OFFICE 202-234-4300)

DEFENSE, MILTARY, NAVAL AND AIR ATTACHE OFFICE
3200 WHITEHAVEN STREET, NW 20008

DJIBOUTI

EMBASSY OF THE REPUBLIC OF DJIBOUTI
Chancery: 1156 15TH STREET, NW, SUITE 515 20005
(EMBASSY 202-331-0270)   (FAX 202-331-0302)

HIS EXCELLENCY ROBLE OLHAYE
MRS. AMINA FARAH AHMED OLHAYE
AMBASSADOR EXTRAORDINARY & PLENIPOTENTIARY

MR. ISSA DAHER BOURALEH
MRS. FOZIA AHMED ABANEH
COUNSELOR

MR. ABDALLAH OMAR ABSIEH
FIRST SECRETARY (ECON, FIN & COM)

MR. SAID MOHAMED FARAH
FIRST SECRETARY (FINANCIAL)

DOMINICA

EMBASSY OF THE COMMONWEALTH OF DOMINICA
Chancery: 3216 NEW MEXICO AVENUE, NW 20016
(EMBASSY 202-364-6781)   (FAX 202-364-6791)

HIS EXCELLENCY HUBERT JOHN CHARLES
DR. SYLVIA M. CHARLES
AMBASSADOR EXTRAORDINARY & PLENIPOTENTIARY

MS. JUDITH ANNE ROLLE
FIRST SECRETARY (DEPUTY CHIEF OF MISSION)

DOMINICAN REPUBLIC

EMBASSY OF THE DOMINICAN REPUBLIC
Chancery: 1715 22ND STREET, NW 20008
(EMBASSY 202-332-6280)   (FAX 202-265-8057)

HIS EXCELLENCY ANIBAL DE CASTRO RODRIGUEZ
AMBASSADOR EXTRAORDINARY & PLENIPOTENTIARY

MRS. ALEJANDRA HERNANDEZ GONZALEZ
MINISTER-COUNSELOR (DEPUTY CHIEF OF MISSION)

MR. WELLINGTON D. BENCOSME CASTANOS
MRS. WALLY MARGARITA NUNEZ DIPP
MINISTER-COUNSELOR

MRS. LIGIA AURISTELA REID BONETTI
MINISTER-COUNSELOR

MRS. CAROLINA CACERES DE HONTSCH
MR. BJOERN THORE HOENTSCH
COUNSELOR

MR. NELSON ADONYS FORTUNA RIVAS
MRS. YAHAIRA JAVIER DE FORTUNA
COUNSELOR

* U.S. Citizen

MR. FELIPE JOSE PEDRO HERRERA CABRAL
COUNSELOR

MR. LEONEL MATEO HERNANDEZ
COUNSELOR

MISS RAISSA M. MELGEN SEMAN
COUNSELOR

MS. CAROLINA PEGUERO FERNANDEZ
COUNSELOR

MISS MARIEL PATRICIA VILCHEZ BOURNIGAL
COUNSELOR

MR. ALEXANDER RAFAEL PEREZ CARRASCO
FIRST SECRETARY

MRS. CHERYBELLE E. GOMEZ DE MITROT
MR. SAULO MITROT
SECOND SECRETARY

MS. DENISE LEONORE BULOS BARCELO
THIRD SECRETARY

ECUADOR

EMBASSY OF ECUADOR
Chancery: 1050 30TH STREET, NW 20007
(EMBASSY 202-234-7200)   (FAX 202-667-3482)

HER EXCELLENCY SASKIA NATHALIE CELY SUAREZ
MR. ALVARO IVAN HERNANDEZ ALVAREZ
AMBASSADOR EXTRAORDINARY & PLENIPOTENTIARY

MR. MAURICIO EFRAIN BAUS PALACIOS
MRS. CARLA MARIA DAVALOS DE BAUS
MINISTER (DEPUTY CHIEF OF MISSION)

MR. ANDRES EFREN MONTALVO
MINISTER

MRS. RULLY JANINA SMITH MINDA
MINISTER & CONSUL GENERAL

MISS SILVIA YOLANDA ESPINDOLA ARELLANO
COUNSELOR

MR. JAVIER TOMAS PASAGUAY LABORDE
MS. NORMA PRISCILA NIVELA GALARZA
FIRST SECRETARY

PETTY OFFICER DIEGO BASSANTE GAVILANES
MISS MARIA ALEJANDRA ESPINOLA MUJICA
THIRD SECRETARY

MS. MARIA DANIELA DAVALOS MUIRRAGUI
MR. DIEGO DANILO BELTRAN BASTIDAS
THIRD SECRETARY

MRS. MAGDALENA MARIA NUNEZ JARAMILLO
MR. DIEGO ARMANDO AGUIRRE OCAMPO
THIRD SECRETARY

MS. ERIKA VANESSA NUNEZ PROANO
MR. ROMULO ANDRES TERREROS BRITO
THIRD SECRETARY

MR. IVAN EDUARDO TORRES DONOSO
THIRD SECRETARY

MRS. NDREA ESTEFANIA VILLALBA CARDENAS
THIRD SECRETARY

MAJOR ANITA ELIZABETH CANELOS ENCALADA
MR. STEVE IVAN VERGARA BAQUERO
ATTACHE & CONSULAR AGENT

COLONEL CARLOS RAFAEL GUERRERO VILLACIS
MRS. SANDRA ILIANA MENDEZ RAMOS
ATTACHE (POLICE)

MR. MILTON FERNANDO ALTAMIRANO MUNOZ
MRS. MARISOL DEL CARMEN NIETO CUEVA
ATTACHE (CIVIL)

MAJOR GALO ALFONSO ERAZO COELLAR
MRS. DEBBYE MADELAINE JARAMILLO RIOS
ASST. ATTACHE (POLICE)

COLONEL JUAN CARLOS CADENA MERLO
MRS. MARIA DOLORES BAQUERO RODRIGUEZ
DEFENSE & MILITARY ATTACHE

COLONEL MAURICIO CAMPUZANO NUNEZ
MS. BETTY PATRICIA ARROYO JARAMILLO
AIR ATTACHE

COLONEL FRANKLIN EDUARDO NIVELO PAREDES
MS. JESSI DE LOS ANGEL CEPEDA YANDUN
ASST. DEFENSE & MILITARY ATTACHE

AIR ATTACHE OFFICE
2535 15TH STREET, NW 20009
(OFFICE 202-234-0601)

AIR ATTACHE OFFICE
2535 15TH STREET, NW 20009

CONSULAR AFFAIRS OFFICE
2535 15TH STREET, NW 20009
(OFFICE 202-234-7166)

CONSULAR AFFAIRS OFFICE
2535 15TH STREET, NW 20009

MILITARY ATTACHE OFFICE
2535 15TH STREET, NW 20009

MILITARY ATTACHE OFFICE
2535 15TH STREET, NW 20009
(OFFICE 202-234-0647)

NAVAL ATTACHE OFFICE
2535 15TH STREET, NW 20009
(OFFICE 202-265-7674)

POLICE ATTACHE OFFICE
2535 15TH STREET, NW 20009
(OFFICE 202-464-9990)   (FAX 202-464-9988)

EGYPT

EMBASSY OF THE ARAB REPUBLIC OF EGYPT
Chancery: 3521 INTERNATIONAL COURT, NW 20008
(EMBASSY 202-895-5400)   (FAX 202-244-4319)

HIS EXCELLENCY MOHAMED MOSTAFA MOHAMED TAWFIK
MRS. AMANI AHMED AMIN
AMBASSADOR EXTRAORDINARY & PLENIPOTENTIARY

MR. YASSER ABOUBAKR ABDELKAD ELNAGGAR
MRS. GIHAN OSSMAN ABDELAZIZ HAFEZ
MINISTER (DEPUTY CHIEF OF MISSION)

MR. ASHRAF MAHMOUD EZZ ELDIN
MRS. MAHA FAWZI ABOU DAHAB
MINISTER

MR. HANI MOHAMED NAGI ABDELHAMID
MRS. OMNIA SHOUKRY A. ABDELRAHMAN
COUNSELOR

MRS. HODA KHAMIS MOHAMED ABDULGHANY
MR. ABDELAZIM MAHMOUD M. ABDELFATTAH
COUNSELOR

DR. SAFWAT ABDELHAMID ELHADDAD AHMED
MRS. LAILA MOURAD SOLTAN MOURAD
COUNSELOR

MR. MOHAMED HELMY ABDELMONEIM ELBORAI
MRS. ALISON ROBERT NORMAN ELBORAI
COUNSELOR

MR. MOHAMED TAREK ABDELHAMED ELGINDY
MRS. NEVINE HUSSEIN ABDELMONEIM TOLBA
COUNSELOR

MR. ABDELAZIZ WAGDY ABDELZIZ ELMANAWY
MRS. MAHA MOUSTAFA KAMAL M. HASSAN
COUNSELOR

MR. KARIM HAGGAG
MRS. SOHA S. A. Z. OMAR
COUNSELOR (PRESS OFFICER)

MR. ALAA MOHAMED SALAHELDIN HEGAZY
MRS. REEM MAGUID AMIN AHMED
COUNSELOR

MR. SAMEH ALFONSE SOLIMAN ISKAROS
COUNSELOR

DR. YASSER MOHAMED ELWY MOHAM MAHMOUD
COUNSELOR

MR. MAHMOUD ELSAYED MAHMOUD MOUSSA
MRS. GIHAN MOHAMED ABDELAAL SAYED
COUNSELOR

MR. AHMED MAHMOUD ABDELHALIM ABU ZEID
MRS. ALIAA ADEL SAADELDEIN ELSHERIF
FIRST SECRETARY

MR. ALLA AHMED EZZELDIN ELBIALLY
MRS. MAHA HASSAN MAHMOUD SALEH
FIRST SECRETARY

MS. MIRANDE CAMILLE VICTOR GOUBRAN
FIRST SECRETARY

MR. FADEL MOHAMED FADEL YACOUB
FIRST SECRETARY

MR. MAHMOUD MOHAMMAD M. EL ASHMAWY
MRS. NADINE OSSAMA ZAKARIA ABOULNASR
SECOND SECRETARY

MR. MOHAMED SALAH A. M. ELKHATIB
MRS. NADA YEHIA ISMAIEL BADRAN
SECOND SECRETARY

MR. KHALED ALI MOHAMED ELMENSHAWY
SECOND SECRETARY

MR. AMGAD AHMED REZK MOHAMED
SECOND SECRETARY

MRS. REHAB ABDEHAK ALI SHAWER
MR. AHMED KHALIL ABDELMONEM KHALIL
SECOND SECRETARY

MR. MOHAMED ABEDEL MONEM ABDEL NABY
ATTACHE

MR. YASSER MOHEELDEN DAWOUD ALI ABED
MRS. REHAM OKASHA HASSAN ALI
ATTACHE (ADMINISTRATIVE)

MR. ABDELQAWY GHARIEB ALI AHMED
ATTACHE

MAJOR ASHRAF AHMED AHMED
MRS. SAFAA MOHAMED KHALIL
ATTACHE (ADMINISTRATIVE)

MR. SALAH ELDIN GHARIB BAYOUMY
MRS. AFIFA MOHAMED ELMAIS
ATTACHE (ADMINISTRATIVE)

MR. WAEL MAHMOUD ABDELAZIZ ELDAHSHAN
MRS. NOHA MOKHTAR ABDELGAWAD ASHARY
ATTACHE

MA SAID MOHAMED SAID ELHAMZAWY
MRS. MAI MOKHTAR ROSTOM AHMED ROSTOM
ATTACHE (ADMINISTRATIVE)

MR. HATEM MOHAMED ABBASS HAMADA
MRS. DINA MOHAMED ABDELWAHAB HASSANEN
ATTACHE

MRS. HODA FOUAD MOHAMED HASSAN
MR. SHABAAN KAMEL MOHAMED SABER
ATTACHE

MR. SABRY ELSAYED ABDELFATTAH HASSAN
MRS. NADIA GALAL MOHAMED ALALFY
ATTACHE

GENERAL ROSHDY ABDELHAMID ABDELAZIZ HGAG
MRS. SEHAM MOHAMED KAMEL MORSY
ATTACHE (PROCUREMENT)

MR. HOSSAMELDIN MOUSTAFA A ISMAIEL
ATTACHE (ADMIN & FINANCIAL)

MR. KHALED IBRAHIM ROSHDY M. S. KAMEL
MRS. HEBATALLAH HASSAN AHMED HASSAN
ATTACHE (ADMINISTRATIVE)

MR. MOHAMED ALY SALEH ALY KERASHA
MS. HODA ABDELGHANY ELSAYED IBRAHIM
ATTACHE (CULTURAL)

MR. MOHAMED KAMEL MOHAMED KHALF
MRS. REHAB HASSAN MAHMOUD MOHAMED
ATTACHE

MR. TAREK FARAH MOHAMED KHALIF
MRS. EMAN ALY MOHAMED TELEB
ATTACHE (ADMINSTRATIVE)

MR. REDA SHAHAT ALY KHATAB
MRS. NOHA MAHMOUD MOHAMED SOLIMAN
ATTACHE

MR. HOSSAM YOUSSEF AHMED KHATER
MRS. ABEER ISMAEL GOMAA ABDELRAHMAN
ATTACHE

MR. AHMED RAMADAN IBRAHIM MOHAMED
ATTACHE (ADMINSTRATIVE)

MR. MAHER MAHMOUD AFIFI MOHAMED
ATTACHE

MR. RAGAB ABDELGAWAD TAHA MORSY
ATTACHE (ADMINSTRATIVE)

MR. AHMED HASSAN IBRAHIM NOSSIER
MRS. SAFAA MAHMOUD MOHAMED HAGGAG
ATTACHE

MR. SAID ABDELFATTAH AHMED RAWASH
MRS. FATMA ABDELSATTAR A. ELGAMAL
ATTACHE

MS. DONIA SAYED SALIM SAID
ATTACHE

MR. ESSAM MOHAMED ABDULLAH SALEM
ATTACHE

MR. GAMAL HAGAG SALEM SHKAWY
MRS. SOAAD ABDELMONIEM ALI MOHAMED
ATTACHE

MR. WAEL TALAAT LOTFY SINGER
MRS. REEM SALAHELDIN ABDELGYED ELSAWY
ATTACHE

MS. DINA EZZAT MAHMOUD SWEILLAM
ATTACHE

WARRANT OFFICER SAAID MOHAMED IBRAHIM AAMR
ASST. ATTACHE

MAJOR AHMED MOHAMED WAGDY A. ABDELAZIM
MRS. SHEREEN MOHAMED MAHYMOUD MOSTAFA
ASST. ATTACHE

WARRANT OFFICER MOUHAMED MOUSTAFA A ABDELRAHMAN
ASST. ATTACHE

MR. ELSAYED ALI AHMED ABO ESMAIL
ASST. ATTACHE (ADMINSTRATIVE)

COMMANDER NABIL ABDEL AZIM ABOUL AZM
MRS. ZEINAB MOHAMED A. ELSESY
ASST. ATTACHE (PROCUREMENT)

COMMANDER AHMED ADEL AHMED ABUELENEIN
MRS. RASHA SHEHATA MOHAMED ABDELHALEM
ASST. ATTACHE

LIEUTENANT COLONEL MOHAMED AHMED YOUSSEF EL ZAYAT
MRS. RANIA MOHAMED M. SAKR
ASST. ATTACHE (MEDICAL)

MR. SAID MAHMOUD MOHAMED AHMED
ASST. ATTACHE

COLONEL ABDELHAMED A. ALLAM
MRS. SANAA AHMED NADA
ASST. ATTACHE

COLONEL KHALED MOHAMED HEIBA ALY
MRS. AMIRA, MOHAMED MOSTAFA SALEH
ASST. ATTACHE

LIEUTENANT COLONEL MOHAMED TAWFIK HASSAN AMIN SAFWAT
MRS. IMAN ANWAR HUSSEIN EL MALAH
ASST. ATTACHE

MR. SALAH SAEED ALY AHMED ELAARABY
ASST. ATTACHE

WARRANT OFFICER HOSNEY FATHY AHMED MOHAMED ELFAKY
ASST. ATTACHE

COLONEL AHMED MOHAMED SALAH ELGOWELY
MRS. SALLY SAMIR IBRAHIM ELMAHROUKY
ASST. ATTACHE

LIEUTENANT COLONEL AHMED HUSSEIN MAHMOUD ELNAYAL
MRS. REEM MAHMOD MAHMOUD ELZAYAT
ASST. ATTACHE

SERGEANT HAFIZ TAWFIK SHEBAH SHABA ELSAWAF
ASST. ATTACHE (ADMINISTRATIVE)

MR. RAMADAN FATHY KOUTOB GADALLA
ASST. ATTACHE (ADMINSTRATION)

LIEUTENANT COLONEL HOSSAM A. S. HASSAN
MRS. REEM I. IBRAHIM
ASST. ATTACHE

LIEUTENANT COLONEL HESHAM MAHMOUD FARID HOSNY
MRS. NADIA ALY MAHMOUD
ASST. ATTACHE

SERGEANT GABIR ELSAID SILIM ALI IBRAHIM
ASST. ATTACHE (ADMINISTRATIVE)

MR. MOHAMED HASSAN ABDELMONEM IBRAHIM
ASST. ATTACHE (ADMINSTRATIVE)

CAPTAIN SAAD ANWAR HASSAN MOHAMMED MANA
ASST. ATTACHE

COLONEL ALI MOHAMED ABDELNAEEM MOHAMED
MRS. GHADA ELSAYED MOHAMED HASHEM
ASST. ATTACHE

WARRANT OFFICER HANI FROUK ZAKI MOHAMED
ASST. ATTACHE

LIEUTENANT COMMANDER LOAIIELDIN YEHIA RAMADAN
MOHAMED
MRS. MENATALLAH MOHSEN MOHAMED HASSAN
ASST. ATTACHE

LIEUTENANT COLONEL MOHAMED AHMED DAHEES MOHAMED
MRS. REHAM MOHAMED ABUBAKR M. HASSAN
ASST. ATTACHE

MAJOR SALAHELDIN HASSAN ABDELFA MOHAMED
MRS. ROLA SHAMSELDIN ZAKI ATAALLAH
ASST. ATTACHE (ADMIN & FINANCIAL)

WARRANT OFFICER ABDELRAHMAN MOHAMMED MOHSEN
ASST. ATTACHE

SERGEANT ABDELRAHMAN ABDELKADER I. OSAMAN
ASST. ATTACHE

WARRANT OFFICER ESMAEEL ABELFATAH M. SHARAFELDEEN
ASST. ATTACHE

LIEUTENANT COLONEL HOSSAM SAMIR ABD EL REHEM TOBAR
MRS. EMAN SROR ABO TALEB MAKLED
ASST. ATTACHE

MAJOR GENERAL MOHAMED ABDELFATTAH A. ELKESHKY
MRS. MALAK MANSOUR YOUSSEF ALY
DEFENSE, MILITARY, NAVAL & AIR ATTACHE

COLONEL MOHAMED MOHAMED MOHAMED ABOUD
MRS. HANAN ELSAYED A. ABDELMOGHEETH
ASST. DEFENSE, MILITARY, NAVAL & AIR ATTACHE

LIEUTENANT COLONEL HATEM HAMDY EMAM HANAFY
MRS. SAJA ELSAYED ELIRAQI SAAD
ASST. DEFENSE, MILITARY, NAVAL & AIR ATTACHE

COMMERCIAL AND ECONOMIC AFFAIRS OFFICE
2232 MASSACHUSETTS AVENUE, NW 20008
(OFFICE 202-265-9111)   (FAX 202-328-4517)

CULTURAL AND EDUCATIONAL BUREAU
1303 NEW HAMPSHIRE AVENUE, NW 20036
(OFFICE 202-296-3888)   (FAX 202-296-3891)

OFFICE OF DEFENSE, MILITARY, NAVAL AND AIR ATTACHE
2590 L STREET, NW 20037
(OFFICE 202-333-1283)   (FAX 202-333-7240)

PRESS AND INFORMATION OFFICE
1666 CONNECTICUT AVENUE, NW, SUITE 440 20009
(OFFICE 202-667-3402)   (FAX 202-234-6827)

PROCUREMENT OFFICE
5500 16TH STREET, NW 20011
(OFFICE 202-726-8006)   (FAX 202-829-4909)

EL SALVADOR

EMBASSY OF EL SALVADOR
Chancery: 1400 16TH STREET, NW, SUITE 100 20036
(EMBASSY 202-265-9671)   (FAX 202-232-3763)

HIS EXCELLENCY FRANCISCO R. ALTSCHUL FUENTES
MRS. MELINDA DELASHMUTT ALTSCHUL*
AMBASSADOR EXTRAORDINARY & PLENIPOTENTIARY

MR. OSCAR OSWALD CHAVEZ VALIENTE
MRS. MARTA ELSA P. MARTINEZ DE CHAVEZ
MINISTER (DEPUTY CHIEF OF MISSION)

MR. GUSTAVO ADOLFO ARGUETA HERNANDEZ
MRS. ALBA MERCEDES LOPEZ DE ARGUETA
MINISTER-COUNSELOR (POLITICAL)

MRS. CLAUDIA BEATRIZ BELTRAN GALVEZ
MR. DANIEL PALACIOS MARCHESINI
MINISTER-COUNSELOR (POLITICAL)

MR. ENILSON SOLANO
MRS. CLAUDIA RIVERA SOLANO
MINISTER-COUNSELOR (ECONOMIC)

MR. LUIS APARICIO BERMUDEZ
MRS. CARMEN DE APARICIO
COUNSELOR (POLITICAL)

MS. GRACE MARY AWAD SAFIEH
DR. TONY MICHAEL CHEHADE*
COUNSELOR (ADMINISTRATIVE)

MR. CARLOS MAURICIO FUENTES FLORES
MRS. MILDRED E. DOMINGUEZ DE FUENTES
COUNSELOR (INFORMATION TECHNOLOGY)

MS. VILMA HERRERA
COUNSELOR (COMMUNITY AFFAIRS)

MRS. CELIA YANETH MEDRANO
COUNSELOR & CONSUL GENERAL

MRS. ROSA ANGELA VALENCIA DE ARGUMEDO
MR. EDUARDO ANTONIO ARGUMEDO ALARCON
COUNSELOR

MR. RICARDO JOSE VALENCIA PINEDA
COUNSELOR (POLITICAL)

MRS. DORA MARIA DE AGUILAR
MR. JOSE M. AGUILAR ARAUJO
FIRST SECRETARY

MR. FREDY ELIANOTH VARGAS RAMIREZ
MS. ANA GERTRUDIS GALEAS DE VARGAS
FIRST SECRETARY & VICE CONSUL

* U.S. Citizen

COLONEL WALTER MAURICIO AREVALO GAVIDIA
MRS. SANDRA ORFILIA FLORES DE GAVIDIA
DEFENSE, MILITARY, NAVAL & AIR ATTACHE

LIEUTENANT COLONEL ENRIQUE ANTONIO ACOSTA BONILLA
MRS. YASMIN REGINA TOBIAS DE ACOSTA
ASST. MILITARY ATTACHE

CONSULATE GENERAL
2332 WISCONSIN AVENUE, NW, FLOOR 1ST 20007
(OFFICE 202-331-4032)   (FAX 202-331-4036)

COUNSELOR FOR ECON., FINANCIAL & COMMERCIAL AFFAIRS
OFFICE
2308 CALIFORNIA STREET 20008

COUNSELOR FOR ECON., FINANCIAL & COMMERCIAL AFFAIRS
OFFICE
2308 CALIFORNIA STREET, NW 20008
(OFFICE 202-265-9671)

DEFENSE ATTACHE OFFICE
2308 CALIFORNIA STREET, NW, FLOOR 4 20036
(OFFICE 202-265-9671)

EQUATORIAL GUINEA

EMBASSY OF THE REPUBLIC OF EQUATORIAL GUINEA
Chancery: 2020 16TH STREET, NW 20009
(EMBASSY 202-518-5700)   (FAX 202-518-5252)

HER EXCELLENCY PURIFICACION ANGUE ONDO
AMBASSADOR EXTRAORDINARY & PLENIPOTENTIARY

MR. ROMAN OBAMA EKUA
SECOND SECRETARY

MRS. PACIENCIA MATA MOHOSO
THIRD SECRETARY

MR. CONSTANTINO NJUE NGUI
ATTACHE (ADMINISTRATIVE)

ERITREA

EMBASSY OF THE STATE OF ERITREA
Chancery: 1708 NEW HAMPSHIRE AVENUE, NW 20009
(EMBASSY 202-319-1991)   (FAX 202-319-1304)

MR. BERHANE GEBREHIWET SOLOMON
MRS. HIWET SEBHATU TESFAZZGHI
FIRST SECRETARY (CHARGE D' AFFAIRES AD INTERIM)

MR. SALIH ABDALLA SAAD
FIRST SECRETARY & CONSUL

ESTONIA

EMBASSY OF ESTONIA
Chancery: 2131 MASSACHUSETTS AVENUE, NW 20008
(EMBASSY 202-588-0101)   (FAX 202-588-0108)

HER EXCELLENCY MARINA KALJURAND
MR. KALLE KALJURAND
AMBASSADOR EXTRAORDINARY & PLENIPOTENTIARY

MR. TANEL SEPP
FIRST SECRETARY (DEPUTY CHIEF OF MISSION)

MR. INDREK KANNIK
MRS. MONIKA REINEM
COUNSELOR

MR. KRISTJAN PRIKK
MRS. LIIS PRIKK
COUNSELOR

MR. OLEG DMITRIJEV
SECOND SECRETARY

MS. MARIA BELOVAS
ATTACHE (PUBLIC AND CULTURAL AFFAIRS)

COLONEL AIVAR SALEKESIN
MRS. INGE SALEKESIN
DEFENSE, MILITARY, NAVAL & AIR ATTACHE

ETHIOPIA

EMBASSY OF ETHIOPIA
Chancery: 3506 INTERNATIONAL DRIVE, NW 20008
(EMBASSY 202-364-1200)   (FAX 202-587-0195)

HIS EXCELLENCY GIRMA BIRRU GEDA
MRS. LYDIA GETANEH BELAY
AMBASSADOR EXTRAORDINARY & PLENIPOTENTIARY

MR. TEBEGE BERHE SHOOK
MRS. HELEN TEKLU GEBRESELASSIE
MINISTER (DEPUTY CHIEF OF MISSION)

MR. WAHIDE BELAY ABITEW
MINISTER-COUNSELOR

MR. SAMSON JOHN ABONG
MRS. ROMAN TEFERA ABEJE
MINISTER-COUNSELOR

MR. TSEGAB KEBEBEW DAKA
MRS. TSIGEREDA MENGESHA AGONAFIR
MINISTER-COUNSELOR

MR. MILKIAS HARASA HANKA
MRS. RAHEL BOGALE BOLCHA
MINISTER-COUNSELOR

MR. MELAKU BEDADA SENBETA
MRS. GENET TEFERI AYIFOKRU
MINISTER-COUNSELOR

MR. YOHANNES GETAHUN YIGZAW
MRS. AGERETU ASFAW CHEKOLE
MINISTER-COUNSELOR

MS. KIDIST YACOB ABIRE
COUNSELOR (POLITICAL DIPLOMACY)

MR. TEGENE MULAT BEYENE
MRS. LIBANOS GIRMA WOGAYEHU
COUNSELOR

MR. ZELEKE NEMERA SHENDU
MRS. SUDAN JALETA DIDI
COUNSELOR (ADMIN. & FINANCE)

MR. TEMESGEN BERHANU TORE
MS. TIRUWORK AWEKE TESEMA
COUNSELOR (INFORMATION TECHNOLOGY)

* U.S. Citizen

MR. DINEKA KORNMA NESREDIN
    MRS. AYNALEM BADENGA BESREMO*
FIRST SECRETARY

MS. EMEBET BIRU HAILE
SECOND SECRETARY

MR. SOLOMON TADESSE G SILASSE
    MRS. KIDAN HAILU ATSBEHA
ATTACHE (SECURITY)

CONSULAR SECTION
    3506 INTERNATIONAL DRIVE, NW 20009

CONSULAR SECTION
    3506 INTERNATIONAL DRIVE, NW 20008
        (OFFICE 202-274-4555)   (FAX 202-686-9621)

ECONOMIC, FINANCIAL AND TRADE OFFICE
    3506 INTERNATIONAL DRIVE, NW 20009

ECONOMIC, FINANCIAL AND TRADE OFFICE
    3506 INTERNATIONAL DRIVE, NW 20008
        (OFFICE 202-364-6385)   (FAX 202-364-6387)

EUROPEAN UNION

DELEGATION OF THE EUROPEAN UNION
Chancery: 2175 K STREET, NW, SUITE 800 20037
(EMBASSY 202-862-9500)   (FAX 202-429-1766)

HIS EXCELLENCY JOAO VALE DE ALMEIDA
    MRS. MARIA ANA RAMOS JARA DE CARVALHO
AMBASSADOR (HEAD OF DELEGATION)

MR. FRANCOIS JEAN MARIE D. RIVASSEAU
    MRS. ELISABETH MARIE M. L. RIVASSEAU
MINISTER (DEPUTY HEAD OF DELEGATION)

MR. ANTONIO DE LECEA FLORES DE LEMUS
    MRS. MONICA MARIA CASTRO GOICOCHEA
MINISTER (ECONOMIC & FINANCIAL)

MR. GEORGES LOUIS GABRIEL PINEAU
    MRS. ANNICK RENEE GILBERT
MINISTER (FINANCIAL)

MR. CARLOS MANUEL ALVAREZ ANTOLINEZ
    MRS. ANA MARIA GALLEGO CASTRO
MINISTER-COUNSELOR (FOOD SAFETY, HEALTH & CONSUMER AFFAIRS)

MS. CATARINA I. CALDEIRA DA SILVA
MINISTER-COUNSELOR

MS. MARIA J CARVALHO DE SOUSA FIALHO
MINISTER-COUNSELOR

MR. JAMES PAUL GAVIGAN
    MRS. JOSEFA PURIFICACION IMEDIO LUENGO
MINISTER-COUNSELOR (SCI/TECH/ED)

MR. GEOFFREY ALAN HARRIS
    MRS. WEI ZHU
MINISTER-COUNSELOR

MS. SILVIA KOFLER
MINISTER-COUNSELOR (PRESS & PUBLIC DIPLOMACY)

MR. BERNARD CHARLES MERKEL
    MRS. DOREEN MERKEL
MINISTER-COUNSELOR (FOOD SAFETY, HEALTH & CONSUMER AFFAIRS)

MR. ANTOINE JACQUES FRANCOIS RIPOLL
    MRS. ILARIA IISABEL LUCE RIPOLL*
MINISTER-COUNSELOR

DR. CHRISTIAN KLAUS BURGSMULLER
    MRS. GABRIELA L. ROMERO ALVAREZ
COUNSELOR (TRANSPORT, ENERGY & ENVIRONMENT)

MRS. BEATRICE COVASSI
    MR. HELDER MANUEL COVASSI ENCARNACAO
COUNSELOR (TRADE)

MR. BRICE RAYMOND MICHEL DE SCHIETERE
    MRS. SLAVITZA DIMITROVA DOBREVA
COUNSELOR (POLITICAL)

MR. RORY ALEXANDER PATTERSON DOMM
    MRS. KRISTINA DOMM
COUNSELOR ((POLITICAL))

MRS. ADELINE HINDERER SAYERS
    MR. BRIAN NEILL SAYERS*
COUNSELOR (TRADE)

MR. GUENTER HOERMANDINGER
    MRS. ANTJE MARGARETE RUHFUS
COUNSELOR (TRANSPORT, ENERGY AND ENVIRONMENT)

MR. HIDDO CARL BEREND JAN HOUBEN
    MS. KARIANN AKEMI YOKOTA*
COUNSELOR (TRADE)

MRS. KARIN HUNDEBOELL
    MR. STEFANO SANTAMATO
COUNSELOR (DEVELOPMENT)

MR. UFFE HOLST JENSEN
COUNSELOR

MR. PETRUS JOANNES CORNELIUS KERSTENS
    MRS. JESSIE JULIE PETRA DEGRYSE
COUNSELOR (ECONOMIC & FINANCIAL)

MR. CRISTIAN MAURIN DE FARINA
COUNSELOR

MR. GIULIO MENATO
    MRS. BELEN PEREZ MANSILLAS
COUNSELOR

MR. JOSE MARIA MURIEL PALOMINO
    MRS. MARIA SONIA LOPEZ LOPEZ
COUNSELOR (POLITICAL)

MR. JEAN LUC PIERRE RAYMOND ROBERT
    MRS. AUDE JEHAN
COUNSELOR

MR. DAVID WHINERAY
COUNSELOR (POLITICAL)

MR. DAVID STEPHEN BATCHELOR
    MRS. EVA RIERA CAROL
FIRST SECRETARY

MR. PATRICK GERARD BYRNE
    MRS. FRANCES PATRICIA BYRNE
FIRST SECRETARY

MR. RAMON GOMEZ SALVADOR
    MRS. MARIA DEL CARMEN PICON AGUILAR
FIRST SECRETARY (FINANCIAL)

MRS. VALERIE ELIZABETH LAXTON
    MR. FRANCOIS XAVIER ROUXEL
FIRST SECRETARY

* U.S. Citizen

MR. FELIX MATTHIAS LEINEMANN
    MS. STEFANIE KRISTIN ARP
FIRST SECRETARY (TRANS/ENERGY/ENV)

MR. ERROL GARFIELD LEVY
FIRST SECRETARY (SCI/TECH/EDU)

MR. GABOR ARPAD PULA
    MRS. ESZTER BONCZ
FIRST SECRETARY (FINANCIAL)

MS. ELIZABETH MARY ROBERTS
FIRST SECRETARY

MS. CLAUDE MARIE HELENE VERON REVILLE
    MR. UFFE HOLST JENSEN
FIRST SECRETARY

MS. EVA HORELOVA
SECOND SECRETARY (PRESS & PUBLIC DIPLOMACY)

MS. KONSTANTINA SLAVCHEVA KOSTOVA
SECOND SECRETARY (POLITICAL)

MRS. MAJBRITT KJAER LE COURTOIS
    MR. GUILLAUME JULIEN LE COURTOIS
SECOND SECRETARY

MRS. EVA PALATOVA
    MR. ALEXANDER RADE
SECOND SECRETARY

MISS ANNA DOMINIKA CISZAK
THIRD SECRETARY (POLITICAL)

MR. TOR JESPER NIKLAS BURMAN
    MRS. ANNA MARGARETA KRISTINA GRUBB
ATTACHE

MR. JULIAN HALL
    MRS. SARAH ELIZABETH GARNER HALL
ATTACHE

MS. ISABEL PASTOR ARENILLAS
ATTACHE (TRADE)

MR. MARIUS VLAICU
ATTACHE

FIJI

EMBASSY OF THE REPUBLIC OF FIJI ISLANDS
Chancery: 2000 M STREET, NW, SUITE 710 20036
(EMBASSY 202-466-8320)   (FAX 202-466-8325)

HIS EXCELLENCY WINSTON THOMPSON
    MRS. QUEENIE PAULINE VERONICA THOMPSON
AMBASSADOR EXTRAORDINARY & PLENIPOTENTIARY

MR. RAY KINI BALEIKASAVU
    MRS. ROBERTA CHAPMAN NAWAQATABU
FIRST SECRETARY

FINLAND

EMBASSY OF FINLAND
Chancery: 3301 MASSACHUSETTS AVENUE, NW 20008
(EMBASSY 202-298-5800)   (FAX 202-298-6030)

HER EXCELLENCY RITVA INKERI KOUKKU RONDE
    MR. HIDDE RONDE
AMBASSADOR EXTRAORDINARY & PLENIPOTENTIARY

MRS. ANNE MARIA VASARA
    MR. MICHEL JEAN LOUIS LODDO
MINISTER (DEPUTY CHIEF OF MISSION)

MS. MARJA ANNA ELINA KUOSMANEN
MINISTER-COUNSELOR

MS. ANN SOFIE ELISABETH HELENA STUDE
MINISTER-COUNSELOR (POLITICAL)

MISS ANNELI KRISTIINA HALONEN
COUNSELOR

MR. SAMI JUHANI HUMALA
    MRS. HEIDI SINIKKA HUMALA
COUNSELOR

MRS. SANNA HELENA KANGASHARJU
    MR. DAVID RIJKAART K. VAN ONGEVALLE
COUNSELOR (PRESS)

MR. MARKKU LAURI SAMULI KAUPPINEN
    MRS. EEVA HELENA KAUPPINEN
COUNSELOR

MRS. SOLVEIG SYNNOEVE ROSCHIER
    MR. MARTTI ILMARI HELAMAA
COUNSELOR (HEAD OF OFFICE)

MR. JUKKA SAKARI SALMINIITTY
COUNSELOR (FINANCIAL)

MR. HEIKKI ANTERO SAVOLA
    MRS. SANNA LEENA SAVOLA
COUNSELOR (DEFENSE)

MS. SANNAMAARIA VANAMO
COUNSELOR

MRS. SANNAMAARIA VANAMO
    MRS. SAMI PETRI JUHANI YLAEOUTINEN
COUNSELOR

MRS. HANNA LEENA KORTENIEMI
    MR. PASI PEKKA TUOMINEN
FIRST SECRETARY

MR. AARETTI KUSTAVI SIITONEN
    MRS. AHU YIGIT
FIRST SECRETARY

MRS. MARIA ANNELI SORSA
SECOND SECRETARY

MS. PAEIVI SISKO HELLEVI CASTREN
ATTACHE

MS. LEA MARITTA PAJULA
ATTACHE (ADMINISTRATIVE)

CAPTAIN TIMO TAPIO JUNTTILA
    MRS. MIRJA HILLEVI JUNTTILA
DEFENSE, MILITARY, NAVAL & AIR ATTACHE

LIEUTENANT COLONEL KIM AARNE JUHALA
    MRS. MAARIT SISKO ANNELI JUHALA
ASST. DEFENSE, MILITARY, NAVAL & AIR ATTACHE

LIEUTENANT COLONEL MARKKU TAPIO VIITASAARI
    MRS. JATTA PAULIINA VIITASAARI
ASST. DEFENSE, MILITARY, NAVAL & AIR ATTACHE

DEFENSE, MILTARY, NAVAL AND AIR ATTACHE OFFICE
3301 MASSACHUSETTS AVENUE, NW 20008
(OFFICE 202-298-5800)

NATIONAL TECHNOLOGY AGENCY OF FINLAND
3301 MASSACHUSETTS AVENUE, NW 20008
(OFFICE 202-298-5837)　　(FAX 202-298-6040)

TRADE AND FINANCE OFFICE
3301 MASSACHUSETTS AVENUE, NW 20008
(OFFICE 202-298-5877)　　(FAX 202-298-6041)

FRANCE

EMBASSY OF FRANCE
Chancery: 4101 RESERVOIR ROAD, NW 20007
(EMBASSY 202-944-6000)　　(FAX 202-944-6166)

HIS EXCELLENCY FRANCOIS MARIE DELATTRE
MRS. MARIE SOPHIE L'HELIAS DELATTRE
AMBASSADOR EXTRAORDINARY & PLENIPOTENTIARY

MR. FREDERIC DORE
MRS. STEPHANIE ALEXANDRA LILIANE DORE
MINISTER-COUNSELOR (DEPUTY CHIEF OF MISSION)

MR. JEAN FRANCOIS BOITTIN
MINISTER-COUNSELOR (ECONOMIC & FINANCIAL)

MS. CLAIRE GISELE BERTHE P AUBIN
COUNSELOR

MS. VERONIQUE SOPHIE MARIA AULAGNON
COUNSELOR (GLOBAL AFFAIRS)

MR. THIERRY BUTTIN
MRS. SYLVIE OUTIN
COUNSELOR (TRANSPORTATION)

MR. DAVID JOSEF CVACH
MRS. ORLANE CYRIAQUE VALENTIN CVACH
COUNSELOR

MRS. CHRISTINE FAGES
COUNSELOR

MR. ARNAUD ALEXANDRE DAMIEN GUILLOIS
MRS. CAROLINE ODETTE S. SAPOR-GUILLOIS
COUNSELOR (PRESS)

MR. NICOLAS YANN GUILLOU
COUNSELOR

MRS. EMMANUELLE MARIE IVANOV
MR. ALEXANDRE IVANOV
COUNSELOR

MR. ALEXIS SERGE LEBLANC
MRS. ANOUK GINIEIS LEBLANC
COUNSELOR

MR. JEAN LOUIS MARTIN
MS. NICOLE JEANNE ESTELLE MARTIN
COUNSELOR (PAYMASTER GENERAL)

MRS. VERONIQUE MASSENET
MR. ALEXIS MASSENET
COUNSELOR (ECONOMIC)

MR. JEAN FRANCOIS PHILIPPE PACTET
COUNSELOR

MR. STEPHANE MICHEL PAILLAUD
MRS. KASUMI IWABUCHI
COUNSELOR

MR. CYRIL PIERRE HENRI PINEL
COUNSELOR ((NUCLEAR))

MRS. CATHERINE JEANNE LOUISE ROGY
MR. MICHEL BERNARD EDOUARD ROGY
COUNSELOR (AGRICULTURE)

MR. FRANCK PATRICK ANDRE ROY
COUNSELOR & DEPUTY CONSUL

MR. OLIVIER SEROT ALMERAS LATOUR
MRS. IRENE AGNES SEROT ALMERAS LATOUR
COUNSELOR & CONSUL GENERAL

MS. ANNICK WEINER
MR. JOHN WEINER*
COUNSELOR

MR. KARIM BEN CHEIKH
FIRST SECRETARY

MR. AYMERIC MARIE CHUZEVILLE
MRS. AUDE MOLIN EP. CHUZEVILLE
FIRST SECRETARY

MR. GILLES HENRI COTTET DUMOULIN
FIRST SECRETARY

MR. FRANCOIS PIERRE ANDRE DELMAS
FIRST SECRETARY

MR. CHARLES ARNAUD FOUAN
MRS. FLORENCE JEANNE BERNADETTE JOSSO
FIRST SECRETARY

MR. OLIVIER DOMINIQUE GAUVIN
FIRST SECRETARY

MS. EMMANUELLE HELENE M. PAVILLON
FIRST SECRETARY

MS. DANA GEORGIANA PURCARESCU
FIRST SECRETARY

MRS. COLOMBE B TAILLANDIER STORME
MR. LOUIS XAVIER MARIE F STORME
FIRST SECRETARY

MR. NICOLAS CHARLES ANTOINE THIRIET
MRS. ALEXANDRA NICOL
FIRST SECRETARY

MR. ARMAND HENRI HENNINOT
SECOND SECRETARY

MRS. NATHALIE BARTHELAT VANNIER
MR. FRANCK ROBERT VANNIER
THIRD SECRETARY

MR. PHILIPPE BRUNBROUCK
THIRD SECRETARY

MR. JOSEPH CATINO
MRS. HELENE EDWIGE NOURRY
THIRD SECRETARY

MR. YANN JEAN EVRARD
MRS. CARINE ANNIE LAURENT EP. EVRARD
THIRD SECRETARY

MR. BENOIT POTOT
MRS. MARIE DOMINIQUE BIKUKI MATONDO
THIRD SECRETARY

* U.S. Citizen

MR. KARING QUACH
    MRS. ROMINA SOLEDAD BLANCO QUACH
THIRD SECRETARY

MR. BERTRAND LOUIS MAURICE CAHUET
    MRS. CHRISTINE BRIGITTE PAGES CAHUET
ATTACHE

MR. MARC PATRICE FRANCOIS DAUMAS
    MRS. FRANCOISE MONIQUE EVELYNE DAUMAS
ATTACHE (SCIENCE & TECHNOLOGY)

MR. JACQUES BRUNO JOSEPH DELFOSSE
    MRS. ESTELLE MARIE ELISE DELFOSSE
ATTACHE

MRS. CLAIRE ALINE DEMONCHY
ATTACHE & DEPUTY CONSUL

MR. PHILIPPE HAZANE
    MS. BEATRICE DOLORES ANNA WAGNER
ATTACHE

MR. CHRISTOPHE VINCENT MALVEZIN
    MS. FANNY AUDE PERUSSE EP. MALVEZIN
ATTACHE (AGRICULTURAL)

MR. ROMUALD MARCEL RENE MULLER
    MRS. MARIE PIERRE ODILE MULLER
ATTACHE (POLICE)

MR. FRANCOIS ROGER RICHARD
    MRS. GENEVIEVE JOSIANE RICHARD
ATTACHE (CUSTOMS)

MR. FLORENT EMILE ANDRE TESSON
    MRS. CAROLINE SYLVIE BOGAERS TESSON
ATTACHE (TAX)

BRIGADIER GENERAL BRUNO ANTOINE CAITUCOLI
DEFENSE ATTACHE

COLONEL JACQUES LAURENT ARAGONES
    MS. PASCALE S. BERTHIAUX EP. ARAGONES
MILITARY ATTACHE

CAPTAIN YVES MARIE ALFRED POSTEC
    MRS. ELIZABETH GENTRY POSTEC*
NAVAL ATTACHE

COLONEL MICHEL DUPONT
AIR ATTACHE

COLONEL NICOLAS MARCEL HUE
    MRS. ANNE MARIE NICOLE LOUBOUTIN
DEFENSE COOPERATION ATTACHE

MR. MATHIEU ARMAND RENAUD B. FOSSAT
    MS. ALEXIA ANDRIVE FOSSAT
    MRS. ALEXIA AN PLANCHENAULT EP. FOSSAT
ASST. DEFENSE COOPERATION ATTACHE

COLONEL GEOFFROY PHILIPPE GASTON LENGLIN
    MS. MURIEL CLAIRE THOMAS LENGLIN
ASST. DEFENSE COOPERATION ATTACHE

MR. FRANCIS LIONEL MATHIOT
    MS. GWENAELLE C. SANCHEZ MATHIOT
ASST. DEFENSE COOPERATION ATTACHE

GABON

EMBASSY OF THE GABONESE REPUBLIC
Chancery: 2034 20TH STREET, NW 20009
(EMBASSY 202-797-1000)   (FAX 301-983-1994)

HIS EXCELLENCY MICHAEL MOUSSA ADAMO
    MRS. BRIGITTE MOUSSA ADAMO
AMBASSADOR EXTRAORDINARY & PLENIPOTENTIARY

MS. REGINE PAULETTE AYANG
COUNSELOR (COMMUN. & PROTOCOL)

MRS. LOUISE HONORINE NATHALIE BA OUMAR
COUNSELOR

MRS. ALBA BIFFOT SALES
    MR. TOMAS JOAO SALES
COUNSELOR (ECONOMIC)

MRS. HUGUETTE MBOUMBA MOUSSODOU
COUNSELOR

MR. ALBERT NGUIA
COUNSELOR

MRS. MIREILLE Y OBAME NGUEMA EKOMVONE
    MR. REGINALD ANTHONY MOORE*
COUNSELOR

MR. FRANCOIS LEON TCHISSAMBO RETENO
    MRS. SONIA EDNA TCHISSAMBO RETENO
COUNSELOR (CULTURAL)

MR. DIEUDONNE WAYI
    MRS. AIMEE WAYI
COUNSELOR (CONSULAR AFFAIRS)

MRS. SUZANNE ABENG MBA EP TROUILLET
FIRST SECRETARY (CULTURAL)

GAMBIA

EMBASSY OF THE GAMBIA
Chancery: 2233 WISCONSIN AVENUE, NW, SUITE 240 20007
(EMBASSY 202-785-1399)   (FAX 202-785-1430)

HIS EXCELLENCY ALIEU MOMODOU NGUM
    MRS. AMINATTA LOIS R. NGUM
AMBASSADOR EXTRAORDINARY & PLENIPOTENTIARY

MR. BABOUCARR JALLOW
    MRS. OUMIE SOWE JALLOW
MINISTER-COUNSELOR (DEPUTY CHIEF OF MISSION)

MRS. FATOUMATA AYO BAYO SIDIBE
    MR. BAKARY K SIDIBE
COUNSELOR (INFORMATION & CULTURAL)

MRS. HENRIETTA JULIAN SYLVA
    MR. SANG MARIE SYLVA
ATTACHE (FINANCE)

GEORGIA

EMBASSY OF THE REPUBLIC OF GEORGIA
Chancery: 2209 MASSACHUSETTS AVENUE, NW 20008
(EMBASSY 202-387-2390)   (FAX 202-387-0864)

MR. MIKHEIL DARCHIASHVILI
    MRS. TAMAR MEDULASHVILI
MINISTER-COUNSELOR (CHARGE D'AFFAIRES AD INTERIM)

MR. DATUNA RAKVIASHVILI
    MRS. SOPIO MAMARDASHVILI
MINISTER (DEPUTY CHIEF OF MISSION)

MRS. MAIA BARTAIA
    MR. MIKHEIL CHIKOBAVA
COUNSELOR & CONSUL

MR. VLADIMER CHACHIBAIA
    MS. BELA CHACHIBAIA
COUNSELOR

MS. JULIETA GIORGADZE
COUNSELOR

MS. THEA KENTCHADZE
COUNSELOR

MR. AKAKI LOMIDZE
    MRS. TEA GAMREKELI
COUNSELOR

MR. MERAB MANJGALADZE
    MRS. EKATERINE DAPKVIASHVILI
COUNSELOR

MR. PAATA MATCHAVARIANI
COUNSELOR

MS. NATELA ZAMBAKHIDZE
    MR. NIKOLOZ LOMASHVILI
COUNSELOR (POLITICAL)

MR. LEVAN BERIDZE
    MS. IRINE ASATIANI
FIRST SECRETARY

MS. TAMAR TCHELIDZE
FIRST SECRETARY

MISS KHATUNA OKROSHIDZE
SECOND SECRETARY

LIEUTENANT COLONEL TEMUR EUBIDZE
    MRS. ELEONORA PHURTSKHVANIDZE
DEFENSE, MILITARY, NAVAL & AIR ATTACHE

LIEUTENANT COLONEL VEPKHVIA CHALABASHVILI
    MRS. MAIA JIBGASHVILI
ASST. DEFENSE, MILITARY, NAVAL & AIR ATTACHE

GERMANY, FED. REP. OF

EMBASSY OF THE FEDERAL REPUBLIC OF GERMANY
Chancery: 2300 M STREET, NW, SUITE 300 20037
(EMBASSY 202-298-4000)   (FAX 202-298-4249)

HIS EXCELLENCY DR. NIELS PETER GEORG AMMON
    MRS. MARLIESE HEIMANN AMMON
AMBASSADOR EXTRAORDINARY & PLENIPOTENTIARY

* U.S. Citizen

MR. JENS HANEFELD
    MRS. PETRA HANEFELD
MINISTER (DEPUTY CHIEF OF MISSION)

MR. ERNST PETER FISCHER
    MRS. MARIA DEL CARMEN FISCHER
MINISTER

MR. LUDGER ALEXANDER SIEMES
    MRS. BARBARA MARGARETE SIEMES
MINISTER

MR. KNUT FRIEDRICH ALEXANDER ABRAHAM
    MRS. MARION ERIKA MARGIT ABRAHAM
MINISTER-COUNSELOR

MR. MANFRED JOSEF KARL BLESS
    MRS. MARTHA KOPP BLESS
MINISTER-COUNSELOR (POLITICAL)

MRS. GESA BRAUTIGAM
    MR. RAINER RUDOLPH
MINISTER-COUNSELOR

MS. CHRISTIANE CONSTANZE HOHMANN
MINISTER-COUNSELOR

MR. MAIK WILHELM KAMMERMANN
    MRS. SABINE KAMMERMANN
MINISTER-COUNSELOR

MR. KARL MATTHIAS KLAUSE
    MRS. SYLVIE CLAUDINE TEISSEIRE KLAUSE
MINISTER-COUNSELOR

MS. ANDREA RENATE NOSKE
MINISTER-COUNSELOR

MR. RAINER RUDOLPH
    MRS. GESA BRAUTIGAM
MINISTER-COUNSELOR

DR. THOMAS SCHMIDT
    MS. ANDREA LORE EGERSDOERFER
MINISTER-COUNSELOR

DR. BERTRAM ANATOL F. C. VON MOLTKE
    MRS. ANNE RUTH MARIA VON MOLTKE
MINISTER-COUNSELOR

MR. DETLEF WAECHTER
    MRS. KATJA MARIA WAECHTER
MINISTER-COUNSELOR

MR. HOLGER UWE GUENTHER ZIEGELER
MINISTER-COUNSELOR

MR. JURIJ DANIEL ASTON
    MRS. HYUN JI ASTON YOU
COUNSELOR

MR. JUERGEN HERBERT BAYER
    MRS. MARTINA LUNINGHAKE
COUNSELOR

MR. PETER JOSEF DEBLON
    MRS. GABI DEBLON
COUNSELOR

MR. TOBIAS FEHLHABER
COUNSELOR

MS. SUSANNE ROSEMARIE FRIEDRICHS
COUNSELOR

MR. PETER MICHAEL GOTZ
    MRS. CHRISTINE GOTZ
COUNSELOR

MR. JORG DIETER MATTHIAS KINNEN
  MRS. FRANZISKA JULIA MARIA KINNEN
COUNSELOR

MS. MARION KNAPPE
COUNSELOR

MR. DANIEL KREBBER
  MRS. CLARA LUISE WIEBKE RUECKERT
COUNSELOR

MR. STEFAN HEINRICH LAETSCH
  MRS. GERDA LAETSCH
COUNSELOR

MR. CHRISTIAN OTTO SIMON
  MRS. CHRISTIANE PETRA ELISABETH SIMON
COUNSELOR

MR. MICHAEL CARL ERICH VOGEL
  MRS. NATHALIE ISABELLE VOGEL
COUNSELOR

MR. HANS MICHAEL AMIN VORLAENDER
  MRS. STEFANIE VORLAENDER
COUNSELOR

MR. DAVID CHRISTOPHER BARTELS
  MRS. SONJA MARTHA BARTELS
FIRST SECRETARY

MRS. ULRIKE BERG HAAS
  MR. WOLF GUNTER HAAS
FIRST SECRETARY

MRS. ANDREA CHRIST
  MR. MICHAEL STOEGER
FIRST SECRETARY

MR. CHRISTOPH HERBERT GRIEBLING
  MRS. SILKE GRIEBLING
FIRST SECRETARY

MS. SILKE CHRISTINA KAUL
FIRST SECRETARY

MRS. NATALIE KAUTHER
  MR. ADRIAN POLLMANN
FIRST SECRETARY

MR. STEPHAN ECKHARD KROGER
  MRS. KIZZIE SHAWON MANNING KROEGER*
FIRST SECRETARY

MR. JAN LOFFLER
  MRS. GRIT LOFFLER
FIRST SECRETARY

MR. GEORG MAUE
FIRST SECRETARY

MR. STEFAN ANTON MESSERER
  MRS. SABINE MESSERER
FIRST SECRETARY

MR. MARIUS OSSWALD
FIRST SECRETARY

MR. ADRIAN POLLMANN
  MRS. NATALIE KAUTHER
FIRST SECRETARY

MR. HELGE POLS
  DR. SYLKE EDITH GEISSENDOERFER
FIRST SECRETARY

MRS. CLARA LUISE WIEBKE RUECKERT
  MR. DANIEL KREBBER
FIRST SECRETARY

MR. HENNING SPECK
  MRS. IRINA KAYE SPECK
FIRST SECRETARY

MRS. IRINA KAYE SPECK
  MR. HENNING SPECK
FIRST SECRETARY

MR. TOBIAS CONRAD THOMA
FIRST SECRETARY

MRS. CHARLOTTE SIGRUN VON FRIEDEBURG
  MR. CHRISTOPH VON FRIEDEBURG
FIRST SECRETARY

MS. BEATE WALTER
FIRST SECRETARY

MS. MARTINA URSULA B BOCK DE OLIVEIRA
  MR. JOAO NEREU DE OLIVEIRA
SECOND SECRETARY

DR. OLINA BURKHARDT
SECOND SECRETARY

MRS. MAIKE FRIEDRICHSEN
  MR. JAVIER SALVADOR MARIN ALVARADO
SECOND SECRETARY

MS. VERA MARIA ELSE GEBHARDT
SECOND SECRETARY

MS. KATJA LINDHOLM ERIKSEN
  MR. GUIDO KRUGER
SECOND SECRETARY

MR. HANS PETER SPEYRER
  MS. LIA CAROL SIEGHART
SECOND SECRETARY

MRS. ANJA CYRIAX
  MR. UWE CYRIAX
THIRD SECRETARY

MRS. SUSANNE HOLZEM
  MR. RALF GOTTFRIED HOLZEM
THIRD SECRETARY & VICE CONSUL

MR. ELMAR UDO KOHLHOFER
  MS. SUSANNE MOECK
THIRD SECRETARY

MR. GEORG CHRISTIAN LOTTERMOSER
  MRS. TERRY MEEL LOTTERMOSER*
THIRD SECRETARY

MR. MARTIN KURT PERTSCH
  MRS. DAGMAR MARGOT MARIA PERTSCH
THIRD SECRETARY

MR. PATRICK SCHUH
  MRS. YVONNE SCHUH
THIRD SECRETARY

MR. RENE SCHULA
  MRS. MICHAELA STRAUCH DE SCHULA
THIRD SECRETARY

MR. ANSGAR BERNHARD SITTMANN
  MRS. HEIKE PETRA SITTMANN
THIRD SECRETARY

* U.S. Citizen

MRS. ANKE WAGNER
    MR. CHRISTIAN THEODOR KOHLROSS
THIRD SECRETARY

MR. TORSTEN MICHAEL WEIDEMANN
    MRS. CLAUDIA WEIDEMANN
THIRD SECRETARY

MRS. ESTHER WEISS
THIRD SECRETARY & VICE CONSUL

MR. THOMAS WIEGEL
    MRS. BARBARA WIEGEL
THIRD SECRETARY

MR. FRANK LOTHAR MORITZ
ATTACHE

MS. WENCKE BERGER
ATTACHE

MR. CHRISTIAN HORST BLINDENBACHER
ATTACHE

MRS. ANDREA ANNA HOLZWARTH CORREA
    MR. TULIO HENRIQUE EMILIO LIMA CORREA
ATTACHE

MR. HANS JUERGEN HUEBNER
ATTACHE

MR. WALTER JONAS
    MRS. MARION JONAS
ATTACHE

MR. MATTHIAS KICK
ATTACHE

MR. THOMAS FRANK KORUS
ATTACHE

MR. MARKUS ROBERT KULOSA
ATTACHE

MR. JOHANN GEORG MANDERLA
ATTACHE

MR. MARCUS OTTE
ATTACHE

MR. ALBERT JOHANNES POERSCHKE
ATTACHE

FIRST LIEUTENANT CARSTEN RAABE
    MRS. PIA MEIER RAABE
ATTACHE (DEFENSE)

MR. LARS ENRICO REISSWECK
ATTACHE

MR. UWE SCHIERBAUM
ATTACHE

MR. MIKE TEICHERT
ATTACHE

MASTER SERGEANT MARKUS TORBRUEGGE
    MRS. STEPHANIE TORBRUEGGE
ATTACHE

MR. KLAUS DIETER TRUDEL
    MRS. SALWA BAROODY TRUDEL
ATTACHE

MRS. BEATRIX MARIA URAN
    MR. MEHMET SAIT URAN
ATTACHE

MR. ALFRED KURT WALTER WAGNER
    MRS. SUZANA ROGINA WAGNER
ATTACHE

MR. ANDREAS HERMANN WEISS
ATTACHE

MR. RAINER WOHLTMANN
ATTACHE

MR. KAI ZEHMKE
ATTACHE (SECURITY)

MS. GERTRUD ANTONI
ASST. ATTACHE

MR. EWALD ARENDS
    MRS. NICOLE ARENDS
ASST. ATTACHE

MRS. TATJANA AUBRAC
    MR. GILLES EDMOND LUC AUBRAC
ASST. ATTACHE

MRS. STEFANIE BARUNKE
ASST. ATTACHE

MRS. INGE GERLINDE BLODIG
ASST. ATTACHE

MR. ECKHARD CURSCHMANN
    MRS. PETRA ERIKA CURSCHMANN
ASST. ATTACHE & VICE CONSUL

MRS. KERSTIN EHSER
    MR. OLIVER EHSER
ASST. ATTACHE

MS. SABINE FINKENZELLER
    MR. GILLES JEAN JACQUES LIGEARD
ASST. ATTACHE

MR. STEFAN FORSTER
ASST. ATTACHE

MS. IRIS BRIGITTE FRANK WUERTZ
    MR. HARALD HANS WUERTZ
ASST. ATTACHE

MS. RUTH ELISABETH FREDRICK
    MR. ANIL ERNEST ARTHUR FREDRICK
ASST. ATTACHE

MS. VANESSA CHARLOTTE URSULA FRITSCH
ASST. ATTACHE

MS. NICOLE FUNKE
ASST. ATTACHE

MRS. MARION GIESLER NIMUBONA
    MR. ARNAUD DIEUDONNE NIMUBONA
ASST. ATTACHE

MR. ALEXANDER GLIENKE
ASST. ATTACHE

MS. KATHARINA GOEPFERT
ASST. ATTACHE

MR. OLIVER WOLFGANG GRUNERT
ASST. ATTACHE

MR. JOHANNES AUGUST HASSNER
ASST. ATTACHE (SECURITY)

MRS. KORNELIA HAU ZILIC
    MR. ELVEDIN ZILIC
ASST. ATTACHE

* U.S. Citizen

MR. MARKO HEIDE
ASST. ATTACHE

MR. STEFFEN HERMANN
ASST. ATTACHE

MS. CAROLIN KEIL
ASST. ATTACHE

MR. ROLAND KLEIN
MRS. ASTRID KLEIN
ASST. ATTACHE

MR. CHRISTIAN KRIPS
ASST. ATTACHE ((SECURITY))

MRS. MELANIE KUNKEL
MR. FRANK KUNKEL
ASST. ATTACHE

MR. KARSTEN MANKE
MRS. NOREEN MANKE
ASST. ATTACHE

MRS. KATHRIN MATHOW
ASST. ATTACHE

MR. LARS HELMUT MELCHER
MRS. JESSICA QUADE
ASST. ATTACHE

MR. MARTIN MEYROSE
MRS. ALONA LEON
ASST. ATTACHE

MS. ANDREA NISSEN
ASST. ATTACHE

MRS. MONIQUE PETERSEN
MR. LARS PETERSEN
ASST. ATTACHE

MS. BIRGIT HELENE PETOECZ
MR. DANIEL FRANZ PETOECZ
ASST. ATTACHE

MR. RALF PICKEL
ASST. ATTACHE

MR. FALK PIWNY
ASST. ATTACHE

MRS. ANKE REED
ASST. ATTACHE

MR. GUENTHER BERNHARD ANDREAS RIEGEL
MRS. SHARON RIEGEL
ASST. ATTACHE

MRS. MONICA MARIA SCHMIDT
ASST. ATTACHE

SERGEANT MAJOR GREGOR SCHULZ
MRS. NINA SCHULZ
ASST. ATTACHE (DEFENSE)

MR. BERND SCHULZE HOLZ
MRS. SYLVIA BARBARA ANGELIKA HOLZ
ASST. ATTACHE

MR. RONALD THIMIAN
ASST. ATTACHE

MRS. NICOLE TORRES Y BULSIEWICZ
MR. ZACARIAS GARCIA GONZALEZ
ASST. ATTACHE

* U.S. Citizen

MRS. BARBARA WIEGEL
MR. THOMAS WIEGEL
ASST. ATTACHE

MR. LOTHAR RUDOLF WILDE
MRS. REGINA MARIA WILDE
ASST. ATTACHE

MR. ERIK WILLIG
ASST. ATTACHE

MR. RALF WOESSNER
MRS. HARDIP KAUR WOESSNER
ASST. ATTACHE

BRIGADIER GENERAL DIRK HEINRICH BACKEN
MRS. KATJA BACKEN
DEFENSE ATTACHE

COLONEL KLAUS WERNER FINCK
MRS. ELISABETH MARIA FINCK
MILITARY ATTACHE & ASST. DEFENSE ATTACHE

COLONEL HUBERT SAUR
MRS. MEIKE TORST SAUR
ASST. DEFENSE & AIR ATTACHE

LIEUTENANT COLONEL ERIC OFFERMANN
MRS. GERIT KATHARINA OFFERMANN
ASST. MILITARY ATTACHE

COMMANDER TOBIAS VOSS
MRS. ELENA KLINKMANN VOSS
ASST. NAVAL ATTACHE

CAPTAIN KARL MICHAEL SETZER
MRS. GABRIELE SETZER
NAVAL ATTACHE & ASST. DEFENSE ATTACHE

LIEUTENANT COLONEL THOMAS FREIHERR VON MALTZAHN
MRS. UTE FREIFRAU VON MALTZAHN
ASST. AIR ATTACHE

GHANA

EMBASSY OF GHANA
Chancery: 3512 INTERNATIONAL DRIVE, NW 20008
(EMBASSY 202-686-4520) (FAX 202-686-4527)

HIS EXCELLENCY DANIEL OHENE AGYEKUM
MRS. ROSE OHENE AGYEKUM
AMBASSADOR EXTRAORDINARY & PLENIPOTENTIARY

MRS. EDITH HAZEL
MR. KODJO HAZEL
MINISTER (DEPUTY CHIEF OF MISSION)

MR. EBENEZER PADI ADJIRACKOR
MRS. LINDA ARABA ABOKUMA ADJIRACKOR
MINISTER (COMMERCIAL)

MS. AMMA ADOMAA TWUM AMOAH
MINISTER

MR. WILLIAM ANANI ABOTSI
MRS. FRANKLYN MARIAN ANANI ABOTSI
MINISTER-COUNSELOR

MR. EMMANUEL OPEKU
MRS. BRENDA AKOSUA OPEKU
MINISTER-COUNSELOR

MR. KWADWO ANTWI BOATENG
    MRS. MILLICENT NAA BOATENG
COUNSELOR

MRS. VANESSA AKOSUA MENSAH ADU
    MR. PHILIP KWASI ADU
COUNSELOR

MS. MAVIS ENYOANM ADZO AKPABLA
FIRST SECRETARY

MR. JOHN ADJEI AMANKWAH
    MRS. PATIENCE AFI AMANKWAH
FIRST SECRETARY

MS. THEODORA DUNCAN OCQUAYE
FIRST SECRETARY

MR. CHRISTIAN NARH
    MS. BRIDGET NARH
FIRST SECRETARY

MRS. GIFTY TAKYIWAA OCRAN
    MR. ALFRED FIIFI OCRAN
FIRST SECRETARY

MS. REBECCA ENYONAM KUDEKOR
THIRD SECRETARY

MR. BENNETT AKANTOA
ATTACHE

BRIGADIER GENERAL GEORGE EDUAM AMAMOO
    MRS. AGNES OPPONG PEPRAH
DEFENSE, MILITARY, NAVAL & AIR ATTACHE

GREECE

EMBASSY OF GREECE
Chancery: 2217 MASSACHUSETTS AVENUE, NW 20008
(EMBASSY 202-939-1300)   (FAX 202-939-1324)

HIS EXCELLENCY CHRISTOS PANAGOPOULOS
AMBASSADOR EXTRAORDINARY & PLENIPOTENTIARY

MRS. SOPHIA PHILIPPIDOU
MINISTER (DEPUTY CHIEF OF MISSION)

MS. IOANNA KRIEBARDI
COUNSELOR

MR. NIKOLAOS KRIKOS
    MRS. MARIA PATILI
COUNSELOR

MR. ANTONIOS MARMARINOS
COUNSELOR (EDUCATIONAL AFFAIRS)

MR. ANTONIOS PAPAKOSTAS
COUNSELOR

MRS. EFTYCHIA XYDIA
    MR. DIMITRIOS VERGITSIS
FIRST SECRETARY

MS. CHRISTINA GEORGIOU
SECOND SECRETARY

MR. ANASTASIOS KEZAS
SECOND SECRETARY

MR. KONSTANTINOS KYRIOU
    MRS. ARTEMIS KONTI
SECOND SECRETARY

MR. CHARALAMPOS PAPADOPOULOS
    MRS. NESTORIA POGKA
THIRD SECRETARY (ECONOMIC & COMMERCIAL)

MRS. ALEXANDRA ADODO
    MR. CHRISTOPHER OGKOGIAFENTO ADODO
ATTACHE

MS. MARIA ARVANITI
ATTACHE

MR. KONSTANTINOS DIMITRIADIS
    MRS. SOFIA KARABATZAKI
ATTACHE (INFORMATION, TECHNOLOGY & TELECOMMUNICATIONS)

MS. MARIA GALANOU
ATTACHE (PRESS)

MRS. ARTEMIS KONTI
    MR. KONSTANTINOS KYRIOU
ATTACHE

MS. MARGO KOUMANAKOS
ATTACHE (PRESS)

MR. NICOLAOS MYLONAS
    MRS. KYRIACOULA MYLONA
ATTACHE (ADMINISTRATIVE)

MR. PERIKLIS PARAPONIARIS
    MRS. IVANA JEANNETTE PARAPONIARI
ATTACHE

COLONEL EVANGELOS PAPADOPOULOS
    MRS. SOFIA ISMIROGLOU
DEFENSE & MILITARY ATTACHE

CAPTAIN GEORGE MATARANGAS
NAVAL ATTACHE

COLONEL GEORGIOS KATSANIS
    MRS. YPERMACHIA KOSMIDOU
AIR ATTACHE

COMMERCIAL, CONSULAR, ED, ECON & PRESS & INFO OFFICES
2211 MASSACHUSETTS AVENUE, NW 20008
(OFFICE 202-232-8222)

DEFENSE, MILITARY, NAVAL AND AIR ATTACHE OFFICE
2228 MASSACHUSETTS AVENUE, NW 20008
(OFFICE 202-234-0561)

GRENADA

EMBASSY OF GRENADA
Chancery: 1701 NEW HAMPSHIRE AVENUE, NW 20009
(EMBASSY 202-265-2561)   (FAX 202-265-2468)

HER EXCELLENCY GILLIAN MARGARET SUSAN BRISTOL
AMBASSADOR EXTRAORDINARY & PLENIPOTENTIARY

MS. PATRICIA DAPHNE MARCELLE CLARKE
COUNSELOR

* U.S. Citizen

GUATEMALA

EMBASSY OF GUATEMALA
Chancery: 2220 R STREET, NW 20008
(EMBASSY 202-745-4952)   (FAX 202-745-1908)

HIS EXCELLENCY JOSE FRANCISCO VILLAGRAN DE LEON
MRS. DONNA SUE EBERWINE VILLAGRAN*
AMBASSADOR EXTRAORDINARY & PLENIPOTENTIARY

MR. FERNANDO DE LA CERDA BICKFORD
CAPTAIN MARIA R. AGUILAR DE DE LA CERDA
MINISTER-COUNSELOR

MS. ANA SOFIA PORRES BUSTAMANTE
COUNSELOR

MR. EDGAR MANUEL VILLANUEVA SOSA
MRS. R. MORENO CARRERA DE VILLANUEVA
COUNSELOR

MR. EDWIN ROLANDO CHACON CORADO
MRS. IRENE FILOMENA CHACON
FIRST SECRETARY & CONSUL

MRS. MIRIAM LETICIA DE LEON ESCOBAR
MR. JORGE JACINTO RODRIGUEZ SANCHEZ
FIRST SECRETARY

MRS. MARIA C. HERNANDEZ
MR. OSCAR MAYNOR HERNANDEZ*
FIRST SECRETARY

MISS DINA LUCIA ZEPEDA FALLA
FIRST SECRETARY

MISS MARIA EUGENIA ALVAREZ RUIZ
SECOND SECRETARY

MRS. KARLA ROBERTHA ARANA DE JUAREZ
MR. DANILO BERNAL JUAREZ*
SECOND SECRETARY

MR. EDGAR MARTIN MEJIA OVANDO
THIRD SECRETARY

MS. AURA ROXANNA MONTERROZA GARCIA
THIRD SECRETARY

MRS. MARTA REGINA FISCHER DE FERNANDEZ
MR. FRANCISCO E. FERNANDEZ HOLLMANN
ATTACHE (CULTURAL)

MR. JOSE GABRIEL LAMBOUR PENALONZO
ATTACHE (COMMERCIAL)

BRIGADIER GENERAL ODBER ENRIQUE ARGUETA MERIDA
MRS. ILMA JANET GALINDO DE ARGUETA
DEFENSE, MILITARY & NAVAL ATTACHE

COLONEL GABRIEL OBDULIO PORTILLO ARRIAZA
MS. ONELIA EDITH ORELLANA DE PORTILLO
AIR ATTACHE

COLONEL GUILLERMO ALFREDO OROZCO RODAS
ASST. DEFENSE, MILITARY & AIR ATTACHE

COMMERICAL ATTACHE OFFICE
2220 R STREET, NW 20008

CONSULAR SECTION
8124 GEORGIA AVENUE
SILVER SPRING, MD 20910
(OFFICE 240-485-5050)

DEFENSE, MILITARY, NAVAL AND AIR ATTACHE OFFICE
2220 R STREET, NW 20008
(OFFICE 202-232-2226)

GUINEA

EMBASSY OF THE REPUBLIC OF GUINEA
Chancery: 2112 LEROY PLACE, NW 20008
(EMBASSY 202-986-4300)   (FAX 202-986-3800)

HIS EXCELLENCY BLAISE CHERIF
MRS. CECILE CHERIF
AMBASSADOR EXTRAORDINARY & PLENIPOTENTIARY

MR. ELHADJ BOUBACAR BARRY
MRS. HADJA OUSSAMATOU BALDE
COUNSELOR

MS. BINTOU CONDE
COUNSELOR (ECONOMIC)

MRS. OUMOU THIAM HANN
COUNSELOR

MRS. AMINATA KOITA
MR. MAMADOU THIAM KASSE
COUNSELOR (POLITICAL AFFAIRS)

MR. THIERNO ABDOURAMAMAN BALDE
MRS. SANTOU TRAORE
FIRST SECRETARY (CULTURAL)

MR. ALY CAMARA
MRS. MABINTY CAMARA
FIRST SECRETARY

MS. CATHERINE SAGNO
FIRST SECRETARY (CULTURAL & SOCIAL AFFAIRS)

GUINEA-BISSAU

EMBASSY OF THE REPUBLIC OF GUINEA-BISSAU
Chancery: P.O. Box 33813 20033
(EMBASSY 301-947-3958)

GUYANA

EMBASSY OF GUYANA
Chancery: 2490 TRACY PLACE, NW 20008
(EMBASSY 202-265-6900)   (FAX 202-232-1297)

HIS EXCELLENCY BAYNEY RAM KARRAN
MRS. DONNA KARRAN
AMBASSADOR EXTRAORDINARY & PLENIPOTENTIARY

MR. FORBES EGERTON JULY
MRS. VALENTINA JULY
FIRST SECRETARY (DEPUTY CHIEF OF MISSION)

MRS. CANDIDA ONEKA DANIELS
FIRST SECRETARY

MS. SONIA ANTOINETTE CALLENDER
ATTACHE (FINANCIAL)

* U.S. Citizen

HAITI

EMBASSY OF THE REPUBLIC OF HAITI
Chancery: 2311 MASSACHUSETTS AVENUE, NW 20008
(EMBASSY 202-332-4090)   (FAX 202-745-7215)

HIS EXCELLENCY PAUL GETTY ALTIDOR
AMBASSADOR EXTRAORDINARY & PLENIPOTENTIARY

MR. ASBOUN JEAN WILLIAM EXANTUS
MRS. GINA EXANTUS BERNARD
MINISTER-COUNSELOR (DEPUTY CHIEF OF MISSION)

MRS. JOCELINE BLEMUR
MINISTER-COUNSELOR

MR. PIERRE MAX CHARLES
MINISTER-COUNSELOR

MR. RALPH RICARDO JEAN PHILIPPE
MRS. ALEXANDRE UDELGARDE*
COUNSELOR (ADMINISTRATION)

MR. SONY ELIAS
MRS. LUCIE ELIAS LORMESTOIR
FIRST SECRETARY

MS. EVICE GUERCIN
FIRST SECRETARY

MRS. MARIE CLAUDE MALEBRANCHE
FIRST SECRETARY (COMMERCIAL)

MRS. WILZA METELLUS FRAZIL
MR. ALFRED FILS METELLUS
FIRST SECRETARY

COMMERCIAL ATTACHE OFFICE
2311 MASSACHUSETTS AVENUE, NW 20008
(OFFICE 202-332-4090)

CONSULAR AFFAIRS OFFICE
2311 MASSACHUSETTS AVENUE, NW 20008
(OFFICE 202-332-4090)

MILITARY ATTACHE OFFICE
2311 MASSACHUSETTS AVENUE, NW 20008
(OFFICE 202-332-4165)

HOLY SEE

APOSTOLIC NUNCIATURE
Chancery: 3339 MASSACHUSETTS AVENUE, NW 20008
(EMBASSY 202-333-7121)   (FAX 202-337-4036)

HIS EXCELLENCY REVEREND CARLO MARIA VIGANO
APOSTOLIC NUNCIO

REVEREND MONSIGNOR ANGELO ACCATTINO
COUNSELOR

REVEREND MONSIGNOR JEAN FRANCOIS LANTHEAUME
COUNSELOR

REVEREND MONSIGNOR FERMIN EMILIO SOSA RODRIGUEZ
COUNSELOR

HONDURAS

EMBASSY OF HONDURAS
Chancery: 3007 TILDEN STREET, NW, SUITE 4-M 20008
(EMBASSY 202-966-2604)   (FAX 202-966-9751)

HIS EXCELLENCY JORGE RAMON HERNANDEZ ALCERRO
MRS. MARIZA VEIGA PINO
AMBASSADOR EXTRAORDINARY & PLENIPOTENTIARY

MR. LUIS FERNANDO SUAZO BARAHONA
MRS. LARISSA KARINA PINEDA DIAZ
MINISTER (DEPUTY CHIEF OF MISSION)

MR. RICARDO GUILLERMO ESTRADA SARAVIA
MRS. ALBA LUZ SOLIS GARRIDO
MINISTER

MR. JORGE ALBERTO MILLA REYES
MINISTER

MRS. NORMA ALLEGRA CERRATO SABILLON
MINISTER-COUNSELOR (LEGAL AFFAIRS)

MRS. TANIA ROBERTA LAZARUS CALLEJAS
MINISTER-COUNSELOR

MR. JOSE RAMON PAZ MORALES
MRS. DANIELA PALACIOS CORRALES
MINISTER-COUNSELOR

MR. LEONARDO IRIAS NAVAS
MRS. NORMA DOLORES UCLES ACOSTA
COUNSELOR (CONSULAR AFFAIRS)

MR. PABLO MARIO ORDONEZ GUZMAN
MRS. CINTHYA MARIA ALVARADO TORRES
COUNSELOR (COMMERCIAL ADVISOR)

MR. ALLAN GILBERTO AGURCIA PAZ
MRS. IRIS ALEJANDRA RAPALO MARTINEZ
FIRST SECRETARY

MISS TANIA VANESSA MARIA A. CASCO RUBI
FIRST SECRETARY

MRS. DANIELA PALACIOS CORRALES
MR. JOSE RAMON PAZ MORALES
FIRST SECRETARY

MR. UILLERMO AUGUSTO PEREZCADALSO PAZ
FIRST SECRETARY

MRS. ISIS AGUILAR ZELAYA
MR. TROY DONNOVAN HAYNES*
SECOND SECRETARY

MRS. SOFIA CERNA RUBINSTEIN
SECOND SECRETARY

MR. LUIS FERNANDO CORDERO MONTOYA
MRS. DANEA DESSHIREE TREJO CARCAMO
SECOND SECRETARY

MISS KAROL MARCELA ESCALANTE HERRERA
SECOND SECRETARY

MR. MARCELINO PINEDA CARCAMO
SECOND SECRETARY (CONSULAR AFFAIRS)

MR. WALTER ROSENDO LEIVA ARDON
ATTACHE (CULTURAL)

* U.S. Citizen

COLONEL ADAN HILARIO SUAZO MOLINA
  MRS. MARCIA MARLENE HERNANDEZ PORTILLO
  DEFENSE, MILITARY, NAVAL & AIR ATTACHE

CONSULAR SECTION
  1014 M STREET, NW, FLOOR 2ND 20001
    (OFFICE 202-682-5947)   (FAX 202-737-2907)

MILITARY ATTACHE
  3007 TILDEN STREET, NW, SUITE 4M 20008
    (OFFICE 202-686-0352)   (FAX 202-966-9751)

HUNGARY

EMBASSY OF HUNGARY
Chancery: 3910 SHOEMAKER STREET, NW 20008
(EMBASSY 202-362-6730)   (FAX 202-966-8135)

HIS EXCELLENCY GYOERGY BELA SZAPARY
  AMBASSADOR EXTRAORDINARY & PLENIPOTENTIARY

MR. ANDRAS TIBOR BACSI NAGY
  MRS. LOTTI LILLA LETANOCZKY
  COUNSELOR (DEPUTY CHIEF OF MISSION)

MRS. KATALIN BALOGNE CSORBA
  MR. LASZLO ISTVAN BALOG
  COUNSELOR

MR. JOZSEF ELEK
  MRS. ILDIKO ELEKNE KAMAN
  COUNSELOR

MR. ISTVAN SANDOR
  MRS. ILDIKO SANDORNE TREFAS
  COUNSELOR & CONSUL

DR. GYORGY RETHAZI
  DR. ESZTER RETHAZI
  FIRST SECRETARY

MR. ANDRAS SZORENYI
  MRS. JUDIT KOZENKOW
  FIRST SECRETARY

MR. PETER VALENTOVICS
  MRS. PETERNE VALENTOVICS
  FIRST SECRETARY (FINANCIAL)

MR. MIHALY DANIEL MANCHIN
  SECOND SECRETARY

MR. FERENC KALMAR
  THIRD SECRETARY

MR. AKOS VEISZ
  THIRD SECRETARY

MR. JOZSEF CZIMER
  ATTACHE (COMMUNICATIONS)

MS. ANNA STUMPF
  ATTACHE

COLONEL ZOLTAN BONE
  MRS. TUNDE MINDSZENTY
  DEFENSE, MILITARY & AIR ATTACHE

MAJOR BALAZS SZEKERES
  MRS. ANDREA MAGDOLNA SZEKERES
  ASST. DEFENSE, MILITARY & AIR ATTACHE

COMMERCIAL OFFICE
  150 E. 58TH STREET, FLOOR 33RD
  NEW YORK, NY 10155--3398
    (OFFICE 212-752-3060)   (FAX 212-486-2958)

MILITARY AND AIR ATTACHE OFFICE
  3910 SHOEMAKER STREET, NW 20008
    (OFFICE 202-362-6730)

ICELAND

EMBASSY OF ICELAND
Chancery: 2900 K STREET, NW, SUITE 509 20007
(EMBASSY 202-265-6653)   (FAX 202-265-6656)

HIS EXCELLENCY GUDMUNDUR ARNI STEFANSSON
  MRS. JONA DORA KARLSDOTTIR
  AMBASSADOR EXTRAORDINARY & PLENIPOTENTIARY

MR. SKAFTI JONSSON
  MRS. KRISTIN THORSTEINSDOTTIR
  COUNSELOR (DEPUTY CHIEF OF MISSION)

MR. ERLINGUR ERLINGSSON
  COUNSELOR

MR. BALDVIN JONSSON
  MRS. MARGRET BJORNSDOTTIR
  ATTACHE (AGRICULTURAL)

MR. TOMAS ARMANN TOMASSON
  MS. HJORDIS GUNNARSDOTTIR
  ATTACHE

INDIA

EMBASSY OF INDIA
Chancery: 2107 MASSACHUSETTS AVENUE, NW 20008
(EMBASSY 202-939-7000)   (FAX 202-483-3972)

HER EXCELLENCY NIRUPAMA RAO
  MR. SUDHAKAR RAO
  AMBASSADOR EXTRAORDINARY & PLENIPOTENTIARY

MR. ARUN KUMAR SINGH
  MRS. MAINA CHAWLA SINGH
  MINISTER (DEPUTY CHIEF OF MISSION)

MRS. BANASHRI BOSE HARRISON
  MR. GARETH ROBERT HARRISON
  MINISTER (COMMERCE)

MR. VINAY MOHAN KWATRA
  MRS. POOJA KWATRA
  MINISTER (COMMERCE)

MR. POOVAKULATH JOSEPH MATHEW
  MRS. JANET MATHEW
  MINISTER (DIRECTOR OF AUDIT)

MR. GOVIND MOHAN
  MRS. MADHAVI CHANDRA
  MINISTER

MR. DATTATRAYA PADSALGIKAR
  MRS. ADITEE PADSALGIKAR
  MINISTER (PERSONNEL&COMM AFFRS)

* U.S. Citizen

MR. PRAVIR PANDEY
     MRS. ANSHU SHUKLA PANDEY
MINISTER

MR. FNU VEDIAPPA SHANMUGHAM SENTHIL
     MRS. FNU SUJATHA RAMDAS
MINISTER

MR. ANKINI PRASAD NALLAPATI
     MRS. RAMADEVI NALLAPATI
MINISTER-COUNSELOR

MR. ALASUBRAMANIAN GANGADHARAN
     MRS. MA BALASUBRAMANIAN
COUNSELOR

MR. RAHUL CHHABRA
     MRS. KAVITA CHHABRA
COUNSELOR

MR. SUDHAKAR DALELA
     MRS. NAMRATA DALELA
COUNSELOR

MR. RANJIT ELIAS
     MRS. ISABELLA ELIAS
COUNSELOR

MRS. SUKRITI LIKHI
     MR. ABHILAKSH LIKHI
COUNSELOR

MR. KUMARAN PERIASAMY
     MRS. RITU KUMARAN
COUNSELOR

MR. RITHWIK RUDRA
     MRS. ANURADHA THAKUR
COUNSELOR

MR. ASHUTOSH SHARMA
     MRS. NIDHI SINGH
COUNSELOR

MR. VIVEK SINGH
     MRS. ANAMIKA SINGH
COUNSELOR

MR. NAVEEN SRIVASTAVA
     MRS. PUNYA SALILA SRIVASTAVA
COUNSELOR

MR. PRANAY KUMAR VERMA
     MRS. MANU VERMA
COUNSELOR (POLITICAL)

MR. AJAY KUMAR
     MRS. NIRMALA AGRAWAL
FIRST SECRETARY

MR. MURLI MANOHAR ISSAR
     MRS. NIVEDITA ISSAR
SECOND SECRETARY

MR. VISHAL VISHWANATH NAIR
THIRD SECRETARY

MRS. SAROJ ARORA
     MR. BALDEV RAJ ARORA
ATTACHE

MR. HARISH BAXLA
     MRS. NIRMALA BAXLA
ATTACHE

MR. ADITYA KUMAR BERWAL
     MRS. SAHIRA BERWAL
ATTACHE

* U.S. Citizen

MR. NIKHILESH MOHAN DHIRAR
     MRS. MADHU DHIRAR
ATTACHE

MR. ANIL GARG
     MRS. MADHURIKA GARG
ATTACHE

MR. MANJISH GROVER
     MRS. SUBEENA GROVER
ATTACHE

MR. KRISHNA NAND JHA
     MRS. ANUDITA JHA
ATTACHE

MR. ALOK KUMAR
     MRS. GEETA SAXENA
ATTACHE

MOST REVEREND FNU LALIT KUMAR
     MRS. PAWAN SHARMA
ATTACHE

MR. NAVEEN MONGA
     MRS. SANGEETA MONGA
ATTACHE

MR. RAJENDRANATHAN NARAYANAN NAIR
     MRS. SNEHALATA RAJENDRAN
ATTACHE

MR. AMAN NARULA
ATTACHE

MR. SANDEEP RAYA PAI
     MRS. SUJATA PAI
ATTACHE (ASSISTANT ACCOUNTS OFFICER)

MR. ISWANATHAN PUTHENPEEDIKAYIL RAMAN
     MRS. USHA VISWANATHAN
ATTACHE

MR. FNU RAJBIR
     MRS. FNU DARSHWATI
ATTACHE

MR. PARAMESWARA PANICKER SANKAR
     MRS. VIJAYA SHANKAR
ATTACHE

MR. ASHOK KUMAR SHARMA
ATTACHE

MRS. DIPALI SHARMA
     MR. ASHOK KUMAR SHARMA
ATTACHE

MR. GAUR CHANDRA TALUKDAR
     MRS. RAMA TALUKDAR
ATTACHE

MR. KIRTICHANDRA JAMES TETE
     MRS. KUSUM TETE
ATTACHE (ADMINISTRATION)

MR. MANOJ BIHARI VERMA
     MRS. POONAM VERMA
ATTACHE

MR. FNU VIJAY KUMAR
     MRS. NEEMA BISHT
ATTACHE

COMMODORE ALOK BHATNAGAR
     MRS. DEEPA BHATNAGAR
NAVAL ATTACHE

AIR COMMODORE SANJAY NIMESH
    MRS. RICHA KHATTAR NIMESH
AIR ATTACHE

COMMERCIAL AND SUPPLY, PASSPORT AND VISA SECTION
2536 MASSACHUSETTS AVENUE, NW 20008
(OFFICE 202-939-9806)

INDONESIA

EMBASSY OF THE REPUBLIC OF INDONESIA
Chancery: 2020 MASSACHUSETTS AVENUE, NW 20036
(EMBASSY 202-775-5200)   (FAX 202-775-5365)

HIS EXCELLENCY DINO PATTI DJALAL
    MRS. ROSA RAI DJALAL
AMBASSADOR EXTRAORDINARY & PLENIPOTENTIARY

MR. WIWIT WIRSATYO
    MRS. ANITA MAGDARINA WIRSATYO
MINISTER (DEPUTY CHIEF OF MISSION)

MR. MOHAMMAD BENYAMIN SCOTT CARNADI
    MRS. ESTHER ZARAH CARNADI
COUNSELOR

MR. SAUD PURWANTO KRISNAWAN
    MRS. DYAH PRAWITA KRISNAWAN
COUNSELOR

MR. CAHYO RAHADIAN MUZHAR
    MRS. KOOSKARDINA ENDANG M. MUZHAR
COUNSELOR

MR. PARTOGI JAN PIETER SAMOSIR
    MRS. JUNI MARDALENA
COUNSELOR (CONSULAR)

MR. HERU HARTANTO SUBOLO
    MRS. SINTA EKAWATI
COUNSELOR (INFORMATION)

MR. ADAM MULAWARMAN TUGIO
    MRS. IRINA EKA MAULIYANTI
COUNSELOR

MR. YUSRON BAHAUDDIN AMBARY
    MRS. RAOKHATI QISTIN YUSRON
FIRST SECRETARY

MS. ZELDA WULAN KARTIKA
FIRST SECRETARY

MR. RIZAL RAHPINUJI RISNAADH WIRAKARA
FIRST SECRETARY

MS. POPPY YEANNY
FIRST SECRETARY

MR. FEBBY ANDRYANANTO
    MS. VALERINA DANIEL
THIRD SECRETARY

MR. ABDUL GAFUR
    MRS. NUNIEK ANDAYANI
THIRD SECRETARY

MR. VAHD NABYL ACHMAD MULACHELA
THIRD SECRETARY

MS. NUR EVI RAHMAWATI
THIRD SECRETARY

MS. NOVIASARI RUSTAM
THIRD SECRETARY

MRS. DARA YUSILAWATI
    MR. MOHAMAD FAISOL AMRULLAH
THIRD SECRETARY

MR. DANY PUS APRIYANTO
ATTACHE

MS. NI MADE AYU MARTHINI
ATTACHE (COMMERCIAL)

MR. ACHMAD RACHMAN
    MRS. INA MUKHAIMINAH
ATTACHE (AGRICULTURE)

MR. SUHASNA ANWAR SANUSI
    MRS. SUSI HANDRIANI
ATTACHE

MR. I WAYAN SUDIARTHA
    MRS. NI MADE SUCIATI
ATTACHE (TRANS AND COMM)

MR. HARYO WINARSO
    MRS. AMENDA MUIS WINARSO
ATTACHE (EDUCATION & CULTURE)

BRIGADIER GENERAL FNU WITJAKSONO
    MRS. SOESETIOWATI WITJAKSONO
DEFENSE & MILITARY ATTACHE

COLONEL FNU HALILI
    MRS. DEWI SRI MARJANI
NAVAL ATTACHE

MR. BENEDICTUS BENNY KOESSETIANTO
    MRS. MARIA REGINA JUITA SETYANINGTYAS
AIR ATTACHE

IRAQ

EMBASSY OF THE REPUBLIC OF IRAQ
Chancery: 3421 MASSACHUSETTS AVENUE, NW 20007
(EMBASSY 202-742-1600)   (FAX 202-462-5066)

HIS EXCELLENCY JABIR HABEB JABIR HEMAIDAWI
    MRS. NAHLAH ABDULATEEF S. AL NUAIMI
AMBASSADOR EXTRAORDINARY & PLENIPOTENTIARY

MR. SAID SHIHAB AHMAD
    MRS. SADIA A. KHAMIS
MINISTER

MR. FAIZ A. K. AL GAILANI
    MRS. GULALA D. A. BABAN
MINISTER

MR. EZZADDIN RASHID HAJI HAJI
COUNSELOR

MS. ALAA HASSAN MOHAMMAD ALOBEIDI
FIRST SECRETARY

MR. MOHSIN ALI RAJAB RAJAB
    MRS. KHILOOD HAMEED HASSAN HASSAN
FIRST SECRETARY (FINANCIAL)

MRS. HALIZ AHMED MOHAMED SEMO
    MR. SALAR ABDOLKAREEM A. AL SHEKH
FIRST SECRETARY

* U.S. Citizen

MR. ZAIDOON A. ABDUL WAHAB
    MRS. SAMAR BASHIR AL KAISI
SECOND SECRETARY

MR. MOHAMMED HUSHAM MALIK AL FITYAN
    MS. SURA ISMAEIL ABDULLAZIZ
SECOND SECRETARY

MR. WAEL G. AL ROBAAIE
    MS. ZENA MAHDY HASOON HASOON
SECOND SECRETARY

MS. RAGHAD ALI HASAN HASAN
SECOND SECRETARY

MR. OSAMA MOHAMMED SAMI SAMI
    MRS. MAY MARROUF IBRAHIM AL RAWI
SECOND SECRETARY

MISS BAIDAA KADHOM A. ABDULKAREEM
THIRD SECRETARY

MS. HIND MOHAMED OMER AL DOSKI
THIRD SECRETARY

MR. HUSSEIN AL FEKEKY
    MRS. OLLA SAMI RAOOF AL ARAJI
THIRD SECRETARY

MR. ISSAM MOHAMMED AL JIBOORI
    MS. VENOS NIAZ TAKI TAKI
THIRD SECRETARY

MR. ATHEER ABOOD SAEED AL SAEDY
    MRS. RASHA FAISAL MAJEED AL RUBAIE
THIRD SECRETARY

MR. MOHAMMAD ADNAN MOHAMMAD AL WAHAIB
THIRD SECRETARY

MR. MOHAMMED ABDULRAHMAN ALAUBIDY
    MRS. ASSMAA KHALID AWAD ALAUBIDY
THIRD SECRETARY

MR. RAWAND ANWAR ABDULLAH DESAI
    MRS. SURA SALAH A. SALAM AL AZZAWI
THIRD SECRETARY

MR. ATHIR HILLAL FLAIH
THIRD SECRETARY

MR. AHMED M. NAJATI MOHSIN M AGHA
    MRS. RIMA A. ABDULRAZZAQ
THIRD SECRETARY

MRS. SAMA SALIM POULES POULES
    MR. SEBASTIAN TALAT SHABU MARCUS
THIRD SECRETARY

MR. AMMAR SABAH MUSTAFA AL DURRA
ATTACHE

MR. ALI ZUHAIR FADHIL AL GHARBAWI
ATTACHE

DR. ABDUL HADI AL KHALILI
    MRS. HANAN SADIQ M SAEED ALKHALILI
ATTACHE (CULTURAL)

MR. ANAS ABDUL LATEEF MOHI AL NEIAMI
ATTACHE

MR. MUSLIM SALMAN HAMZAH AL OBAIDI
ATTACHE (COMMERCIAL)

MR. AMJAD ABDULHAMED JAAFER RAJEB
    MRS. WASAN MOHAMED KUDHER AL AUKAILI
ATTACHE (COMMERCIAL)

* U.S. Citizen

MR. JALAL MAJEED SHAREEF SHAREEF
    MRS. GASHAW MOHAMMED FARAJ FAQI SHALLY
ATTACHE (CULTURAL)

MR. AMMAR AZEEZ MOHAMMED A AL SAHRAWI
    MRS. QABAS HUSSEIN MOHAMMED AL HELLI
ASST. ATTACHE (CULTURAL)

BRIGADIER GENERAL ALI M SALIM ALI BAHJAT AL AARAGY
    MRS. IBTIHAL H. MAJEED MAJEED
DEFENSE, MILITARY, NAVAL & AIR ATTACHE

BRIGADIER GENERAL RAMADHAN M. ABDAL AL KOCHER
    MRS. DILSHAD M. MOMEN
MILITARY ATTACHE

COLONEL MAZIN SUHIL MOHAMMED S. AL JAAF
    MRS. IBTISAM RIDHA JASIM ALGANMI
ASST. DEFENSE & MILITARY ATTACHE

COLONEL KHALID ABBAS MAHMOOD AL JANABI
    MRS. SUHA KADHIM SADEQ AL OBAIDI
ASST. DEFENSE & MILITARY ATTACHE

CULTURAL OFFICE
    1101 14TH STREET, NW, SUITE 710 20005
      (OFFICE 202-986-2626)

MILITARY OFFICE
    2600 VIRGINIA AVENUE, NW, SUITE 600 20037

IRELAND

EMBASSY OF IRELAND
Chancery: 2234 MASSACHUSETTS AVENUE, NW 20008
(EMBASSY 202-462-3939)   (FAX 202-232-5993)

HIS EXCELLENCY MICHAEL COLLINS
    MRS. MARIE COLLINS
AMBASSADOR EXTRAORDINARY & PLENIPOTENTIARY

MR. KEVIN FRANCIS CONMY
    MS. SIOBHAN MARY CAMPBELL
COUNSELOR (DEPUTY CHIEF OF MISSION)

MR. NIALL PATRICK BRADY
FIRST SECRETARY

MR. JOHN VINCENT DARDIS
    MS. CAOIMHE DARDIS
FIRST SECRETARY (AGRICULTURE)

MR. DEREK HANNON
FIRST SECRETARY (POLITICAL)

MS. CATHERINE OCONNOR
    MR. COLM MCCABE
FIRST SECRETARY (INFORMATION & COMMUNICATION)

MR. EAMON JOHN SAUNDERS
    MS. BRIDE SAUNDERS
FIRST SECRETARY (JUSTICE)

MR. RALPH JAMES VICTORY
    MRS. KAREN ANNE VICTORY
FIRST SECRETARY (PRESS & INFO.)

MS. DEIRDRE BOURKE
THIRD SECRETARY

MS. LYNDA CARROLL
ATTACHE (ADMINISTRATIVE)

ISRAEL

EMBASSY OF ISRAEL
Chancery: 3514 INTERNATIONAL DRIVE, NW 20008
(EMBASSY 202-364-5500)   (FAX 202-364-5607)

HIS EXCELLENCY MICHAEL SCOTT OREN
    MRS. SALLY ANN OREN*
AMBASSADOR EXTRAORDINARY & PLENIPOTENTIARY

MR. BARUKH BINAH
    MRS. SHULAMIT BINAH
MINISTER (DEPUTY CHIEF OF MISSION)

MR. BOONI COHAVI
    MRS. NAAMA ZUSSMAN COHAVI
MINISTER (ADMIN.) & CONSUL

MR. ELIYAHU GRONER
    MRS. TAMAR GRONER*
MINISTER (ECONOMIC AFFAIRS)

MR. NOAM KATZ
    MRS. EINAT ETEL KATZ
MINISTER (PUBLIC DIPLOMACY)

MR. LAURENT JOSHUA ZARKA
    MRS. ESTHER ZARKA
MINISTER (CONGRESSIONAL AFFAIRS)

MRS. AMIRA ILANY
    MR. EHUD ILANY
MINISTER-COUNSELOR

MRS. ANAT KATZ KARNI
    MR. TAL KARNI
MINISTER-COUNSELOR (ECONOMIC)

MRS. TAMAR SHARON RAHAMIMOFF HONIG
    MR. YEHUDA ARIEL HONIG RAHAMIMOFF
MINISTER-COUNSELOR

MRS. IFAT RESHEF
    MR. DANIEL ROBERT ZISENWINE*
MINISTER-COUNSELOR

MR. AARON SAGUI
    MS. LIHI SHAVIT SAGUI
MINISTER-COUNSELOR (PRESS)

MR. RAM BEN BARAK
    MRS. AYELET AMISHAV BEN BARAK
COUNSELOR

MR. ELIAV BENJAMIN
    MRS. EFRAT BENJAMIN
COUNSELOR

MR. AVIV EZRA
    MRS. EINAT ANETA EZRA
COUNSELOR

MRS. MALI GAL
    MR. AVRAHAM GAL
COUNSELOR (ADMINISTRATION)

MR. YEHONADAV DAFI HERTZ
    MRS. ORIT HERTZ
COUNSELOR

MR. CHAGAI YEHUDA TZURIEL
    MRS. ALIZA TZURIEL
COUNSELOR

MRS. ESTHER AVITAL HERSHCOVITZ
    MR. RAFAEL HERSHCOVITZ
FIRST SECRETARY

MR. ERAN LEVI
    MRS. RAVIT LEVI
FIRST SECRETARY

MR. OREN MARMORSTEIN
    MRS. MICHAL PAULA MARMORSTEIN
FIRST SECRETARY

MR. SHAI PEER
    MRS. LIBI PEER
FIRST SECRETARY

MRS. ADVA BAR NATAN
    MR. NETANEL BAR NATAN
SECOND SECRETARY

MS. MERAV YAFFA HORSANDI
SECOND SECRETARY

MR. MORDEKHAY ALAJEM
ATTACHE (DEPUTY CHIEF OF SECURITY)

MR. LIDOR AMSELLEM
    MRS. MALI AMSELLEM
ATTACHE

BRIGADIER GENERAL MENASHE ARVIV
    MS. SIGAL PERES
ATTACHE (POLICE & PUBLIC SECURITY)

COLONEL ELIEZER ZVI BEN MEIR
    MRS. GALIT BEN MEIR
ATTACHE

MR. MOSHE ELMALEH
    MRS. PAOLA SILVA MARINO
ATTACHE

MR. MICHAEL GIRIN
    MRS. ANGELINA CHURIKOVA
ATTACHE

MRS. DALIA LAZAROF
    MR. YOSI LAZAROF
ATTACHE

MR. YANIV MENAHEM
ATTACHE

MR. MOSHE MORADOV
ATTACHE

MR. NAOR NISIM PERETZ
ATTACHE

MR. NADAV PERI
    MRS. IRINA PERI
ATTACHE

MR. ASAF RUDNER
    MRS. KAREN MALKA RUDNER
ATTACHE

MR. SHAHAR SHALOM
    MRS. SHANY SHALOM
ATTACHE

MAJOR GENERAL YAACOB AYISH
    MRS. DALIA AYISH
DEFENSE & DEFENSE COOPERATION ATTACHE

COLONEL EYAL ROZEN
    MRS. ANAT ROZEN
MILITARY ATTACHE

* U.S. Citizen

CAPTAIN RONEN NISIM NIMNI
MRS. OSNAT NIMNI
NAVAL ATTACHE

BRIGADIER GENERAL YAKOV SHAHARABANI
MRS. KEREN CARP SHAHARABANI
AIR ATTACHE

MAJOR NADAV MORDEHAY FREEDMAN
MRS. NAAMA BAT SHEVA FREEDMAN
ASST. DEFENSE ATTACHE

LIEUTENANT COLONEL ASSAF NAVOT
MRS. REVITAL NAVOT
ASST. DEFENSE & MILITARY ATTACHE

COLONEL ITZHAK ELIMELECH
MRS. NAOMI ELIMELECH
ASST. DEFENSE COOPERATION, MILITARY, NAVAL & AIR ATTACHE'

LIEUTENANT COLONEL ALON HAIM GAL
MRS. NURIT GAL
ASST. MILITARY ATTACHE

LIEUTENANT COLONEL GIL SHEN
MRS. DAFNA SHEN
ASST. AIR ATTACHE

ITALY

EMBASSY OF ITALY
Chancery: 3000 WHITEHAVEN STREET, NW 20008
(EMBASSY 202-612-4400)   (FAX 202-518-2151)

HIS EXCELLENCY CLAUDIO BISOGNIERO
MRS. AURA DENISE NOCE BENIGNI OLIVIERI
AMBASSADOR EXTRAORDINARY & PLENIPOTENTIARY

MR. LUCA FRANCHETTI PARDO
MRS. MARTA AZEVEDO
MINISTER (DEPUTY CHIEF OF MISSION)

MR. PIER GIORGIO ALIBERTI
MRS. FRANCESCA BARONIO
COUNSELOR

MR. ANTONIO ENRICO BARTOLI
MRS. ESTER MARIA DENARO
COUNSELOR

MR. FABRIZIO BUCCI
MRS. CARLA CAPRIATI
COUNSELOR

MR. LORENZO GALANTI
MRS. FRANCESCA ANDREINI
COUNSELOR

MR. LUCA GORI
MRS. EUGENIA GRESTA
COUNSELOR

MR. CRISTIANO MAGGIPINTO
MRS. TAMARA ANN HARDIKAR*
COUNSELOR

MR. MICHELE PALA
MRS. MARCIA ANDRADE
COUNSELOR

MR. CARLO ROMEO
MRS. ANTONELLA DE FURIA
COUNSELOR

MS. ANTONELLA UNEDDU
COUNSELOR

MR. NICOLA VEROLA
MRS. SUSANNA BONINI
COUNSELOR

MR. THOMAS BOTZIOS
FIRST SECRETARY

MR. FRANCESCO FEDELE
FIRST SECRETARY

MR. BENEDETTO GIUNTINI
MRS. FRANCESCA BIANUCCI
FIRST SECRETARY (ECONOMIC)

MR. FRANCO IMPALA
MRS. INGRID BOUILLE
FIRST SECRETARY

MR. PIERFRANCESCO TAURELLI SALIMBENI
ATTACHE

MS. NADIA BRAMA NICOLI
MR. MARCO NICOLI
ATTACHE (ADMINISTRATION)

MR. GIULIO MARIA BUSULINI
MRS. FEDERIGA BINDI
ATTACHE (SCIENTIFIC)

MR. NICOLA CARBONE
MRS. FRANCESCA AZZARITI
ATTACHE (COMMERCIAL)

MS. DOMENICA CARRABBIA
ATTACHE (ADMINISTRATIVE, CONSULAR & SOCIAL AFFAIRS)

MR. RANIERO GUERRA
MRS. ANNA MARIA DE SANTI
ATTACHE (SCIENTIFIC)

MR. ALBERTO PIETRO AURELIO MANAI
ATTACHE (CULTURAL)

MR. RENATO MIRACCO
ATTACHE (CULTURAL)

MRS. ANDREINA NARDINI
ATTACHE (CONSULAR)

MRS. CLARA ROSE
ATTACHE (COMMERCIAL)

MR. GIANNICOLA SINISI
MRS. LOREDANA TARRICONE
ATTACHE

MR. MASSIMO TATULLI
MRS. FRANCESCA PITRUZZELLA
ATTACHE

MR. ALDO VALEO
MRS. EUGENIA CURATOLO
ATTACHE (HEAD OF ADMINISTRATION)

MR. CARLO VILLANACCI
MRS. CARLA MANNESE
ATTACHE (ECONOMIC)

MR. PAOLO VIOLINI
MRS. TERESA DE SIMONE
ATTACHE (COMMUNICATIONS)

* U.S. Citizen

MR. ROBERTO VITTORI
ATTACHE (SPACE AFFAIRS)

MR. UMBERTO VIVIANI
ATTACHE (FINANCIAL)

MR. SERGIO ZAMPOGNARO
MRS. CARMELA CRISTOFARO
ATTACHE

MAJOR GENERAL GIOVANNI FANTUZZI
DEFENSE & DEFENSE COOPERATION ATTACHE

COLONEL PIETRO TORNABENE
MRS. ALESSANDRA MESINI
MILITARY ATTACHE

CAPTAIN FABRIZIO SIMONCINI
MRS. TIZIANA COCCOLI
NAVAL ATTACHE

COLONEL FLAVIO DANIELIS
MRS. VITTORIA TIBERINI
AIR ATTACHE

LIEUTENANT COLONEL GIUSEPPE BATTAGLIA
MRS. FRANCESCA MASCELLINI
ASST. DEFENSE COOPERATION ATTACHE

AIR ATTACHE OFFICE
3000 WHITEHAVEN STREET, NW 20008
(OFFICE 202-612-4400)

COMMERCIAL OFFICE
3000 WHITEHAVEN STREET, NW 20008
(OFFICE 202-612-4400)

CULTURAL ATTACHE OFFICE
3000 WHITEHAVEN STREET, NW 20008
(OFFICE 202-612-4400)

DEFENSE ATTACHE OFFICE
3000 WHITEHAVEN STREET, NW 20008
(OFFICE 202-612-4400)

MILITARY ATTACHE OFFICE
3000 WHITEHAVEN STREET, NW 20008
(OFFICE 202-612-4400)

NAVAL ATTACHE OFFICE
3000 WHITEHAVEN STREET 20008
(OFFICE 202-612-4400)

SCIENCE ATTACHE OFFICE
3000 WHITEHAVEN STREET, NW 20008
(OFFICE 202-612-4400)

JAMAICA

EMBASSY OF JAMAICA
Chancery: 1520 NEW HAMPSHIRE AVENUE, NW 20036
(EMBASSY 202-452-0660)   (FAX 202-452-0081)

HIS EXCELLENCY STEPHEN CHARLES VASCIANNIE
MRS. LISA ANN VASCIANNIE
AMBASSADOR EXTRAORDINARY & PLENIPOTENTIARY

MRS. JULIA ELIZABETH HYATT
MINISTER

MRS. ARIEL ESTELLA BOWEN
MR. MARK ALTON BOWEN
MINISTER-COUNSELOR

MR. ANDREW PAUL FRANCIS
FIRST SECRETARY

MR. SHELDON JAMES DEROY BROWN
MRS. KADIA ALECIA BROWN
ATTACHE & VICE CONSUL

MRS. ATHLENE WINNOVA GABAY
MR. ROBERT GEORGE GABAY
ATTACHE

MISS STACY ANN GREEN
ATTACHE

MRS. CHERYL ANGELA HAMILTON
ATTACHE

MISS HOPE ANN JARRETT
ATTACHE & VICE CONSUL

MISS SHARON MAXINE MARSTON
ATTACHE

MR. GLADSTONE MICHAEL ANTHONY MOORE
MRS. JOAN ELIZABETH PEART MOORE
ATTACHE & VICE CONSUL

JAMAICAN CENTRAL LABOUR ORGANIZATION
1812 R STREET, NW 20009

JAPAN

EMBASSY OF JAPAN
Chancery: 2520 MASSACHUSETTS AVENUE, NW 20008
(EMBASSY 202-238-6700)   (FAX 202-328-2187)

HIS EXCELLENCY KENICHIRO SASAE
MRS. NOBUKO SASAE
AMBASSADOR EXTRAORDINARY & PLENIPOTENTIARY

MR. KOJI TOMITA
MS. NORIKO TOMITA
MINISTER (DEPUTY CHIEF OF MISSION)

MR. YASUSHI AKAHOSHI
MRS. CHIE AKAHOSHI
MINISTER

MR. AKIRA CHIBA
MS. YUKO CHIBA
MINISTER

MR. TOSHINORI DOI
MINISTER

MR. NAOFUMI HASHIMOTO
MRS. MARI HASHIMOTO
MINISTER

MR. HIDEAKI MIZUKOSHI
MINISTER

MR. TAKEO MORI
MRS. KYOKO MORI
MINISTER

MR. MASATO OTAKA
MINISTER

MR. SHIGEO YAMADA
MINISTER

DR. TAKAHISA ASAKA
        MRS. CHIKAKO ASAKA
COUNSELOR (MEDICAL)

MR. KAZUYA ENDO
        MRS. AKIKO ENDO
COUNSELOR

MR. YUKIYA HAMAMOTO
        MRS. MAMI HAMAMOTO
COUNSELOR

MR. SHIGENORI HIRAOKA
COUNSELOR

MR. JINICHI KADOWAKI
        MRS. MIKIKO KADOWAKI
COUNSELOR

MR. KENTARO KAIHARA
        MS. CHIERI KAIHARA
COUNSELOR

MR. YUTAKA KASHIWABARA
        MRS. REIKO KASHIWABARA
COUNSELOR

MR. SHINGO MIYAMOTO
        MRS. KUNIKO MIYAMOTO
COUNSELOR

MR. KAZUTAKA NAKAMIZO
        MRS. NAOKO NAKAMIZO
COUNSELOR

MR. KAORU NISHIYAMA
        MRS. TOMIE NISHIYAMA
COUNSELOR

MR. KATSUHIRO SAKA
        MS. AKIKO SAKA
COUNSELOR

MS. IZUMI SEKI
COUNSELOR

MR. KENKO SONE
        MRS. MAMI SONE
COUNSELOR

MR. YOSHIYUKI TAHARA
        MRS. YUMIKO TAHARA
COUNSELOR

MR. TAKAHIRO TAJIRI
        MS. MARIKO TAJIRI
COUNSELOR

MR. HIROSHI TAKAHASHI
COUNSELOR

MR. AKIRA TSUGITA
        MRS. SATOKO TSUGITA
COUNSELOR

MR. AKIHIRO TSUJI
        MRS. CHIE TSUJI
COUNSELOR

MR. HIROKI TSUTSUI
        MS. MASAYO TSUTSUI
COUNSELOR

MR. YOSHIYUKI YAMADA
        MRS. AKIKO YAMADA
COUNSELOR

MR. TADASHI YOKOYAMA
        MRS. JINKO YOKOYAMA
COUNSELOR

MR. TAKAHIRO YOSHIDA
        MRS. HARUKO YOSHIDA
COUNSELOR

MR. HIROAKI BABA
        MS. KIKUKO BABA
FIRST SECRETARY

MR. SHINGO FUKUI
        MRS. MICHIKO FUKUI
FIRST SECRETARY

MS. MAYU HAGIWARA
FIRST SECRETARY

MS. NORIKO MIYAKAWA
        MR. TAKUYA MIYAKAWA
FIRST SECRETARY

MR. NORIO MIYAKAWA
        MRS. MIZUHO MIYAKAWA
FIRST SECRETARY

MR. NORIO NAKADA
        MRS. MIKIKO NAKADA
FIRST SECRETARY

MR. TSUTOMU NAKANE
FIRST SECRETARY & CONSUL

MR. TOMOSHIGE NAMBU
        MRS. FUMI NAMBU
FIRST SECRETARY

MR. DAISUKE NIHEI
        MS. MIKIKO NIHEI
FIRST SECRETARY

MR. SHINICHI NOZAKI
        MRS. HARUMI NOZAKI
FIRST SECRETARY

MR. CHIAKI OKAWARA
        MRS. MASUMI OKAWARA
FIRST SECRETARY

MR. EIICHIRO OMATA
        MRS. RIE OMATA
FIRST SECRETARY

MS. KAYO ROKUMOTO
FIRST SECRETARY

MR. TAKASHI SADAKANE
        MRS. YUKAKO SADAKANE
FIRST SECRETARY

MR. SEIICHI SHIMASAKI
        MS. MAYUMI SHIMASAKI
FIRST SECRETARY

MR. KIYOYUKI SUGAHARA
        MRS. MAKIKO SUGAHARA
FIRST SECRETARY

MR. MASAKAZU TAKAHASHI
        MS. YOSHIE TAKAHASHI
FIRST SECRETARY

* U.S. Citizen

MR. TAKESHI TOYODA
    MRS. CHIKAKO TOYODA
FIRST SECRETARY

MR. NAOKI WATANABE
    MRS. AYUKO WATANABE
FIRST SECRETARY

MR. TETSUJI WATANABE
    MRS. YUKO WATANABE
FIRST SECRETARY

MR. TAKAHISA YAMAGUCHI
    MS. YOKO YAMAGUCHI
FIRST SECRETARY

MR. HIROKI YAMAMOTO
    MRS. NORIKO YAMAMOTO
FIRST SECRETARY

MR. RYUJI YAMANOUCHI
    MRS. MINA YAMANOUCHI
FIRST SECRETARY

MR. SATORU YATSUKA
    MRS. MIYO YATSUKA
FIRST SECRETARY

MR. HIROAKI YOSHINO
FIRST SECRETARY

MR. TOSHIAKI ABE
SECOND SECRETARY

MR. TOSHIYUKI ABE
    MRS. AYUMI ABE
SECOND SECRETARY

MS. YOKO ANAZAWA
SECOND SECRETARY

MS. KAZUKO HIKAWA
SECOND SECRETARY

MR. SHINJIRO HOSHINO
    MRS. MAKI HOSHINO
SECOND SECRETARY

MR. TAKESHI ISHIHARA
    MRS. AYA ISHIHARA
SECOND SECRETARY

MR. MITSUHIKO IYOTA
    MRS. MIYUKI IYOTA
SECOND SECRETARY

MR. HIROYUKI KAJITA
SECOND SECRETARY

MR. MASAYUKI KAMEDA
SECOND SECRETARY

MS. MAYUMI KOBAYASHI
SECOND SECRETARY

MR. JIRO KODERA
    MRS. FUMI KODERA
SECOND SECRETARY

MS. MAKI MACHIYAMA
    MR. SHUN MACHIYAMA
SECOND SECRETARY

MR. SHINSUKE MATSUI
    MRS. YOKO MATSUI
SECOND SECRETARY

MS. NAOKO MATSUTANI
SECOND SECRETARY

MR. DAIJU MITA
    MRS. MACHIKO MITA
SECOND SECRETARY

MR. YOSUKE MURASE
    MS. AYANO MURASE
SECOND SECRETARY

MR. YOSHIKATSU NAGANO
    MRS. MEGUMI NAGANO
SECOND SECRETARY

MR. TAKAMICHI NAKAI
SECOND SECRETARY

MR. NOBUAKI NORIZUKI
    MS. MAYU HAGIWARA
SECOND SECRETARY

MR. HIKOHITO OISHI
    MRS. KYOKO OISHI
SECOND SECRETARY

MR. TAKUO SATO
SECOND SECRETARY

MR. MASAYUKI UENO
    MRS. FUMIKO UENO
SECOND SECRETARY

MR. KATSUNORI YANO
SECOND SECRETARY

MR. SHINJI KIKUCHI
THIRD SECRETARY

MR. AKIRA KOKUBUN
THIRD SECRETARY

MS. MIZUHO KURANAGA
THIRD SECRETARY

MS. NAO OI
THIRD SECRETARY

MS. HIROMI TAKASE
THIRD SECRETARY

MR. KAZUNORI YAMAHOKA
THIRD SECRETARY

MR. MASAYUKI YOKOBORI
    MRS. KARI YOKOBORI
THIRD SECRETARY

MR. NAOKI YOSHINO
THIRD SECRETARY & VICE CONSUL

MS. YOSHIE DOMYO
ATTACHE

MR. MASAKI HASHIMOTO
ATTACHE

MR. HITOSHI IKEDA
    MRS. ERIKO IKEDA
ATTACHE

MR. KEI ISHII
    MRS. KAZUMI ISHII
ATTACHE

MR. KEIICHI KAJIWARA
    MRS. HIROKO KAJIWARA
ATTACHE

* U.S. Citizen

MR. KAZUNORI NAKAGAWA
MS. JUNKO NAKAGAWA
ATTACHE

MR. KOSUKE NAKAJIMA
ATTACHE

MR. KENJI OE
MRS. YURI OE
ATTACHE

MR. KAZUTO SAKEMI
ATTACHE

MR. HIROSHI UDA
ATTACHE

MR. DAIKI YAMAGUCHI
ATTACHE

MS. MIKI YOKOYAMA
ATTACHE

MAJOR GENERAL ATSUSHI HIKITA
MRS. ETSUKO HIKITA
DEFENSE & AIR ATTACHE

LIEUTENANT COLONEL KAZUNORI SAITO
MS. MANAMI SAITO
ASST. DEFENSE & AIR ATTACHE

COLONEL YOSHIHIRO ISERI
MRS. AKIKO ISERI
ASST. DEFENSE & MILITARY ATTACHE

CAPTAIN IZURU IKEUCHI
MRS. TAKAKO IKEUCHI
ASST. DEFENSE & NAVAL ATTACHE

LIEUTENANT COLONEL KANAME YAMASHITA
MRS. KAZU YAMASHITA
ASST. MILITARY ATTACHE

COMMANDER HIROSHI SEKINO
MRS. MAMIKO SEKINO
ASST. NAVAL ATTACHE

CHANCERY ANNEX
1150 18TH STREET, NW, SUITE 100 20036
(OFFICE 202-238-6900)   (FAX 202-822-6524)

JORDAN

EMBASSY OF HASHEMITE KINGDOM OF JORDAN
Chancery: 3504 INTERNATIONAL DRIVE, NW 20008
(EMBASSY 202-966-2664)   (FAX 202-966-3110)

HER EXCELLENCY DR. ALIA MOHAMAD ALI HATOUGH BOURAN
MR. ISHAQ MOUSA AHMAD BOURAN
AMBASSADOR EXTRAORDINARY & PLENIPOTENTIARY

MR. MAHMOUD DAIFALLAH MAHMOUD HMOUD
MRS. KIRSTY ANN GEORGE ROBIN REID
MINISTER (DEPUTY CHIEF OF MISSION)

HER ROYAL HIGHNESS PRINCESS FIRYAL AL MOHAMMAD
MINISTER

HIS ROYAL HIGHNESS PRINCE TALAL BIN MOHAMMED
HER ROYAL HIGHNESS PRINCESS GHIDA TALAL
MINISTER

MR. AMJAD HATEM ABDUL K AL MBIDEEN
MRS. LAMA MUSTAFA OMAR HAJ-KHALEEL
COUNSELOR

MR. FAWAZ FAROUK ABDEL KARIM BILBEISI
MRS. FUTOUN MOHD HISHAM A. AL ATTAR
COUNSELOR (ECONOMIC)

HER ROYAL HIGHNESS PRINCESS GHIDA TALAL
HIS ROYAL HIGHNESS PRINCE TALAL BIN MOHAMMED
COUNSELOR

MR. QAIS MOHD AKEL EID BILTAJI
FIRST SECRETARY

MR. ADI GHASSAN MOHD KHAIR
FIRST SECRETARY

MR. RAMI MASHHOUR A. ALKHARABSHEH
SECOND SECRETARY

MR. ZAID ABDEL KARIM SAAD AL EDWAN
MRS. RIMA SALEEM ABDEL AZIZ ALBARARI
ATTACHE (FINANCIAL)

MR. KAMAL AHMAD NAYEF M. K. NANAAH
MRS. NORMA MOHD SHAWQI BADRI ASFOUR
ATTACHE (FINANCIAL)

BRIGADIER GENERAL AISHA BINT AL HUSSEIN
DEFENSE, MILITARY, NAVAL & AIR ATTACHE

COLONEL MOHD H M ABU HASHISH
MRS. THIKRA J. I. MASARANI
ASST. DEFENSE, MILITARY, NAVAL & AIR ATTACHE

INFORMATION BUREAU
3504 INTERNATIONAL DRIVE, NW 20008
(OFFICE 202-966-1009)   (FAX 202-667-0777)

MILITARY, AIR AND NAVAL ATTACHE OFFICE
3504 INTERNATIONAL DRIVE, NW 20008
(OFFICE 202-966-1009)

KAZAKHSTAN

EMBASSY OF THE REPUBLIC OF KAZAKHSTAN
Chancery: 1401 16TH STREET, NW 20036
(EMBASSY 202-232-5488)   (FAX 202-232-5845)

HIS EXCELLENCY KAIRAT UMAROV
MRS. GALIYA UMAROVA
AMBASSADOR EXTRAORDINARY & PLENIPOTENTIARY

MR. DASTAN YELEUKENOV
MRS. DILOROM YELEUKENOVA
MINISTER-COUNSELOR

MR. TOLEUGAZY M. ABZHANOV
MRS. DINA ABZHANOVA
COUNSELOR

MR. ALMAT AIDARBEKOV
MRS. DINARA AIDARBEKOVA
COUNSELOR & CONSUL

MS. MERUYERT SAUDABAY
MR. DAULET ORYNBAYEV
COUNSELOR

MR. NURGALI ARYSTANOV
MRS. DILYARA ARYSTANOVA
FIRST SECRETARY

* U.S. Citizen

MR. ANDREY KIM
    MRS. YEVGENIYA PAK
FIRST SECRETARY

MR. ZHANAT KUANDYKOVICH SHAIMERDENOV
    MRS. MILANA KANATOVNA SHAIMERDENOVA
FIRST SECRETARY

MR. AMIR SULTANGOZHIN
    MRS. ALIYA SULTANGOZHINA
FIRST SECRETARY

MR. DAUREN KABIYEV
    MRS. ANELIYA KABIYEVA
SECOND SECRETARY

MR. KAISAR KOPISH
    MS. GAZIZA KOPISH
SECOND SECRETARY

MR. ANUAR KURZHIKAYEV
SECOND SECRETARY

MR. ERNAR SERIKOV
    MS. DINARA BERDIGULOVA
SECOND SECRETARY

MR. NURZHAN AITMAKHANOV
    MRS. RADA MAKHAMBETOVA
THIRD SECRETARY

MR. RAKHIM ZHAN AKHMETOV
    MRS. ZHANAR AKHMETOVA
THIRD SECRETARY & CONSUL

MRS. DANA KHUSSAINOVA
    MR. YERBOL KEMELBEKOV
THIRD SECRETARY

MRS. DANA MASALIMOVA
    MR. ARDAK MASALIMOV
THIRD SECRETARY

MR. ASKHAT ABLAISSOV
    MRS. DILYA ABLAISSOVA
ATTACHE

MR. ALIBEK ALDAMZHAROV
    MRS. MAIRA ALDAMZHAROVA
ATTACHE

MR. ZHASSULAN SADVAKASSOV
    MRS. ASSEMGUL SADVAKASSOVA
ATTACHE

GENERAL BAKHTIYAR SYZDYKOV
    MRS. URZHAMAL SYZDYKOVA
DEFENSE, MILITARY, NAVAL & AIR ATTACHE

MR. NURKEN URMANTAYEV
    MRS. ZHANAR SMAILOVA
ASST. DEFENSE, MILITARY, NAVAL & AIR ATTACHE

CONSULAR SECTION
    1401 16TH STREET, NW 20036
        (OFFICE 202-232-5488)   (FAX 202-232-3541)

KENYA

EMBASSY OF THE REPUBLIC OF KENYA
Chancery: 2249 R STREET, NW 20008
(EMBASSY 202-387-6101)   (FAX 202-462-3829)

HIS EXCELLENCY ELKANAH ODEMBO ABSALOM
    MRS. AOKO MIDIWO ODEMBO
AMBASSADOR EXTRAORDINARY & PLENIPOTENTIARY

MRS. LUCY NJERI KIRUTHU
    MR. FELIX MACHARIA KIRUTHU
MINISTER-COUNSELOR

MR. JON CHESSONI
    MRS. MARY NYAGUTHII CHESSONI
COUNSELOR (ADMINISTRATION)

MS. NAIRIMAS SHARON OLE SEIN
    MR. AMIT TYAGI
COUNSELOR

MR. WILLIAM NJOROGE MUGO
    MRS. CELESTINE NJAMBI NJOROGE
FIRST SECRETARY (IMMIGRATION)

MR. CHARLES MUTUKU MUNYAO
    MRS. JANE NGUNYA MUNYAO
FIRST SECRETARY (IMMIGRATION)

MR. PETER MWITA GESOWAN
    MRS. MIRIAM NYOKABI KARURI
SECOND SECRETARY (ECONOMIC)

MR. DENNIS MILIMO MUHAMBE
    MS. MICHELLE AMONDI LANGI
SECOND SECRETARY

MS. WAITHIRA NJUGUNA
SECOND SECRETARY

MRS. EVELYN CHELUGET
    MR. MIKE KIPKORIR TOO CHELUGET
ATTACHE (IMMIGRATION)

MR. JAMES MWANGI KIIRU
ATTACHE (COMMERCIAL)

MRS. RAHEL MWANAKE MUREITHI
    MR. BENSON MURIITHI MURIMI
ATTACHE (ADMINISTRATIVE)

MR. CHARLES MUEMA MUTUA
    MRS. FAITH KIVINYA MUEMA
ATTACHE (FINANCIAL)

COLONEL HESBON ODANGA MALWEYI
    MRS. RUTH KHAMALI ODANGA
DEFENSE, MILITARY, NAVAL & AIR ATTACHE

KOREA

EMBASSY OF THE REPUBLIC OF KOREA
Chancery: 2450 MASSACHUSETTS AVENUE, NW 20008
(EMBASSY 202-939-5600)   (FAX 202-387-0250)

HIS EXCELLENCY YOUNGJIN CHOI
    MRS. HEEWON LEE
AMBASSADOR EXTRAORDINARY & PLENIPOTENTIARY

MR. HYUNDONG CHO
    MINISTER (DEPUTY CHIEF OF MISSION)

MR. SUWHAN CHOE
    MISS SEUNGAH LEE
MINISTER

MR. GHEEWHAN KIM
    MISS JIHYUN KANG
MINISTER

* U.S. Citizen

MR. JIN CHUL BAE
    MRS. HYE KYUNG AHN
MINISTER-COUNSELOR

MR. BYUNG GOO CHOI
    MRS. HEEJEONG SUH
MINISTER-COUNSELOR

MR. KUN IL HWANG
    MISS JEONG IN KIM
MINISTER-COUNSELOR

MR. YOUNG JIN JANG
    MISS SUNMIN LEE
MINISTER-COUNSELOR

MR. KYEONG KYU KIM
    MISS EUN SUNG LEE
MINISTER-COUNSELOR

MR. KI BONG LEE
    MISS HEE JIN HAN
MINISTER-COUNSELOR

MR. YOUNG HO LEE
    MRS. HYUN JIN CHO
MINISTER-COUNSELOR

MR. JONG IN YOON
    MISS SONGWON KIM
MINISTER-COUNSELOR

MR. SOON GU YOON
    MISS CHAN SOON PARK
MINISTER-COUNSELOR & CONSUL GENERAL

MR. HYOUNG CHAN CHOE
    MISS HYEJUNG KIM
COUNSELOR

MR. HAE KWAN CHUNG
    MRS. YOUNG SUK LIM
COUNSELOR

MR. SANG WOOK HAM
    MISS JA OK PAE
COUNSELOR

MR. SEOK IN HONG
    MISS KYEONG OK JEONG
COUNSELOR

MR. JI HOON JANG
    MRS. SOO KYUNG KU
COUNSELOR

MR. JANGWON JO
    MISS JUNGOCK SOHN
COUNSELOR

MR. DAE RYOUN KANG
    MRS. KICHA CHO
COUNSELOR

MR. CHOON GOO KIM
    MRS. EUNSOOK CHUNG
COUNSELOR

MR. JINWOOK KIM
    MRS. KYUNGSOOK YUN
COUNSELOR

MR. KYUNG HAN KIM
    MISS YU JUNG KIM
COUNSELOR

MR. TAEJIN KIM
    MS. SUYEON KIM
COUNSELOR

MR. SOOKWON LEE
    MISS CHI EUN KIM
COUNSELOR

MR. WOONJU LEE
    MISS HYERYUNG YU
COUNSELOR

MR. BONG HYUN NAM
    MRS. YOUNG HEE LEE
COUNSELOR

MR. YUN KYU PARK
    MRS. YUNKYUNG O
COUNSELOR

MR. JEONGHYUN RYU
    MRS. YOUNGSUN PARK
COUNSELOR

MR. BYOUNGCHOUL SONG
    MISS SUNG HYE KIM
COUNSELOR

MR. JOO CHEON UM
    MRS. MEE HEE LEE
COUNSELOR

MR. TAEYUN UM
    MRS. EUI HYANG KIM
COUNSELOR

MR. SUN HAK CHO
    MRS. SE WON CHO
FIRST SECRETARY

MR. JOON HONG JEON
    MISS JUNG A. KANG
FIRST SECRETARY

MR. BYUNGMIN JEONG
    MISS JUNGSOON HWANG
FIRST SECRETARY

MR. ILBUM KIM
    MS. SUNYEONG PARK
FIRST SECRETARY

MR. JONGMIN KIM
    FIRST SECRETARY

MR. JUNPYO KIM
    MISS EUNAH SHIN
FIRST SECRETARY

MR. SUNGHOON KIM
    FIRST SECRETARY

MR. YOUNG TAE KIM
    MISS HYUN SOO YOO
FIRST SECRETARY

MR. JONGHO KYUN
    MISS YUKYUNG CHOI
FIRST SECRETARY

MR. CHANGHO LEE
    MISS JINSOOK KIM
FIRST SECRETARY

MR. DONGWON LEE
    MS. YOUNJOUNG CHO
FIRST SECRETARY

* U.S. Citizen

MISS JONGJOO LEE
    MR. SE HYEON CHA
    FIRST SECRETARY

MR. SANGGUN LEE
    MISS SUJUNG JUNG
    FIRST SECRETARY

MR. WONDOO LEE
    MISS HA YOUNG SHIN
    FIRST SECRETARY

MR. HOHYOUNG PARK
    MRS. HYEMI KIM
    FIRST SECRETARY

MR. JAE HUN RYU
    MISS HYO JUNG LEE
    FIRST SECRETARY

MR. CHAN SIK SONG
    MS. KYUNG JIN LEE
    FIRST SECRETARY

MR. SEUNGMIN YOO
    MISS SU IN MOON
    FIRST SECRETARY

MR. CHU SOK YOON
    FIRST SECRETARY

MISS DAYOUN CHOI
    SECOND SECRETARY

MR. WOOYONG HAN
    SECOND SECRETARY

MR. CHEOL SANG KIM
    MISS SOOKKYUNG SUH
    SECOND SECRETARY

MR. DONG YOUNG KIM
    MRS. KI YEON CHOI
    SECOND SECRETARY

MR. HYUNSOO KIM
    MISS YEYOUNG SOHN
    SECOND SECRETARY

MR. JAEMIN KIM
    MISS YEONGMI KIM
    SECOND SECRETARY

MISS MYOUNSUN KIM
    SECOND SECRETARY

MISS DOYEON KWON
    MR. GYUNGSU JANG
    SECOND SECRETARY

MISS YUN JOO LEE
    SECOND SECRETARY

MR. TAEHO UHM
    MISS WONJOUNG CHANG
    SECOND SECRETARY

MR. SEOJIN YANG
    SECOND SECRETARY

MR. CHANG HO SHIN
    MISS JIYOUN OH
    THIRD SECRETARY

COLONEL YONG GWAN BYUN
    ATTACHE (RESEARCH & DEVELOPMENT)

* U.S. Citizen

COLONEL SUNYUP CHOI
    MISS SOONHEE CHO
    ATTACHE (DEFENSE LOGISTICS)

MR. YONGSANG KIM
    MRS. SUNGWON LEE
    ATTACHE (VETERINARY)

BRIGADIER GENERAL SEOYOUNG LEE
    MISS KYOUNG YEON CHOI
    DEFENSE ATTACHE

COLONEL SANG HAE LEE
    MISS EUNHEE HWANG
    MILITARY ATTACHE

CAPTAIN HOYJE KIM
    MRS. YOUNGSOOK LEE
    NAVAL ATTACHE

COLONEL CHONGPHIL LIM
    MRS. EUNKYUNG KIM
    AIR ATTACHE

LIEUTENANT COLONEL IN WOONG YEO
    MRS. HYUN SOOK LEE
    ASST. DEFENSE & MILITARY ATTACHE

LIEUTENANT COLONEL MOON HO KANG
    MISS KYEI SOOK KWON
    ASST. DEFENSE & NAVAL ATTACHE

CONSULAR OFFICE
    2320 MASSACHUSETTS AVENUE, NW 20008
        (OFFICE 202-939-5657)   (FAX 202-342-1597)

EDUCATION OFFICE
    2320 MASSACHUSETTS AVENUE, NW 20008
        (OFFICE 202-939-5634)   (FAX 202-342-1597)

INFORMATION OFFICE
    2370 MASSACHUSETTS AVENUE, NW 20008
        (OFFICE 202-797-6343)   (FAX 202-387-0413)

OFFICE OF THE DEFENSE AND LOGISTICS
    2400 WILSON BOULEVARD
    ARLINGTON, VA 22201
        (OFFICE 703-524-5505)

KOSOVO REPUBLIC

EMBASSY OF THE REPUBLIC OF KOSOVO
Chancery: 1101 30TH STREET, NW, SUITE 330/340 20007
(EMBASSY 202-380-3581)   (FAX 202-380-3628)

HIS EXCELLENCY AKAN ISMAILI
    MRS. FITORE ISMAILI
    AMBASSADOR EXTRAORDINARY & PLENIPOTENTIARY

MR. JETISH JASHARI
    MRS. LEONORE KRASNIQI JASHARI
    MINISTER-COUNSELOR (DEPUTY CHIEF OF MISSION)

MS. GJENEZA BUDIMA
    COUNSELOR

BRIGADIER GENERAL XHAVIT GASHI
    MRS. VALENTINA GASHI
    ATTACHE (SECURITY)

KUWAIT

EMBASSY OF THE STATE OF KUWAIT
Chancery: 2940 TILDEN STREET, NW 20008
(EMBASSY 202-966-0702)   (FAX 202-966-0517)

HIS EXCELLENCY SHEIKH SALEM ABDULLAH AL JABER AL SABAH
MRS. RIMA FARES AL SABAH
AMBASSADOR EXTRAORDINARY & PLENIPOTENTIARY

MR. ABDULAZIZ S.M. ALQADFAN
MRS. MANAL M.F.S. ALFEHAID
FIRST SECRETARY (DEPUTY CHIEF OF MISSION)

MR. ABDULAZEEZ ALOMAR
MS. ASEEL M. S. A. S. A. ALTABTABAE
COUNSELOR (CULTURAL)

MR. KHALED B KH F A AL KHULIFAH
SECOND SECRETARY

MR. FAISAL GH A T M ALENEZI
SECOND SECRETARY

MR. FAWAZ A S M BOURISLY
MRS. HESSAH S F S ALFAHAD
SECOND SECRETARY

DR. HAMAD A. H. ALADWANI
MRS. MASHAEL KH A.S ALBRAIKAN
ATTACHE (CULTURAL)

MR. YOUSEF SALAH E A ALAWADHI
MRS. FAJER OTHMAN I. A. ALAWADHI
ATTACHE

MR. ABDULWAHAB MOHAMMAD J ALDHAFIRI
MRS. FATIMA MOHAMMAD H M S ALAWADHI
ATTACHE (CULTURAL)

MR. SALEH M. A. J. ALFAYLAKAWI
MRS. MAHA H. M. ALJERAN
ATTACHE

MRS. ALYAA A. H. M. H. ALHAYEN
ATTACHE (CULTURAL)

MR. KHALED H. H. A. ALMAJED
MRS. ASMA M. ALSALEH
ATTACHE

MR. ADNAN M.A.E. ALSAIF
MRS. ASMA S.A. AL-SAMAKAH
ATTACHE

MR. ABDULLAH H R J ALWETAIB
MRS. MAALI R M J ALAJMI
ATTACHE (HEALTH)

MRS. HANAN N A SHARAF
MR. ALI I. GH. S. MOHAMMAD
ATTACHE (HEALTH)

MR. MARZOUQ HASAN M. H. ALBADER
MRS. HANAN ABDULAZIZ F AL THUWAINI
DEFENSE, MILITARY, NAVAL & AIR ATTACHE

COLONEL MAZEN KHALIFAH A KH ALABWAH
MRS. MAHA MAAMOUN ALTAYEB
ASST. MILITARY ATTACHE

LIEUTENANT COLONEL FAWAZ KHALEEL E E ALSHARHAN
MRS. GHADIR N A A ALOMANI
ASST. MILITARY ATTACHE

* U.S. Citizen

COLONEL AMER MOHAMMAD H. M. ALZAID
MRS. HUDA ABDUALMOHSEN S. ALDHUWAIHI
ASST. MILITARY ATTACHE

MR. BASHAR ABDULHUSAIN AWADH
MRS. EBTESAM HUSSAIN H J SHAGHOULI
ASST. MILITARY ATTACHE

KUWAIT CULTURAL, UNIVERSITY, LIAISON OFFICES
3500 INTERNATIONAL DRIVE, NW 20008
(OFFICE 202-363-8055)

KUWAIT DEFENSE ATTACHE OFFICE
3500 INTERNATIONAL DRIVE, NW 20008

KUWAIT HEALTH OFFICE
4201 CONNECTICUT AVENUE, NW, SUITE 502 20008
(OFFICE 202-686-4304)

KYRGYZSTAN

EMBASSY OF THE KYRGYZ REPUBLIC
Chancery: 2360 MASSACHUSETTS AVENUE, NW 20008
(EMBASSY 202-449-9823)   (FAX 202-386-7550)

HIS EXCELLENCY MUKTAR DJUMALIEV
MS. ASEL AKENEEVA
AMBASSADOR EXTRAORDINARY & PLENIPOTENTIARY

MR. ARSLAN ANARBAEV
MRS. INAIATKHAN BAIEVA
MINISTER-COUNSELOR (DEPUTY CHIEF OF MISSION)

MR. MARATBEK DUVANAEV
MRS. CHINARA AIDRALIEVA
COUNSELOR

MR. AIBEK OMOKEEV
MRS. DAMIRA MURZAGAZIEVA
COUNSELOR

MR. RAKHMAN ADANOV
MRS. AIZHAN SYDYKOVA
FIRST SECRETARY

MR. ZHANYBEK ERALIEV
MRS. CHOLPON MAMYROVA
FIRST SECRETARY

MR. RUSLAN BEKBOLOTOV
MRS. GULBARA ARSLANBEKOVA
SECOND SECRETARY & CONSUL

MR. CHOLPONBEK IMANALIEV
MRS. BERMET DJUMASHALIEVA
ATTACHE & VICE CONSUL

CONSULAR SECTION
1511 K STREET, NW 20005
(OFFICE 202-628-0433)

LAOS

EMBASSY OF THE LAO PEOPLE'S DEMOCRATIC REPUBLIC
Chancery: 2222 S STREET, NW 20008
(EMBASSY 202-332-6416)   (FAX 202-332-4923)

HIS EXCELLENCY SENG SOUKHATHIVONG
MRS. SOMDY SOUKHATHIVONG
AMBASSADOR EXTRAORDINARY & PLENIPOTENTIARY

MR. MAI SAYAVONGS
MRS. SOUMALY SAYAVONGS
MINISTER-COUNSELOR (DEPUTY CHIEF OF MISSION)

MRS. BOUAPHA PHOMMASENG
FIRST SECRETARY (ADMINISTRATIVE)

MR. THONGMOON PHONGPHAILATH
MRS. VIENGVILAY THAMMAVONGSA
FIRST SECRETARY

MR. CHANTHAVISOUK CHANTHASANE
MRS. PHONESAVANH CHANTHASANE
SECOND SECRETARY (PROTOCOL)

MR. SOMXAI KITTANOUVONG
MRS. BANG ORN KITTANOUVONG
SECOND SECRETARY (CONSULAR)

MR. YHALATH SINGHANAKHONE
SECOND SECRETARY (CONSULAR)

MR. NANTHANAKHONE KEOVONGVICHITH
THIRD SECRETARY (PROTOCOL)

MR. VIENGKHAM SAENBOUTTALATH
MRS. THONGLEUANG CHANHTHALATH
THIRD SECRETARY

MR. KERLOR YANGKO
MRS. YEKYANG YANGKO
THIRD SECRETARY (POLITICAL, ECONOMIC & CULTURE)

MR. SOUNTHONE DUANGXATY
ATTACHE (POLITICAL, ECONOMIC & CULTURE)

COLONEL KENEKEO PHOLSENA
MRS. SOUKANTHA PHOLSENA
DEFENSE & MILITARY ATTACHE

LIEUTENANT COLONEL BOUNMYVIENG VIENGNHOUTTHASAT
MRS. BOUNPHENG VIENGNOUTTHASAT
ASST. DEFENSE & MILITARY ATTACHE

LATVIA

EMBASSY OF LATVIA
Chancery: 2306 MASSACHUSETTS AVENUE, NW 20008
(EMBASSY 202-328-2840)   (FAX 202-328-2860)

HIS EXCELLENCY ANDRIS RAZANS
MRS. GUNTA RAZANE
AMBASSADOR EXTRAORDINARY & PLENIPOTENTIARY

MR. JURIJS POGREBNAKS
MRS. KRISTINE KRIGERE
COUNSELOR (DEPUTY CHIEF OF MISSION)

MS. VINETA MEKONE
COUNSELOR

MR. VALTS VITUMS
MRS. ILZE VITUMA
FIRST SECRETARY

MISS BAIBA KINE
THIRD SECRETARY

MRS. ILZE VITUMA
MR. VALTS VITUMS
THIRD SECRETARY

COMMERCIAL OFFICE
1776 K STREET, NW, SUITE 814 20006

LEBANON

EMBASSY OF LEBANON
Chancery: 2560 28TH STREET, NW 20008
(EMBASSY 202-939-6300)   (FAX 202-939-6324)

HIS EXCELLENCY ANTOINE CHEDID
MRS. AFIFE NICOLE CHEDID
AMBASSADOR EXTRAORDINARY & PLENIPOTENTIARY

MISS CARLA JAZZAR
FIRST SECRETARY (DEPUTY CHIEF OF MISSION)

MRS. REINA CHARBEL
MR. MAROUN FARHAT
FIRST SECRETARY

MR. HUSSEIN HAIDAR
MRS. TALA EL HAJJ SLEIMAN
FIRST SECRETARY

BRIGADIER GENERAL ALBERT KARAM
MRS. SUZANNE ABI SAMRA
DEFENSE, MILITARY, NAVAL & AIR ATTACHE

LESOTHO

EMBASSY OF THE KINGDOM OF LESOTHO
Chancery: 2511 MASSACHUSETTS AVENUE, NW 20008
(EMBASSY 202-797-5533)   (FAX 202-234-6815)

HIS EXCELLENCY PROFESSOR ELIACHIM MOLAPI SEBATANE
MRS. LOIS ANNE SEBATANE*
AMBASSADOR EXTRAORDINARY & PLENIPOTENTIARY

MR. MOLEFI CHRISTOPHER NYAKA
MRS. MATSEPO MARETHA NYAKA
COUNSELOR (DEPUTY CHIEF OF MISSION)

MRS. MATOKA CORINA PHORI
MR. JOSHUA REENTSENG PHORI
FIRST SECRETARY

MRS. MAJANE ANNA NTSALA
THIRD SECRETARY

LIBERIA

EMBASSY OF THE REPUBLIC OF LIBERIA
Chancery: 5201 16TH STREET, NW 20011
(EMBASSY 202-723-0437)   (FAX 202-723-0436)

HIS EXCELLENCY JEREMIAH CONGBEH SULUNTEH
MRS. KABEH GORNOR PEWU SULUNTEH
AMBASSADOR EXTRAORDINARY & PLENIPOTENTIARY

MR. EDWIN F. SELE
MRS. ESTELLA D. SELE
MINISTER (DEPUTY CHIEF OF MISSION)

MR. WILLIAM V. S. BULL
MINISTER

* U.S. Citizen

MR. JEFF GONGOER DOWANA
MINISTER (DEPUTY CHIEF OF MISSION)

MR. GABRIEL I. H. WILLIAMS
MRS. NEIKO I. WILLIAMS
MINISTER-COUNSELOR (PUBLIC AFFAIRS)

MS. MARGARET C. ANSUMANA
COUNSELOR (MARITIME)

MR. CHRISTOPHER JUGBE NIPPY SR
MS. OLIVE M. B. NIPPY
FIRST SECRETARY & CONSUL

MR. DOLIAKEH QUOIMIE
MRS. TINA YAMAH QUOIMIE
FIRST SECRETARY

MRS. CATHERINE J. NMAH
SECOND SECRETARY & VICE CONSUL

MRS. KATHLEEN M. K. DEMMAH
ATTACHE

LIBYA

EMBASSY OF LIBYA
Chancery: 2600 VIRGINIA AVENUE, NW, SUITE 705 20037
(EMBASSY 202-944-9601)   (FAX 202-944-9606)

HIS EXCELLENCY ALI SULEIMAN AUJALI
MRS. NAIMA MUFTAH BSEIKRI
AMBASSADOR EXTRAORDINARY & PLENIPOTENTIARY

MR. SULEIMAN S. H. ABULHUL
MRS. ZEINAB S S ABULHUL
MINISTER-COUNSELOR

MR. AHMED F. ABULGASEM
MRS. HANA O. M. ABDANNABI
COUNSELOR (FINANCIAL)

MR. SALEH A. S. BUFRNINA
MRS. NEVEN SAAD A. HASSAN
COUNSELOR

MR. EMAD M. S. ABUGOSSA
MRS. AIDA A. M. JATELLI
FIRST SECRETARY

MR. FAISL B M ALSHARIF
MRS. SHAALA M A ELMILADI
FIRST SECRETARY

MRS. SANIA O R ELFORJANI
FIRST SECRETARY (POLITICAL AFFAIRS)

MR. SAMI K A ELGHODBAN
MRS. WESAL N. B. NEBBAL
FIRST SECRETARY

MR. ALSUDIK S. ALI
SECOND SECRETARY

MR. ASSAD TAJEDDIN ALI ALJERBI
THIRD SECRETARY

MR. NURI M S ABDULWAHAB
MRS. MUNIRA A. S. WHEBA
ATTACHE (ADMINISTRATIVE)

MR. MOHAMED L ABUGHRARA
MRS. IMAN A AYALA
ATTACHE (ADMINISTRATIVE)

* U.S. Citizen

MR. RIAD O A ALMOGHRABI
ASST. ATTACHE (MEDICAL)

CULTURAL OFFICE
666 11TH STREET, NW, SUITE 600 20001

ECONOMIC AND CONSULAR OFFICE
2600 VIRGINIA AVENUE, NW, SUITE 711 20037

LIECHTENSTEIN

EMBASSY OF THE PRINCIPALITY OF LIECHTENSTEIN
Chancery: 2900 K STREET, NW, SUITE 602B 20007
(EMBASSY 202-331-0590)   (FAX 202-331-3221)

HER EXCELLENCY CLAUDIA FRITSCHE
AMBASSADOR EXTRAORDINARY & PLENIPOTENTIARY

LITHUANIA

EMBASSY OF THE REPUBLIC OF LITHUANIA
Chancery: 2622 16TH STREET, NW 20009
(EMBASSY 202-234-5860)   (FAX 202-328-0466)

HIS EXCELLENCY ZYGIMANTAS PAVILIONIS
MRS. LINA PAVILIONIENE
AMBASSADOR EXTRAORDINARY & PLENIPOTENTIARY

MR. SIMONAS SATUNAS
MRS. ZIVILE SATUNIENE
MINISTER-COUNSELOR (DEPUTY CHIEF OF MISSION/ POLITICAL)

MR. ROLANDAS KACINSKAS
MRS. DEIMANTE KACINSKIENE
MINISTER (POLITICAL AFFAIRS)

MR. ARTURAS VAZBYS
MINISTER-COUNSELOR

MRS. LIANA VAZBIENE
FIRST SECRETARY

MR. MARIUS ATROSKA
THIRD SECRETARY (CONSULAR)

MS. JUSTINA KRUTULYTE
THIRD SECRETARY

MR. EVALDAS STANKEVICIUS
MRS. NERILE URBONAITE
ATTACHE (CULTURE)

COLONEL JUOZAS KACERGIUS
MRS. LINA KACERGIENE
DEFENSE, MILITARY, NAVAL & AIR ATTACHE

LIEUTENANT COLONEL MINDAUGAS ABALIKSTA
MRS. JURGITA ABALIKSTIENE
ASST. DEFENSE, MILITARY, NAVAL & AIR ATTACHE

LUXEMBOURG

EMBASSY OF THE GRAND DUCHY OF LUXEMBOURG
Chancery: 2200 MASSACHUSETTS AVENUE, NW 20008
(EMBASSY 202-265-4171)   (FAX 202-328-8270)

HIS EXCELLENCY JEAN LOUIS WOLZFELD
AMBASSADOR EXTRAORDINARY & PLENIPOTENTIARY

MR. OLIVIER BALDAUFF
MRS. MURIEL FEIDT
MINISTER (DEPUTY CHIEF OF MISSION)

MR. MARIO WIESEN
MRS. LADA TURBINA
FIRST SECRETARY

MACEDONIA

EMBASSY OF THE REPUBLIC OF MACEDONIA
Chancery: 2129 WYOMING AVENUE, NW 20008
(EMBASSY 202-667-0501)   (FAX 202-667-2131)

HIS EXCELLENCY ZORAN JOLEVSKI
MRS. SUZANA JOLEVSKA
AMBASSADOR EXTRAORDINARY & PLENIPOTENTIARY

MISS SONJA BAJDESKA
COUNSELOR (POLITICAL)

MRS. ELI BOJADJIESKA RISTOVSKI
MR. DRAGAN RISTOVSKI
COUNSELOR

MR. SERDJIM MUHAMED
MRS. GERTA MUHAMED JAHJA
COUNSELOR

MR. SASHA GRUJEVSKI
MRS. KATJA GRUJEVSKA
THIRD SECRETARY

MR. BAJRAM IBRAIMI
MRS. MIRLINDA IBRAIMI
ATTACHE (CIVIL)

COLONEL JORDANCHO MILADINOVSKI
DEFENSE, MILITARY, NAVAL & AIR ATTACHE

MADAGASCAR

EMBASSY OF THE REPUBLIC OF MADAGASCAR
Chancery: 2374 MASSACHUSETTS AVENUE, NW 20008
(EMBASSY 202-265-5525)   (FAX 202-265-3034)

MRS. VELOTIANA RAKOTOANOSY RAOBELINA
MR. QUERRY RAOBELINA
COUNSELOR (CHARGE D'AFFAIRES AD INTERIM)

MR. MAMIHARILALA RASOLOJAONA
MRS. BODOHARIMA RANOROMARO RASOLOJAONA
COUNSELOR (DEPUTY CHIEF OF MISSION)

MR. ARISON HONORE CLAIR ANDRIAMALALA
MRS. H S RAZAFIMAHAZO ANDRIAMALALA
COUNSELOR

MR. ANDRIATSITOHAINA JAONA
MRS. EVA RAHASIMBOLAMANANALITERA JAONA
COUNSELOR (COMMERCIAL)

MR. PHILIBERT RABESANDRAT RATIANARIVO
MRS. FNU NORO VOAHANGY
ATTACHE (ACCOUNTING)

MALAWI

EMBASSY OF MALAWI
Chancery: 2408 MASSACHUSETTS AVENUE, NW 20008
(EMBASSY 202-721-0270)   (FAX 202-721-0288)

HIS EXCELLENCY STEPHEN DICK TENNYSON MATENJE
MRS. ISABEL CHIWALITSO MATENJE
AMBASSADOR EXTRAORDINARY & PLENIPOTENTIARY

MS. JANE FRANCES NANKWENYA
MINISTER (DEPUTY CHIEF OF MISSION)

MR. RHINO GRANT MCHENGA
MRS. LISSY JACQUILINE MCHENGA
COUNSELOR

MS. YVONNE TINYADE KALUMO
FIRST SECRETARY (COMMUNICATIONS)

MR. GEORGE MUTUWASUNTCHE LAMYA
MRS. KETTIE COLLEN LAMYA
FIRST SECRETARY

MR. RENOX WILLIAM MALUWA
MRS. BEATRICE MALUWA
FIRST SECRETARY (ADMINISTRATION)

MR. PATRICK MPHEPO
MRS. MATANDA MPHEPO
FIRST SECRETARY (INVESTMENTS)

MALAYSIA

EMBASSY OF MALAYSIA
Chancery: 3516 INTERNATIONAL COURT, NW 20008
(EMBASSY 202-572-9700)   (FAX 202-572-9882)

HIS EXCELLENCY DATO OTHMAN BIN HASHIM
DATIN ROHAYAZAM BINTI KAMARUZAMAN
AMBASSADOR EXTRAORDINARY & PLENIPOTENTIARY

MR. SHAHRIL EFFENDI BIN ABD GHANY
MRS. SURIYAH BINTI ABDULLAH
MINISTER (DEPUTY CHIEF OF MISSION)

MR. HAIRUL REAZA BIN HAROUN AL RASHID
MRS. WAN ALIZA BINTI WAN MOHAMED
MINISTER-COUNSELOR

MR. HAIRIL YAHRI BIN YAACOB
MRS. NARIZAN BINTI NAWAWI
MINISTER-COUNSELOR (ECONOMICS)

MR. SHAHABUDEEN BIN ADAM SHAH
MRS. ANITA BINTI NOOR MOHAMED
COUNSELOR

MR. NAIM MAJDI BIN SULAIMAN
MRS. NURUL AMAL BINTI AHMAD FAIZAL
COUNSELOR (AGRICULTURE)

* U.S. Citizen

MR. MOHD HADTAMIZI BIN ABU BAKAR
    MRS. ANIZAH BINTI OMAR
    SECOND SECRETARY (CONSULAR)

MR. KHAIRUL AZAM BIN BANI
    MRS. NAZLYN BINTI ROSLI
    SECOND SECRETARY

MR. FNU SYED EDWAN ANWAR
    MRS. RAJA ZARINA BINTI RAJA SALLEHUDIN
    SECOND SECRETARY

MRS. NOR SYAREENA BINTI YEM
    MR. SHAHRI IZHAR BIN ABDUL KARIM
    SECOND SECRETARY (AGRICULTURE)

MR. KHAIR BAHARI BIN AHMAD
    THIRD SECRETARY (ADMIN & FINANCE)

MR. RAZAK BIN AZIZ
    MRS. JUMAILIAH BINTI A. JAMIL
    ATTACHE (EDUCATION)

MR. MOHD NAZROL BIN MARZUKE
    MRS. KHAIRUN NISA BINTI MD KHUZAIMAH
    ATTACHE (EDUCATION)

MR. JOHARI BIN MINAL
    MRS. MASTURA BINTI YUSOP
    ATTACHE (SCIENCE)

DR. POSIAH BINTI MOHD ISA
    ATTACHE (EDUCATION)

MR. MOHD SHUHAILY BIN MOHD ZAIN
    MRS. ENNIE SALINA BINTI ROSELI
    ATTACHE (POLICE)

MR. ABD RAHIM BIN MASUM
    MRS. AIDAH BINTI MISDAN
    ASST. ATTACHE (EDUCATION)

MR. AZIM BIN HARUN
    MRS. EMI FAIRUZ BINTI SUPARMAN
    ASST. ATTACHE (EDUCATION)

MR. AEMRAN BIN MUSTAFA
    MRS. NORLIZA BINTI AB KAHAR
    ASST. ATTACHE (POLICE)

BRIGADIER GENERAL JAAFAR BIN KASIM
    MRS. AZMIYATUL SHIMA B. ZAINOL ABIDIN
    DEFENSE, MILITARY, NAVAL & AIR ATTACHE

LIEUTENANT COLONEL MOHD HAFIZAR BIN MD IDRIS
    MRS. ZETI AKHTAR BINTI MUSTAFA
    ASST. DEFENSE, MILITARY, NAVAL & AIR ATTACHE

CONSULAR SECTION
    3516 INTERNATIONAL COURT, NW 20008
        (OFFICE 202-572-9755)

DEFENSE, MILITARY, NAVAL AND AIR ATTACHE OFFICE
    3516 INTERNATIONAL COURT, NW 20008
        (OFFICE 202-572-9711)   (FAX 202-572-9884)

ECONOMIC COUNSELOR OFFICE
    3516 INTERNATIONAL COURT, NW 20008
        (OFFICE 202-572-9735)   (FAX 202-572-9782)

MALAYSIAN RUBBER EXPORT PROMOTION COUNCIL
    3516 INTERNATIONAL COURT, NW 20008
        (OFFICE 202-572-9771)   (FAX 202-572-9787)

MALAYSIAN STUDENTS OFFICE
    3516 INTERNATIONAL COURT, NW 20008
        (OFFICE 202-572-9765)   (FAX 202-572-9784)

MARA STUDENTS OFFICE
    1501 18TH STREET, NW 20036
        (OFFICE 202-328-2777)   (FAX 202-462-6851)

SCIENTIFIC ATTACHE
    3516 INTERNATIONAL COURT, NW 20008
        (OFFICE 202-572-9768)   (FAX 202-572-9783)

MALDIVES

EMBASSY OF THE REPUBLIC OF MALDIVES
Chancery: 800 SECOND AVENUE, SUITE 400 E
NEW YORK, NY 10017
(EMBASSY 212-599-6195)   (FAX 212-661-6405)

HIS EXCELLENCY AHMED SAREER
    MRS. FATHIMATH ATHIFA
    AMBASSADOR EXTRAORDINARY & PLENIPOTENTIARY

MALI

EMBASSY OF THE REPUBLIC OF MALI
Chancery: 2130 R STREET, NW 20008
(EMBASSY 202-332-2249)   (FAX 202-332-6603)

HIS EXCELLENCY AL-MAAMOUN BABA LAMINE KEITA
    MRS. THERESE KEITA
    AMBASSADOR EXTRAORDINARY & PLENIPOTENTIARY

MR. AHMADOU BARAZI MAIGA
    MRS. HAOUA MAIGA EPS MAIGA
    COUNSELOR

MR. MOHAMED OUZOUNA MAIGA
    MRS. FATOUMATA MAIGA
    COUNSELOR

MR. SALIF SANOGO
    MRS. SIRA SANOGO
    COUNSELOR (COMMUNICATION)

MR. MAHAMA DAOUDA DICKO
    MRS. MAIMOUNA ARBY DICKO
    ATTACHE (FINANCIAL)

COLONEL BOURAMA SANGARE
    MRS. AISSATA SANGARE
    DEFENSE, MILITARY & AIR ATTACHE

MALTA

EMBASSY OF MALTA
Chancery: 2017 CONNECTICUT AVENUE, NW 20008
(EMBASSY 202-462-3611)   (FAX 202-387-5470)

HIS EXCELLENCY JOSEPH COLE
    MRS. BERNARDINA COLE
    AMBASSADOR EXTRAORDINARY & PLENIPOTENTIARY

MR. DENNIS GRECH
    FIRST SECRETARY (DEPUTY CHIEF OF MISSION) & CONSUL

MARSHALL ISLANDS

EMBASSY OF THE REPUBLIC OF THE MARSHALL ISLANDS
Chancery: 2433 MASSACHUSETTS AVENUE, NW, FLOOR
1ST 20008
(EMBASSY 202-234-5414)   (FAX 202-232-3236)

HIS EXCELLENCY CHARLES RUDOLPH PAUL
AMBASSADOR EXTRAORDINARY & PLENIPOTENTIARY

MS. DIXIE LOMAE
FIRST SECRETARY

MAURITANIA

EMBASSY OF THE ISLAMIC REPUBLIC OF MAURITANIA
Chancery: 2129 LEROY PLACE, NW 20008
(EMBASSY 202-232-5700)   (FAX 202-319-2623)

HIS EXCELLENCY MOHAMED LEMINE EL HAYCEN
MS. LAAZIZA HOUZALI
AMBASSADOR EXTRAORDINARY & PLENIPOTENTIARY

MR. DHEHBI ALARBI
MRS. GHADA HAMDAN
COUNSELOR (DEPUTY CHIEF OF MISSION)

MR. DJIBRIL CISSE
MRS. JEMILA DOUMBIA
COUNSELOR

MRS. MARIEM DAH
COUNSELOR

MRS. AMINETOU DEIHI
MR. DIDI BIHA
COUNSELOR (ACCOUNTANT)

MR. MOUSSA OUMAR DIOP
MRS. AMINATA MAMADOU DIOP
COUNSELOR

MR. MOHAMED EL MOCTAR A. OULD YOUBA
MRS. FATIMETOU MINT MOCTAR ALAOUI
COUNSELOR

MAURITIUS

EMBASSY OF REPUBLIC OF MAURITIUS
Chancery: 1709 N STREET, NW 20036
(EMBASSY 202-244-1491)   (FAX 202-966-0983)

HIS EXCELLENCY SOMDUTH SOBORUN
MRS. OMILA DEVI SOBORUN
AMBASSADOR EXTRAORDINARY & PLENIPOTENTIARY

MR. HANS IRVIN ANTISH BHUGUN
FIRST SECRETARY

MR. SAMEEM GAFFAR
MRS. PRITTY TEELUCK GAFFAR
SECOND SECRETARY

MR. DHANANDJAY GOBOODUN
MRS. RADIKA GOBOODUN
SECOND SECRETARY

MEXICO

EMBASSY OF MEXICO
Chancery: 1911 PENNSYLVANIA AVENUE, NW 20006
(EMBASSY 202-728-1600)   (FAX 202-728-1698)

HIS EXCELLENCY EDUARDO TOMAS MEDINA MORA ICAZA
AMBASSADOR EXTRAORDINARY & PLENIPOTENTIARY

MRS. MABEL DEL PILAR GOMEZ OLIVER
MR. MANUEL DOMINGUEZ MENENDEZ
MINISTER (DEPUTY CHIEF OF MISSION)

MR. MARIO GILBERTO AGUILAR SANCHEZ
MINISTER (FISHERY)

MR. RICARDO ALDAY GONZALEZ
MINISTER

MR. EDUARDO CHAILLO ORTIZ
MRS. FABIOLA LIZARRAGA RUZ
MINISTER (TOURISM)

MS. BRENDA ESTEFAN MARTINEZ
MINISTER

MR. GUILLERMO FONSECA LEAL
MS. MARIA FERNANDA ALVA HERNANDEZ
MINISTER (ATTORNEY'S GENERAL OFFICE)

MR. JOSE MARTIN GARCIA SANJINES
MRS. PATRICIA GOMEZ HINOJOSA
MINISTER (TAX & CUSTOMS)

MR. JORGE LOPEZ PEREZ
MRS. ADRIANA CHAVEZ ITURBE
MINISTER (TRADE & INVESTMENT)

MR. ANTONIO ORTIZ MENA LOPEZ NEGRETE
MRS. MARIANA MARTINEZ BERLANGA
MINISTER (ECONOMIC)

MR. ALEJANDRO POSADAS URTUSUASTEGUI
MRS. PERLA LILIANA NAVA RAMIREZ
MINISTER (ENVIRONMENTAL AFFAIRS)

MR. KENNETH PATRICK SMITH RAMOS
MRS. AMY LYN GLOVER*
MINISTER

MR. CARLOS VAZQUEZ OCHOA
MRS. EDMI H. CLAUDIA RAMOS CUEVAS
MINISTER (AGRICULTURAL)

MR. SALVADOR BEHAR LAVALLE
MRS. ADRIANA ISABEL KADO SEGOVIA
COUNSELOR (ECONOMIC)

MR. ENRIQUE BRAVO ESCOBAR
COUNSELOR (CHIEF OF STAFF)

MR. JESUS ENRIQUE ESCAMILLA NUNEZ
MRS. XIAO WU
COUNSELOR

MR. ENRIQUE ERNESTO ESCORZA ZAMUDIO
MRS. ANA ELIZABETH RODRIGUEZ BEDOY
COUNSELOR (POLITICAL)

MISS MARTHA JOSEFINA GAYTAN FRETTLOHR
COUNSELOR

MR. ANIBAL GOMEZ TOLEDO
MRS. YESENIA CONTRERAS LOPEZ
COUNSELOR (HEAD OF CONSULAR SECTION)

* U.S. Citizen

MR. JUAN CARLOS LARA ARMIENTA
    MRS. MARIA ALEJANDRA EZETA BAGNIS
COUNSELOR

MR. DAVID ALEJANDRO MACEDO SANTOS
COUNSELOR (ATTORNEY GENERAL'S OFFICE)

MR. MIGUEL ANGEL MENDEZ BUENOS AIRES
    MRS. ELMA ALICIA OVIEDO GALDEANO
COUNSELOR (ATTORNEY'S GENERAL OFFICE)

MR. MARGARITO JESUS OCAMPO MARTINEZ
COUNSELOR

MR. JOSE ANTONIO ORTIZ PEDRAZA
    MS. FLOR DE MARIA A. DIAZ GONZALEZ
COUNSELOR

MR. JOSE LUIS PAZ VEGA
    MRS. GEORGINA PASTELIN ISLAS
COUNSELOR (ECONOMIC)

MR. MIGUEL EDUARDO REA FALCON
    MRS. KARLA IVETTE NIETO NEVAREZ
COUNSELOR

MR. SAUL SALVADOR RONQUILLO GARCIA
    MRS. IRENE BECERRIL RUBIO
COUNSELOR (PUBLIC SECURITY)

MR. JOSE L. STEIN VELASCO G. CASANOVA
COUNSELOR (FINANCIAL INTELLIGENCE)

MR. GERARDO TAMAYO CASTROPAREDES
    MRS. DAYUMA AVELINA RUIZ VILAR
COUNSELOR (POLITICAL AFFAIRS)

MR. VICTOR MANUEL URIBE AVINA
COUNSELOR (LEGAL AFFAIRS)

MR. MOISES JOEL ZAVALETA LOPEZ
COUNSELOR

MS. PAOLA ARCE RODRIGUEZ
FIRST SECRETARY (TAX & CUSTOMS)

MRS. ANA PAOLA BARBOSA FERNANDEZ
FIRST SECRETARY

MR. JOSE V. BORJON LOPEZ COTERILLA
    MRS. BLANCA LILIA VALLEJO GOMEZ
FIRST SECRETARY (LATINO AFFAIRS)

MR. MARTIN TEODORO CARO SANCHEZ
FIRST SECRETARY

MR. TOMAS DIAZ DIAZ
    MRS. DOLORES JIMENEZ HERNANDEZ
FIRST SECRETARY

MRS. URSULA REGINA DOZAL ALVARADO
FIRST SECRETARY (POLITICAL)

MRS. ILSE LILIAN FERRER SILVA
    MR. DOUGLAS PETER SMURR*
FIRST SECRETARY

MR. JOSE RAMON LARA ZAMARRIPA
FIRST SECRETARY (TAX & CUSTOMS)

MS. MARIANA MARRON ESNAURRIZAR
FIRST SECRETARY

MRS. MARIA FERNANDA PEREZ GALINDO
FIRST SECRETARY

MR. RICARDO F. ROJAS GRANADOS
    MRS. BRENDA ESTHELA MARTINEZ VERGARA
FIRST SECRETARY

MRS. LETICIA MAKI TERAMOTO SAKAMOTO
    MR. WILBERT TORRE RAMIREZ
FIRST SECRETARY

MRS. LYDIA ANTONIO DE LA GARZA
    MR. CARLOS MARQUEZ AQUIQUE
SECOND SECRETARY

MS. VANESSA CALVA RUIZ
SECOND SECRETARY

MR. JULIAN ESCUTIA RODRIGUEZ
    MRS. PAOLA ABAD SARQUIS
SECOND SECRETARY

MR. JORGE LUIS LEYVA VAZQUEZ
    MRS. GISELA GARCIA DE LA ROSA
SECOND SECRETARY (AGRICULTURAL)

MR. CARLOS IVAN MENDOZA AGUIRRE
SECOND SECRETARY

MS. FERNANDA ISABEL MONTANO VALDES
    MR. JOSHUA NEAL KLATZKIN*
SECOND SECRETARY

MS. ORENA MARIA NILZA PADILLA AGUILAR
SECOND SECRETARY (ECONOMIC)

MR. FRANCISCO SANDOVAL SAQUI
SECOND SECRETARY

MR. JORGE ALVARO TORRES OROZCO
    MRS. MAGDA ROCA*
SECOND SECRETARY

MS. MARIA DEL ROCIO VAZQUEZ ALVAREZ
SECOND SECRETARY

MS. CYNTHIA MARTINEZ CORTES
THIRD SECRETARY (PRESS)

MR. SERGIO ALONSO MENDEZ LARA
THIRD SECRETARY

MS. MARIA DELCARMEN AGUIRRE LE VINSON
ATTACHE

MRS. ELSA BORJA RUY SANCHEZ
    MR. FERNANDO SEPULVEDA AMOR
ATTACHE

MRS. LILIANA CAPETILLO ALCEDA
    MR. ALEJANDRO ROMERO AGUIRRE
ATTACHE

MRS. MARINES CERVANTES MAYAGOITIA
ATTACHE (CONSULAR)

MS. ARCELIA DOMINGUEZ MEDINA
    MR. JUAN LOBERA GONZALEZ
ATTACHE & CONSUL

MR. HECTOR MANUEL DOMINGUEZ SANCHEZ
    MRS. HELENA WIDGREN DOMINGUEZ
ATTACHE (ADMINISTRATOR)

MISS LOURDES ESTEBA
ATTACHE (CONSULAR)

MRS. LUZ MARIA GARCIA HERRERA MAGANA
ATTACHE (ADMINISTRATIVE)

* U.S. Citizen

MR. DANIEL SERVANDO GARDUNO BOLANOS
ATTACHE (CONSULAR)

MR. JAIME JIMENEZ MORENO
MRS. MARICELA MORENO DE JIMENEZ
ATTACHE (CULTURAL AFFAIRS)

MRS. MARGARITA IVONNE LASTIRI JIMENEZ
ATTACHE (CONSULAR)

BRIGADIER GENERAL ARTURO CORONEL FLORES
MS. TERESA DOLORES CONTRERAS MAGANA
DEFENSE, MILITARY & AIR ATTACHE

COLONEL ROMAN CARMONA LANDA
MRS. GUADALUPE AVILA MENDEZ
ASST. DEFENSE ATTACHE

LIEUTENANT COLONEL RICARDO HERNANDEZ VELASCO
MRS. LORENA PENUELAS MARTINEZ
ASST. DEFENSE ATTACHE

LIEUTENANT COLONEL RUBEN MONTESINOS TORRES
MRS. ALMA DELIA VALERIO ACEVES
ASST. MILITARY ATTACHE

LIEUTENANT COLONEL DARWIN PUC ACOSTA
MRS. YURIXHI GONZALEZ SARMIENTO
ASST. MILITARY ATTACHE

LIEUTENANT COLONEL DAVID ALEJANDRO TREJO FLORES
MRS. NIVIA CARAVEO MERINO
ASST. MILITARY ATTACHE

CAPTAIN RAUL GARCIA ALTAMIRANO
MS. BEATRIZ RUEDA MARQUEZ
ASST. NAVAL ATTACHE

LIEUTENANT COMMANDER FELIPE MENDEZ MARTINEZ
MRS. LUZ DEL CARMEN DE LUNA LOPEZ
ASST. NAVAL ATTACHE

COMMANDER MIGUEL ANGEL NAVA VILLAVICENCIO
MRS. MARIA LAURA NAVA ROSADO
ASST. NAVAL ATTACHE

MR. JOSE RAYMUNDO TUNON JAUREGUI
MRS. GABRIELA BASILISA ORTIZ AGUILAR
ASST. NAVAL ATTACHE

LIEUTENANT COLONEL HUMBERTO OLASCOAGA GRANADOS
MS. MARIA DEL CARMEN GONZALEZ JUAREZ
ASST. AIR ATTACHE

AGRICULTURAL AND FORESTY MINISTER
1911 PENNSYLVANIA AVENUE, NW 20006
(OFFICE 202-728-1687)   (FAX 202-728-1728)

CONSULAR OFFICE
2827 16TH STREET, NW 20009
(OFFICE 202-736-1000)

DEFENSE, MILITARY AND AIR OFFICE
1911 PENNSYLVANIA AVENUE, NW 20006
(OFFICE 202-728-1687)   (FAX 202-728-1741)

FINANCIAL COUNSELOR OFFICE
1615 L STREET, NW, SUITE 310 20005
(OFFICE 202-338-9010)   (FAX 202-338-9244)

MEXICAN CULTURAL INSTITUTE
2829 16TH STREET, NW 20009

NAVAL ATTACHE
1911 PENNSYLVANIA AVENUE, NW 20006
(OFFICE 202-728-1760)   (FAX 202-728-1767)

* U.S. Citizen

TOURISM BOARD
2829 16TH STREET, NW 20009
(OFFICE 202-728-1600)   (FAX 202-728-1698)

TOURISM MINISTER
1911 PENNSYLVANIA AVENUE, NW 20006
(OFFICE 202-728-1687)   (FAX 202-728-1758)

TRADE NEGOTIATIONS
1911 PENNSYLVANIA AVENUE, NW 20006
(OFFICE 202-728-1687)   (FAX 202-296-4904)

MICRONESIA

EMBASSY OF THE FEDERATED STATES OF MICRONESIA
Chancery: 1725 N STREET, NW 20036
(EMBASSY 202-223-4383)   (FAX 202-223-4391)

HIS EXCELLENCY ASTERIO R TAKESY
MRS. JUSTINA YANGILMAU TAKESY
AMBASSADOR EXTRAORDINARY & PLENIPOTENTIARY

MR. JAMES AMANDO NAICH
MRS. ANGELINA PRESTIPINO NAICH*
MINISTER (DEPUTY CHIEF OF MISSION)

MR. DOMINIC R. MALUCHMAI
MRS. MARYANN R. MALUCHMAI
FIRST SECRETARY

MOLDOVA

EMBASSY OF THE REPUBLIC OF MOLDOVA
Chancery: 2101 S STREET, NW 20008
(EMBASSY 202-667-1130)   (FAX 202-667-1204)

HIS EXCELLENCY IGOR MUNTEANU
MRS. ANGELA MUNTEANU
AMBASSADOR EXTRAORDINARY & PLENIPOTENTIARY

MR. DORIN PANFIL
MRS. LUCIA PANFIL
MINISTER-COUNSELOR (DEPUTY CHIEF OF MISSION)

MRS. TATIANA MUNTEANU
MR. ANDREI MUNTEANU
COUNSELOR

MR. VEACESLAV PITUSCAN
MRS. DIANA GRICIUC
COUNSELOR

MRS. CARINA BLANOVSCHI
MR. TUDOR BLANOVSCHI
FIRST SECRETARY

MR. SERGIU LUCA
MRS. RODISLAVA LUCA
FIRST SECRETARY

MR. NICOLAE POPA
MRS. TATIANA POPA
SECOND SECRETARY & CONSUL

MS. CORINA PRIGORSCHI
SECOND SECRETARY

MONACO

EMBASSY OF MONACO
Chancery: 3400 INTERNATIONAL DRIVE, NW, SUITE 2K-100
20008
(EMBASSY 202-234-1530)   (FAX 202-244-7656)

HIS EXCELLENCY GILLES ALEXANDRE NOGHES
MRS. ELLEN JANE NOGHES*
AMBASSADOR EXTRAORDINARY & PLENIPOTENTIARY

MR. LORENZO LIVIO MARIA RAVANO
MRS. SOPHIE MARGUERITE DE SIGALDY
COUNSELOR

MR. CHRISTIAN LOUIS R. BARON DE MASSY
ATTACHE (ECONOMICS)

MONGOLIA

EMBASSY OF MONGOLIA
Chancery: 2833 M STREET, NW 20007
(EMBASSY 202-333-7117)   (FAX 202-298-9227)

HIS EXCELLENCY ALTANGEREL BULGAA
MRS. CHULUUNTSETSEG ERDENEE
AMBASSADOR EXTRAORDINARY & PLENIPOTENTIARY

MR. BAATAR CHOISUREN
MRS. ENKHJARGAL BEKH OCHIR
MINISTER-COUNSELOR (DEPUTY CHIEF OF MISSION)

MR. JAMBALDORJ TSERENDORJ
MRS. DULAMSUREN GOMBO
MINISTER-COUNSELOR

MRS. BOLORMAA BATSAIKHAN
MR. ARIUNBAT TSERENDASH
COUNSELOR

MR. MUNKHJARGAL BYAMBA
COUNSELOR

MR. ANAND AMGALAN
MRS. BAYARMAA JARGALSAIKHAN
SECOND SECRETARY

MR. ERDENBAYAR ZAGDRAGCHAA
MRS. SARANTSETSEG TSEEBAATAR
SECOND SECRETARY & CONSUL

MR. ODMUNKH ENKHBOLD
MRS. ZOLJARGAL AMARSAIKHAN
ATTACHE

MRS. MYAGMARGARMAA MANDAKH
MR. GANTOGTOKH TOGOO
ATTACHE

MONTENEGRO

EMBASSY OF THE REPUBLIC OF MONTENEGRO
Chancery: 1610 NEW HAMPSHIRE AVENUE, NW 20009
(EMBASSY 202-234-6108)   (FAX 202-234-6109)

HIS EXCELLENCY PROFESSOR SRDAN DARMANOVIC
MRS. ANETA SPAIC
AMBASSADOR EXTRAORDINARY & PLENIPOTENTIARY

* U.S. Citizen

MRS. MARIJA PETROVIC
MR. IVAN PETROVIC
FIRST SECRETARY

LIEUTENANT COLONEL VELIBOR BAKRAC
MRS. OLIVERA BAKRAC
DEFENSE, MILITARY, NAVAL & AIR ATTACHE

MOROCCO

EMBASSY OF THE KINGDOM OF MOROCCO
Chancery: 1601 21ST STREET, NW 20009
(EMBASSY 202-462-7980)   (FAX 202-462-7643)

HIS EXCELLENCY MOHAMMED RACHAD BOUHLAL
MRS. FATIHA BENNANI
AMBASSADOR EXTRAORDINARY & PLENIPOTENTIARY

MR. ABDERRAHIM RAHHALY
MRS. HALIMA AMEZIAN
MINISTER-COUNSELOR (DEPUTY CHIEF OF MISSION)

PRINCE MOULAY SOULEIMANE CHERKAOUI
MRS. HIND HRIDA
MINISTER-COUNSELOR

MR. FOUAD KADMIRI
MRS. SALIMA LAZRAQ
MINISTER-COUNSELOR (POLITICAL)

MR. MAHFOUD BAHBOUHI
MRS. NADIA AIBOUDI
COUNSELOR

MRS. BADIA BENADI
COUNSELOR

MR. NOUR EDDINE BOURANJA
COUNSELOR (PAYMASTER GENERAL)

MR. NABIGHA HAJJI
COUNSELOR

MR. MOUAAD IBRIZ
COUNSELOR (POLITICAL)

MR. TALAL JENNANE
MRS. MOUNIA ALAOUI
COUNSELOR (CONSULAR AFFAIRS)

MRS. LATIFA LOUALI
COUNSELOR

MR. ALI RAH
MRS. NAJAT ADDOU
COUNSELOR (CONSULAR)

MR. HAKIM SAYAH
COUNSELOR

MS. AMINA SELMANE
COUNSELOR (CONSULAR AFFAIRS)

MRS. SAIDA ZAID
COUNSELOR

MS. LALLA LAILA EL ALAOUI LAMDAGHRI
FIRST SECRETARY

MR. JAWAD CHERRAT
MRS. HAYAT TOUHAMI
ATTACHE

MR. NAJIB TAZI
ATTACHE

COLONEL MOHAMMED ANESRIF
MRS. BOUCHRA ZAKI
DEFENSE, MILITARY, NAVAL & AIR ATTACHE

CHANCERY ANNEX
1211 CONNECTICUT AVENUE, NW, SUITE 312 20036
(OFFICE 202-457-0012)   (FAX 202-452-0106)

MOZAMBIQUE

EMBASSY OF THE REPUBLIC OF MOZAMBIQUE
Chancery: 1525 NEW HAMPSHIRE AVENUE, NW 20036
(EMBASSY 202-293-7146)   (FAX 202-835-0245)

HER EXCELLENCY AMELIA NARCISO MATOS SUMBANA
MR. ADRIANO FERNANDES SUMBANA
AMBASSADOR EXTRAORDINARY & PLENIPOTENTIARY

MS. ANA MARIA RAQUEL D. ALBERTO
COUNSELOR (COMMERCIAL)

MR. EDUARDO CANDIDO ALBINO ZAQUEU
MRS. MARIA ISABEL ANGELO TITO
COUNSELOR

MR. ANTONIO TAUZENE
MRS. ANTONIETA BENE MOIANE TAUZENE
SECOND SECRETARY

MRS. MARIA DO CEU SAMBO
ATTACHE (FINANCIAL AND ADMINISTRATIVE)

MRS. ANTONIETA BENE MOIANE TAUZENE
MR. ANTONIO TAUZENE
ATTACHE (ADMINISTRATIVE)

NAMIBIA

EMBASSY OF THE REPUBLIC OF NAMIBIA
Chancery: 1605 NEW HAMPSHIRE AVENUE, NW 20009
(EMBASSY 202-986-0540)   (FAX 202-986-0443)

HIS EXCELLENCY MARTIN ANDJABA
MRS. CAROLINE PENGEVALI ANDJABA
AMBASSADOR EXTRAORDINARY & PLENIPOTENTIARY

MS. ANNA NENGENGE
COUNSELOR (DEPUTY CHIEF OF MISSION)

MR. ULRICH FREDDIE GAOSEB
MRS. MONIKA GAOSES
COUNSELOR (COMMERCIAL)

MR. O'BRIEN SIMASIKU SIMASIKU
FIRST SECRETARY

MR. ISAI KEJA
MRS. DIANA KEJA
SECOND SECRETARY

NAURU

EMBASSY OF THE REPUBLIC OF NAURU
Chancery: 800 SECOND AVENUE
NEW YORK, NY 10017
(EMBASSY 212-937-0074)   (FAX 212-937-0079)

HER EXCELLENCY MARLENE INEMWIN MOSES
AMBASSADOR EXTRAORDINARY & PLENIPOTENTIARY

NEPAL

EMBASSY OF NEPAL
Chancery: 2131 LEROY PLACE, NW 20008
(EMBASSY 202-667-4550)   (FAX 202-667-5534)

HIS EXCELLENCY SHANKAR PRASAD SHARMA
MRS. KALPANA SHARMA
AMBASSADOR EXTRAORDINARY & PLENIPOTENTIARY

MR. ARJUN KANT MAINALI
MRS. SUMEDHA MAINALI
MINISTER-COUNSELOR (DEPUTY CHIEF OF MISSION)

MR. LEKH NATH GAUTAM
MRS. PRAMILA GAUTAM
SECOND SECRETARY

MR. HAKIM BAHADUR BHANDARI
MRS. JANUKI DEVI BHANDARI
THIRD SECRETARY

MR. JIT BAHADUR KARKEE
MRS. RIMA KUMARI KARKEE
THIRD SECRETARY

COLONEL JASWANT SHAMSHER J. B. RANA
MRS. NEETU RANA
DEFENSE & MILITARY ATTACHE

NETHERLANDS

ROYAL NETHERLANDS EMBASSY
Chancery: 4200 LINNEAN AVENUE, NW 20008
(EMBASSY 202-244-5300)   (FAX 202-362-3430)

HIS EXCELLENCY RUDOLF SIMON BEKINK
MRS. GABRIELLE DE KUYPER SHESHUNOFF
AMBASSADOR EXTRAORDINARY & PLENIPOTENTIARY

MR. PIETER MOLLEMA
MRS. HARMANNA MARTHA VEGT
MINISTER (DEPUTY CHIEF OF MISSION)

MRS. JOCELYN MARIE M CROES DE HERONIMO
MR. RENWICK FRANCIS JOHN HERONIMO
MINISTER (ARUBA)

MR. STEPHAN ERIC PAUL RAES
MRS. AILEEN ELIZABETH LONIE
MINISTER

MR. ROBBERT JOHN ANDERSON
COUNSELOR

MR. PIETER ANNE BOOTSMA
MRS. MARJORIE GEERS
COUNSELOR

* U.S. Citizen

MR. MARCEL JACCO DE VINK
COUNSELOR (POLITICAL)

MRS. JANKE SYTSKE DE VRIES
MR. JOOST RENE VAN DAAL
COUNSELOR

MRS. ANNETTA JOHANNA F.M. DECKERS
MR. ROBERT VAN DER GRAAF
COUNSELOR (FINANCIAL)

MR. ROGER KLEINENBERG
MRS. CATHARINA VAN DER MEER
COUNSELOR (INNOVATION)

MR. PELGROM JOHAN LANGENBERG
COUNSELOR (TRANSPORTATION&TELECOMMUNICATIONS)

MR. MARTINUS WILHELMUS OLDE MONNIKHOF
MRS. JACQUELINE CORNELIA C. GREVEN
COUNSELOR (AGRICULTURAL)

MR. HENRICUS PAULUS SCHREINEMACHERS
MRS. CHANTAL DENISE MAES
COUNSELOR (POLICE & JUDICIAL AFFAIRS)

MR. ANDRIES FRANK VAN DER MEULEN
MRS. BIRGITTA LOUISE JOHANNA SMITS
COUNSELOR

MR. PETER JOHN VAN MECHELEN
MRS. DENISE MARIE RYAN
COUNSELOR

MRS. ELISABETH MARIA H VAN OVERVELD
MR. MARTIJN JAN NAGTEGAAL
COUNSELOR

MRS. ELISABETH PETRONELLA M. BERKERS
MR. JOSEPHUS WOUTERUS H HURKMANS
FIRST SECRETARY & VICE CONSUL

MR. ALEXANDER CHRISTIAN KOFMAN
MRS. CELESTA JUDITH BOS
FIRST SECRETARY (POLITICAL)

MRS. MIRJAM ADRIANA JOHANNA KRIJNEN
MR. AREND STEUNENBERG
FIRST SECRETARY (POLITICAL)

MR. JOB VAN DEN BERG
MRS. KAREN BURBACH
FIRST SECRETARY

MR. FLORIS VAN EIJK
FIRST SECRETARY

MR. MAARTEN VAN ROSSUM
MRS. ARINDA ADRIENNE J VAN DER MEER
FIRST SECRETARY

MR. RONALD ERIC GENEMANS
MRS. OSIRA AMILDA VAN DER VOORT
ATTACHE (DEFENSE)

MRS. MARGARETHA ELISABETH KUBBE
ATTACHE (POLICE)

MS. KARIN LYDIA LOUZADA
ATTACHE (SCIENCE & TECHNOLOGY)

MRS. JACQUELINE ANN TEERLINK
MR. DANIEL EMILE GAREAU
ATTACHE (ADMINISTRATIVE)

MISS LOBKE KOOLEN
ASST. ATTACHE

* U.S. Citizen

AIR COMMODORE RALPH WILFRED REEFMAN
MRS. LIANNE ELSJE BREURE
DEFENSE ATTACHE

COLONEL ANTON DEN DRIJVER
MRS. SANDRA FATIMA HOVENIER
AIR ATTACHE

COLONEL ARIE OOMS
MRS. ELISABETH MARIA VAN BREE
ASST. DEFENSE ATTACHE

COLONEL JOSEPH CHRISTIAAN COUMANS
MRS. LUCIA PHILOMENA FRANCISCA HUTTER
NAVAL ATTACHE & ASST. DEFENSE ATTACHE

MR. MARTIN NOORDZIJ
MRS. CHARLOTTE CORNELIA WALTHER
ASST. DEFENSE COOPERATION ATTACHE & ASST. NAVAL ATTACHE

LIEUTENANT COLONEL MARC LEO SLEVEN
ASST. DEFENSE COOPERATION ATTACHE & ASST. AIR ATTACHE

NEW ZEALAND

EMBASSY OF NEW ZEALAND
Chancery: 37 OBSERVATORY CIRCLE, NW 20008
(EMBASSY 202-328-4800)   (FAX 202-667-5227)

HIS EXCELLENCY MICHAEL KENNETH MOORE
MRS. YVONNE DANIELLA MARIA MOORE
AMBASSADOR EXTRAORDINARY & PLENIPOTENTIARY

DR. ANTHONY LINCOLN SMITH
MRS. CATHERINE JANE CHURCHILL SMITH
COUNSELOR (DEPUTY CHIEF OF MISSION)

DR. TRAVIS LLOYD BENSON
MRS. JALEH VIRGINIA BENSON
COUNSELOR

MR. GARRY PHILIP COLLINS
MRS. CHRISTINE ANNE COLLINS
COUNSELOR (CUSTOMS)

MR. GRANT JOSEPH FLETCHER
MS. MARTA ELIZABETH VOS
COUNSELOR

MS. ROWENA CHRISTINE HUME
MR. SAM HOBEN
COUNSELOR (TRADE AND ECONOMIC)

MS. LESLEY JANE MCCONNELL
COUNSELOR (SCIENCE & TECHNOLOGY)

MR. MICHAEL KELVIN PANNETT
MRS. DENISE PANNETT
COUNSELOR (POLICE LIAISON)

MR. DEAN TAYLOR STOUT
MS. KATHLEEN MARY BRAND*
COUNSELOR

MR. MATTHEW STUART ROBERT HAWKINS
MRS. PANIZ FIROUZABADI
FIRST SECRETARY

MS. BELINDA JANE
MR. JAMES PATRICK MOLNAR
FIRST SECRETARY (LIAISON OFFICER)

MR. RICHARD JOHN PRENDERGAST
    MS. ELENA CARVALHO CREMM PRENDERGAST
FIRST SECRETARY (POLITICAL)

MR. STEPHEN DOUGLAS PRENTICE
    MRS. ANNE MARIE PRENTICE*
FIRST SECRETARY

MR. DAVID JOHN REARDON
    MRS. FRANCES HELEN REARDON
FIRST SECRETARY

MR. MICHAEL EDWARD APPLETON
SECOND SECRETARY (POLITICAL)

MR. WILLEM DANIE BEUKMAN
SECOND SECRETARY

MR. GARY RAYMOND FORSYTH
    MRS. NATALIE KAY FORSYTH
ATTACHE

AIR VICE MARSHAL GRAHAM BRIAN LINTOTT
    MRS. DIANNE JOY LINTOTT
DEFENSE, NAVAL & AIR ATTACHE

COMMANDER MATHEW CHARLES WILLIAMS
    MRS. CLAIRE WILLIAMS
NAVAL ATTACHE

LIEUTENANT COLONEL DUNCAN GEORGE ROY
    MRS. NICOLA JANE ROY
ASST. DEFENSE & MILITARY ATTACHE

WING COMMANDER ALLAN WILLIAM JENKINSON
    MRS. ELVIE KATRINA JENKINSON
ASST. AIR ATTACHE

WING COMMANDER NIGEL MARK SAINSBURY
ASST. AIR ATTACHE

NICARAGUA

EMBASSY OF THE REPUBLIC OF NICARAGUA
Chancery: 1627 NEW HAMPSHIRE AVENUE, NW 20009
(EMBASSY 202-939-6570)   (FAX 202-939-6545)

HIS EXCELLENCY FRANCISCO OBADIAH CAMPBELL HOOKER
    MRS. MIRIAM ELINOREE HOOKER COE
AMBASSADOR EXTRAORDINARY & PLENIPOTENTIARY

MR. ALCIDES J. MONTIEL BARILLAS
    MRS. ISOLDA DEL CARMEN MONTIEL*
MINISTER-COUNSELOR (DEPUTY CHIEF OF MISSION)

MR. OSCAR ALEJANDRO ZAMORA HINOJOS
    MS. NADINE EUDILIA LACAYO RENNER
COUNSELOR & CONSUL GENERAL

MISS SAMMIA ALICIA HODGSON MCKENZIE
ATTACHE (CULTURAL & EDUCATION)

MR. ARTURO MCFIELDS YESCAS
    MRS. RAQUEL NOHEMI VARGAS DE MCFIELDS
ATTACHE (PRESS)

LIEUTENANT COLONEL ARMANDO JOSE ALANIZ NOGUERA
    MRS. JULIA ISABEL CASTELLON DE ALANIZ
DEFENSE, MILITARY, NAVAL & AIR ATTACHE

NIGER

EMBASSY OF THE REPUBLIC OF NIGER
Chancery: 2204 R STREET, NW 20008
(EMBASSY 202-483-4224)   (FAX 202-483-3169)

HIS EXCELLENCY MAMAN SAMBO SIDIKOU
    MRS. FATIMA DJIBO SIDIKOU
AMBASSADOR EXTRAORDINARY & PLENIPOTENTIARY

MR. MOUSSA RILLA BOUBACAR
    MRS. TIDARI D. BOUBACAR MOUSSA RILLA
COUNSELOR

MRS. FATIMA DJIBO SIDIKOU
COUNSELOR

MR. HASSANE DOULLA
    MRS. KADIDJATOU DOULLA HASSANE
FIRST SECRETARY (FINANCIAL)

MR. HASSANE TAHER
    MRS. FADOUMA S. TAHER
FIRST SECRETARY

COLONEL ABDOULAYE BADIE
    MRS. TAJIRA AICHATOU ABDOULAYE BADIE
DEFENSE & AIR ATTACHE

NIGERIA

EMBASSY OF THE FEDERAL REPUBLIC OF NIGERIA
Chancery: 3519 INTERNATIONAL COURT, NW 20008
(EMBASSY 202-986-8400)   (FAX 202-362-6541)

HIS EXCELLENCY ADEBOWALE IBIDAPO ADEFUYE
    MRS. CATHERINE ADESOLA ADEFUYE
AMBASSADOR EXTRAORDINARY & PLENIPOTENTIARY

MR. BASSEY EFFIOM ARCHIBONG
    MRS. ASARI BASSEY ARCHIBONG
MINISTER (DEPUTY CHIEF OF MISSION)

MR. ZANGO ABDUSSAMADU ABDU
    MRS. ASIYA ZANGO ABDU
MINISTER (ECONOMIC)

MR. YUSUF SAULAWA ABDULLAHI
    MRS. AMINA AHMADU ABDULLAHI
MINISTER

MR. ABDU WANGARA ADO
MINISTER (ECONOMIC)

MR. CLEMENT ONOJA ADUKU
MINISTER (CULTURE AND WELFARE)

MR. DEMENONGU APOLLONIUS AGEV
    MRS. TERLUMUN THERESA AGEV
MINISTER

MR. IBRAHEEM FOLORUNSHO AJADI
    MRS. MARYAM MERO AJADI
MINISTER

MR. STEPHEN AKIN AKINGBOLASAN
MINISTER (POLITICAL)

MR. EYO ASUQUO
    MRS. EKEI EYO EPHRAIM ASUQUO
MINISTER (PROTOCOL & INFORMATION)

MR. STEPHEN MOMOH BABA
    MRS. ESTHER OLOBO BABA
MINISTER (TRADE AND INVESTMENT)

MR. WASEEU BABATUNDE BALOGUN
MINISTER (SPECIAL DUTIES)

MS. LARABA ELSIE BINTA BHUTTO
MINISTER

MR. FRANCIS ASUQUO EYO
    MRS. CARISSA OMO EYO
MINISTER (POLITICAL)

MR. OBARIJIMA GOMBA
    MRS. ESTHER GOMBA
MINISTER (POLITICAL)

MR. OLUWASEGUN IBIDAPO OBE
MINISTER

MR. ENARUNA E. IMOHE
    MRS. PHILOMENA O. IMOHE
MINISTER (ECONOMIC & COMMERCIAL)

MRS. HADIZA MUSTAPHA
MINISTER (TRADE AND INVESTMENT)

MRS. INGEKEM REGINA OCHENI
    MR. STEPHEN IKANI OCHENI
MINISTER (ADMINISTRATION)

MRS. VIVIAN NWUNAKU ROSE OKEKE
    MR. SIMON NSOBUNDU OKEKE
MINISTER (ECONOMICS)

DR. GREGORY UWEMEDIMO OKON
MINISTER (ECONOMICS)

MR. OLUSANYA OLUGBOYEGA OLUKOYA
MINISTER (PROTOCOL)

MR. PATRICK OLUSOLA ONADIPE
MINISTER (POLITICAL)

MR. BELLO SHEHU RINGIM
    MRS. RAIYA BELLO RINGIM
MINISTER (ECONOMIC)

MR. HARRISON OLUWATOYIN SOLAJA
    MRS. MARGARET OLUBUNMI SOLAJA
MINISTER

MRS. WOSILAT ABIMBOLA ADEDEJI
    MR. MUSTAPHA INAOLAJI ADEDEJI
MINISTER-COUNSELOR

MR. ALEX INEMOH EBIMIEBO
    MRS. CATHERINE OPURUZIFAGHA EBIMIEBO
MINISTER-COUNSELOR (POLITICAL)

MRS. MARTHA OLA OKPI NNOLI
MINISTER-COUNSELOR

MR. OJEMAME OLUSOLA OREVBA
    MRS. THERESA OLUWAYEMISI OREVBA
MINISTER-COUNSELOR

MR. SHEHU ILU BARDE
    MRS. HALIMA SHEHU
COUNSELOR

MR. MOHAMMED BELLO
    MRS. MAIMUNA MOHAMMED BELLO
COUNSELOR (COMMUNICATIONS)

MRS. SARAH EMMANUEL ISONG
FIRST SECRETARY

MR. GBADEBO HASSAN KAREEM
    MRS. MORIDIYAT MOTUNRAYO KAREEM
FIRST SECRETARY

MR. ADEWUNMI OLANREWAJU MAFE
    MRS. OMOLABAKE OMOBOWALE MAFE
FIRST SECRETARY (PROTOCOL)

MR. OKECHUKWU EMMANUEL IDEGWU
    MRS. BLESSING IDEGWU
SECOND SECRETARY

MR. OMAR ABDULRASHEED LAWAL
    MRS. BASIRAT SHADE AIYELESO LAWAL
SECOND SECRETARY

MRS. ROSE OKOH YAKOWA
    MR. PRINCE EHIS MICHAEL OKOH
SECOND SECRETARY

MRS. ADEOLA ANNE ADESOKAN
    MR. BABATUNDE ADEBOWALE ADESOKAN
ATTACHE (IMMIGRATION)

MRS. DORIS IBHADE BRAIMAH
ATTACHE (IMMIGRATION)

LIEUTENANT COLONEL EZRA JAHADI JAKKO
    MRS. GRACE OLUBUNMI KKYETTI JAKKO
ATTACHE (FINANCE)

LIEUTENANT COLONEL ABUBAKAR SULAIMAN MAIKANO
    MRS. ZUWAIRA MAIKANO
ATTACHE (FINANCE)

LIEUTENANT COLONEL JULIUS EHIOZE OSIFO
    MS. AMENAGHAWON ANDREA EHIOZE OSIFO
ATTACHE (FINANCE)

MR. IKECHI JASON OZOEMELAM
ATTACHE (IMMIGRATION)

GROUP CAPTAIN ALIYU GAYA BELLO
    MRS. SADIYA NUHU BELLO
DEFENSE, MILITARY, NAVAL & AIR ATTACHE

COLONEL SULEIMAN ABUBAKAR DAMBO
    MRS. ZALIHA SULEIMAN DAMBO
AIR ATTACHE & ASST. MILITARY ATTACHE

LIEUTENANT COLONEL ALIYU ADANOGU
ASST. DEFENSE ATTACHE

LIEUTENANT COLONEL ABUBAKAR NURA MOHAMMED
    MRS. ZAINAB NURA MOHAMMED
ASST. DEFENSE ATTACHE

LIEUTENANT COLONEL KINGSLEY NWANNE NWOKO
    MRS. ENDURANCE CHIZOBA NWOKO
ASST. DEFENSE ATTACHE

CAPTAIN ADEFEMI POPOOLA KAYODE
    MRS. ABIOLA FUNMILAYO KAYODE
ASST. DEFENSE, MILITARY, NAVAL & AIR ATTACHE

CHANCERY ANNEX
    2201 M STREET, NW 20037

(FAX 202-362-6541)

* U.S. Citizen

NORWAY

ROYAL NORWEGIAN EMBASSY
Chancery: 2720 34TH STREET, NW 20008
(EMBASSY 202-333-6000)   (FAX 202-459-3990)

HIS EXCELLENCY WEGGER CHRISTIAN STROMMEN
REVEREND MRS. CECILIE JOERGENSEN STROMMEN
AMBASSADOR EXTRAORDINARY & PLENIPOTENTIARY

MRS. LAJLA BRANDT JAKHELLN
MR. LEIF GUNNAR JOHANNESSEN KJOEITA
MINISTER-COUNSELOR (DEPUTY CHIEF OF MISSION)

MRS. BERIT ENGE
MR. DONALD JEROME RIDINGS JR*
MINISTER-COUNSELOR

MR. LARS PETTER HENIE
MRS. TOVE IREN BERG
MINISTER-COUNSELOR

MS. LINKEN NYMANN BERRYMAN
MR. NICHOLAS GAY BERRYMAN*
COUNSELOR

MR. KEITH FRODE EIKENES
MRS. JOHANNE FJELLESTAD EIKENES
COUNSELOR

MRS. KIRSTEN HAMMELBO
MR. SVEND SOEYLAND
COUNSELOR (SHIPPING & CIVIL AVIATION)

MRS. MARYANN LOECKA
MR. DAG ALF LOECKA
COUNSELOR (PETROLEUM & ENERGY)

MR. OLA OEIANGEN
COUNSELOR

MS. GRETHE JENSINE PAULSEN
COUNSELOR

MR. RICHARD LORENTZ PEDERSEN
COUNSELOR

MRS. MARI ARCHER SAETHER
MR. EIVIND ROLL
COUNSELOR (ENVIRONMENTAL)

MRS. KIRSTI SKJERVEN
MR. ARILD KOVDAL
COUNSELOR (DEFENSE & SECURITY POLICY)

MR. LARS GUNSTEIN WAHL
MRS. HELENE WAHL
COUNSELOR

MR. ARILD WEGENER
MRS. TORUNN HOLST
COUNSELOR (COMMERCE)

MR. TOMMY FLAKK
MRS. CHRISTINE NORDTOMME SURLIEN
FIRST SECRETARY

MR. EINAR IRGENS GUSTAFSON
MS. TONYA MICHELLE OHNSTAD*
FIRST SECRETARY

MR. DAG OLAV HEIAN ENGDAL
MRS. MARTE HEIAN ENGDAL
FIRST SECRETARY

MR. LARS KJETIL KOEBER
MRS. INGVILD NAESS STUB
FIRST SECRETARY

MRS. MARITA SOERHEIM RENSVIK
MRS. HANNE SOERHEIM RENSVIK
FIRST SECRETARY

MS. RAGNHILD WIKEBY
FIRST SECRETARY

MS. AQSA NOREEN
ATTACHE

REAR ADMIRAL TROND GRYTTING
MRS. HILDE MERETE GRYTTING
DEFENSE ATTACHE

COLONEL ROY ABELSEN
MRS. AASHILD SYNNOEVE ABELSEN
ASST. DEFENSE & MILITARY ATTACHE

CAPTAIN BJORN EGENBERG
MRS. HILDE EGENBERG
NAVAL ATTACHE & ASST. DEFENSE ATTACHE

MAJOR ANN KARIN KRISTENSEN SONDOV
COLONEL RAGNAR TORMOD SONDOV
ASST. DEFENSE COOPERATION ATTACHE & ASST. AIR ATTACHE

COLONEL HELGE TORE MARKUSSEN
MRS. MONA LOFTHUS MARKUSSEN
AIR & DEFENSE COOPERATION ATTACHE & ASST. DEFENSE ATTACHE

OMAN

EMBASSY OF THE SULTANATE OF OMAN
Chancery: 2535 BELMONT ROAD, NW 20008
(EMBASSY 202-387-1980)   (FAX 202-745-4933)

HER EXCELLENCY HUNAINA SULTAN AHMED AL MUGHAIRY
MR. FUAD MUBARAK ALI AL HINAI
AMBASSADOR EXTRAORDINARY & PLENIPOTENTIARY

MR. ABDULLAH HAMED SAIF AL RIYAMI
MRS. LATIFA HAMDAN SAID AL HINAI
MINISTER (DEPUTY CHIEF OF MISSION)

MR. AHMED ALI SHAHDAD
MRS. FATIMA MOHAMED DAD ALLAH AL RAISI
MINISTER

MR. ABDUL HAKEEM ALI ISSA AL SABBAGH
MRS. NAJAT DADRAHMAN F. M. AL BALUSHI
MINISTER-COUNSELOR

MS. ZAINAB MOHAMMED ALI AL BALUSHI
COUNSELOR

MR. JUMA RASHID SAIF AL JAHWARI
MRS. SALWA GHASSAN SALIM AL JAHWARI
COUNSELOR

MR. SALIM AHMED MOHAMED AL KINDI
MRS. RAHMA AHMED ABDULLAH AL GHAZALI
FIRST SECRETARY

MR. AHMED DAWOOD ALI AL ZADJALI
MRS. AWATIF ABDUL HAMEED A. AL ZADJALI
FIRST SECRETARY

* U.S. Citizen

MR. SALIM MOHAMMED SALIM AL IBRAHIM
SECOND SECRETARY

MS. HANAN ABDUL AZIZ YAHYA AL KINDI
ATTACHE (INFORMATION)

DR. ASYA MOHAMED SULAIMAN AL LAMKI
DR. HARITH MOHAMED AL GHASSANI
ATTACHE (CULTURAL)

MS. SHIREEN ABDUL QADER YOUSUF
ATTACHE (COMMERCIAL)

MS. AISHA HAMAD MOHAMMED AL HAJRI
MR. AHMED SAID MASAAOD AL HABSI
ASST. ATTACHE (CULTURAL)

COMMODORE MOHAMED SAID MUSALLAM AL RAWAHI
MRS. FAKHRIYA ALI OMRAN AL MARHUBI
DEFENSE, MILITARY, NAVAL & AIR ATTACHE

COMMANDER MOHAMMED SALIM MOHAMME AL KHARUSI
MRS. RAHAMA SAUD KHALAF AL KHARUSI
ASST. DEFENSE, MILITARY, NAVAL & AIR ATTACHE

CULTURAL OFFICE
8381 OLD COURTHOUSE ROAD, SUITE 130
VIENNA, VA 22182
(OFFICE 571-722-0000)   (FAX 571-722-0001)

DEFENSE OFFICE
2535 BELMONT ROAD, NW 20008
(OFFICE 202-232-8816)   (FAX 202-232-8818)

PAKISTAN

EMBASSY OF PAKISTAN
Chancery: 3517 INTERNATIONAL COURT, NW 20008
(EMBASSY 202-243-6500)   (FAX 202-686-1544)

HER EXCELLENCY SHERRY REHMAN
MR. SYED NADEEM HUSSAIN
AMBASSADOR EXTRAORDINARY & PLENIPOTENTIARY

MR. ASAD MAJEED KHAN
MRS. ZUNAIRA ASAD KHAN
MINISTER (DEPUTY CHIEF OF MISSION)

MR. MOHSIN MUSTAQ CHANDNA
MS. MUSARAT MOHSIN BOZAI
MINISTER (ECONOMIC)

MR. SYED MOHAMMAD IMRAN GARDEZI
MRS. IFFAT IMRAN GARDEZI
MINISTER

MR. MUHAMMAD HASSAN
MRS. RUQIA HASSAN
MINISTER

MRS. MOMINA BANDEY RATHORE
MR. AMEER KHURRAM RATHORE
MINISTER

COLONEL MUHAMMAD KAMRAN AFSAR
MRS. RABIA KAMRAN
COUNSELOR

MS. MUMTAZ ZAHRA BALOCH
COUNSELOR

MR. MUHAMMAD SYRUS SAJJAD QAZI
MRS. SHAZA SYRUS
COUNSELOR

* U.S. Citizen

MR. SHUJJAT ALI RATHORE
MRS. UZMA SHUJJAT
COUNSELOR

MR. MUHAMMAD MUDASSIR TIPU
MRS. FATIMA MUDASSIR
COUNSELOR

MR. SHAIKH MUHAMMAD UMAR
MRS. FARIDA KHANAM
COUNSELOR (COMMUNITY AFFAIRS)

MR. MUHAMMAD ALEEM AKHTAR
MRS. ZAHIDA KANWAL
FIRST SECRETARY (FINANCE & ACCOUNTS)

MR. NAVEED SAFDAR BOKHARI
MRS. AMNA BOKHARI
FIRST SECRETARY

MR. BILAL HAYEE
MRS. SHAMYLA BILAL
FIRST SECRETARY

MR. ZAMAN MEHDI
MRS. MARYAM AFNAN AHMED
FIRST SECRETARY

MR. SALMAN SHARIF
MRS. SADIA SALMAN
FIRST SECRETARY

MS. FOZIA FAYYAZ
SECOND SECRETARY

MR. MUHAMMAD TAUSEEF KHAWAR
MRS. SAIRA NAZ QURESHI
THIRD SECRETARY

GROUP CAPTAIN MUDDASSIR AHMAD
MRS. NISHAT MUDDASSIR
ATTACHE (PROCUREMENT)

MR. AHMAD NADEEM SADIQ
MRS. SHAHZANA NADEEM
ATTACHE (PRESS)

MR. MUHAMMAD FAISAL ILYAS
ASST. ATTACHE (PRESS)

BRIGADIER GENERAL ABDULLAH DOGAR
MRS. AYESHA DOGAR
DEFENSE & MILITARY ATTACHE

MR. ADNAN AHMED
MRS. KAMILA ADNAN
NAVAL ATTACHE

GROUP CAPTAIN MUHAMMAD HASEEB PARACHA
MRS. ROBINA PARACHA
AIR ATTACHE

ATTACHE DEFENSE PROCUREMENT OFFICE
3517 INTERNATIONAL COURT, NW 20008
(OFFICE 202-243-2845)   (FAX 202-686-7614)

PALAU

EMBASSY OF THE REPUBLIC OF PALAU
Chancery: 1701 PENNSYLVANIA AVENUE, NW, SUITE 300
20036
(EMBASSY 202-452-6814)   (FAX 202-452-6281)

HIS EXCELLENCY HERSEY KYOTA
MRS. LYDIA SHMULL KYOTA
AMBASSADOR EXTRAORDINARY & PLENIPOTENTIARY

PANAMA

EMBASSY OF THE REPUBLIC OF PANAMA
Chancery: 2862 MCGILL TERRACE, NW 20007
(EMBASSY 202-483-1407) (FAX 202-483-8413)

HIS EXCELLENCY MARIO ERNESTO JARAMILLO CASTILLO
MRS. ELSA MARIE JARAMILLO*
AMBASSADOR EXTRAORDINARY & PLENIPOTENTIARY

MS. LAURA GRACIELA CASTRO GRIMALDO
COUNSELOR (LEGAL)

MR. GIAMPAOLO RENATO CALCAGNO BURILLO
ATTACHE (CULTURAL)

MS. LOURDES PATRICIA CUEVAS SUBARA
MR. FRANCISCO SEVERO ALVAREZ SERRANO
ATTACHE & VICE CONSUL

MISS GINA DELLA TOGNA NIETO
ATTACHE (CULTURAL AND SCIENTIFIC ATTACHE)

MS. MARIA LUCHIA FABREGA VIRZI
ATTACHE (POLITICAL)

MR. ROY ANTONIO GALAN PEREZ
ATTACHE (COMMERCIAL)

MS. KARLA PATRICIA GONZALEZ RODRIGUEZ
ATTACHE (COMMERCIAL)

MR. OMAR ARIEL PINZON MARIN
MRS. NACELIS D ULLOA FABREGA DE PINZON
ATTACHE (POLICE)

PAPUA NEW GUINEA

EMBASSY OF PAPUA NEW GUINEA
Chancery: 1779 MASSACHUSETTS AVENUE, NW, SUITE 805
20036
(EMBASSY 202-745-3680) (FAX 202-745-3679)

MR. ELIAS RAHUROMO WOHENGU
MRS. RELVIE WOHENGU
MINISTER (CHARGE D'AFFAIRES AD INTERIM)

MS. HELEN ELIZABETH SANNY
THIRD SECRETARY

PARAGUAY

EMBASSY OF PARAGUAY
Chancery: 2400 MASSACHUSETTS AVENUE, NW 20008
(EMBASSY 202-483-6960) (FAX 202-234-4508)

HIS EXCELLENCY FERNANDO ANTONIO PFANNL CABALLERO
AMBASSADOR EXTRAORDINARY & PLENIPOTENTIARY

MR. FRANCISCO MARIA BARREIRO PERROTTA
MRS. LARISA MARIEL GUILLEN DE BARREIRO
MINISTER (DEPUTY CHIEF OF MISSION)

* U.S. Citizen

MR. RUBEN DARIO BENITEZ PALMA
MINISTER

MR. VICTOR LUIS BENITEZ RODRIGUEZ
COUNSELOR

MR. JORGE BRIZUELA PEREZ
MRS. LOURDES C. ALONZO CAMPOS VARELA
FIRST SECRETARY

MS. NORMA CARDOZO SALDIVAR
SECOND SECRETARY

MRS. KUNI CAROLINA HASHIMOTO AMARILLA
MR. FRANCISCO JAVIER HAMMERSLEY ROJAS
SECOND SECRETARY

GENERAL NICASIO RIOS MARTINEZ
MRS. RITA KRAUSKOPF DE RIOS
AIR ATTACHE & ASST. DEFENSE & MILITARY ATTACHE

COMMERICAL AND ECONOMIC AFFAIRS OFFICE
2400 MASSACHUSETTS AVENUE, NW 20008

DEFENSE ATTACHE
2400 MASSACHUSETTS AVENUE, NW 20008

PRESS AND INFORMATION AFFAIRS
2400 MASSACHUSETTS AVENUE, NW 20008
(OFFICE 202-483-6962)

VISA AND CONSULAR AFFAIRS
2400 MASSACHUSETTS AVENUE, NW 20008
(OFFICE 202-483-6960)

PERU

EMBASSY OF PERU
Chancery: 1700 MASSACHUSETTS AVENUE, NW 20036
(EMBASSY 202-833-9860) (FAX 202-659-8124)

HIS EXCELLENCY HAROLD WINSTON FORSYTH MEJIA
MRS. MARIA V SOMMER MAYER DE FORSYTH
AMBASSADOR EXTRAORDINARY & PLENIPOTENTIARY

MS. CECILIA ZUNILDA GALARRETA BAZAN
MINISTER (DEPUTY CHIEF OF MISSION)

MRS. MARIA EUGENIA CHIOZZA BRUCE
MR. HUGO CLAUDIO DE ZELA MARTINEZ
MINISTER & DEPUTY CONSUL GENERAL

MR. CESAR AUGUSTO JORDAN PALOMINO
MRS. CONSUELO DEL C CARBAJAL DE JORDAN
MINISTER & CONSUL GENERAL

MR. PEDRO ANTONIO BRAVO CARRANZA
MS. ELIDA TRINIDAD GASTANAGA DE BRAVO
MINISTER-COUNSELOR (POLITICAL)

MR. LUIS CHANG BOLDRINI
MINISTER-COUNSELOR (POLITICAL)

MR. MIJAIL AUGUSTO QUISPE SANDOVAL
MRS. ROCIO SANCHEZ CACERES
MINISTER-COUNSELOR

MR. JORGE RENATO REYES TAGLE
MRS. TEIJA JALASKOSKI DE REYES
MINISTER-COUNSELOR

MR. OSCAR RAFAEL SUAREZ PENA
MRS. DORIS CRISTINA SEMBERA DE SUAREZ
MINISTER-COUNSELOR

MS. ERIKA VIOLETA LIZARDO GUZMAN
COUNSELOR (ECONOMIC)

MR. RODOLFO AUGUSTO PEREIRA TERRONES
COUNSELOR (PRESS)

MR. FERNANDO ALFONSO MAYTA GALARZA
MRS. IRYNA LAVDANSKA
FIRST SECRETARY

MR. RODRIGO HERNAN BOLUARTE CHAVEZ
MRS. MAYA TERESA SOTO
SECOND SECRETARY

MS. MARIA CAROLINA CARRANZA NUNEZ
SECOND SECRETARY (PUBLIC DIPLOMACY)

MR. RICARDO MALCA ALVARINO
SECOND SECRETARY & VICE CONSUL

MR. JUAN ALEJANDRO MONTOYA VALDERRAMA
SECOND SECRETARY

COLONEL JORGE FERNANDO G. BROATCH JACOBI
ATTACHE (POLICE)

MR. JOSE RAUL CORBERA TENORIO
ATTACHE (CIVIL)

MRS. FLOR MARIA DIAZ HONORES
MR. HERNAN ALVARO LIZARRAGA SUAREZ
ATTACHE (CULTURAL)

MR. LUIS ENRIQUE GONZALES BUSTAMANTE
MRS. FLORENCIA MARINA VIOLENTA VARGAS
ATTACHE (AGRICULTURAL)

COMMANDER VICTOR MANUEL GALARRETA SANDOVAL
ASST. ATTACHE (POLICE)

MAJOR GENERAL RODOLFO GARCIA ESQUERRE
MRS. EMMY DOYLITH G. MONTERO DE GARCIA
ASST. DEFENSE & AIR ATTACHE

COMMANDER EDWARD OMAR LOPEZ CAZORLA
MRS. LLEY SIGRID CORAL HIDALGO
ASST. NAVAL ATTACHE

MR. GUILLERMO MEDRANDA ESPINOSA
MRS. LORELLA ELENA K. ROCHA NICOLETTI
ASST. NAVAL ATTACHE

CAPTAIN HUGO RENZO ROSPIGLIOSI MELGAR
MRS. GIANINA CIRIANI GALVEZ
ASST. NAVAL ATTACHE

COLONEL ELIAZAR DAVID SCHRADER SCHLAEFLI
MRS. JUANA L URIBE RAMO DE SCHRADER
ASST. AIR ATTACHE

AIR ATTACHE OFFICE
2141 WISCONSIN AVENUE, NW, SUITE A 20007
(OFFICE 202-333-1528)

CONSULAR OFFICE
1225 23RD STREET, NW 20037
(OFFICE 202-462-1081)

JOINT FIGHT AGAINST DRUGS OFFICE
1511 K STREET 20005
(OFFICE 202-737-5484)

MILITARY ATTACHE OFFICE
2141 WISCONSIN AVENUE, NW, SUITE F 20007
(OFFICE 202-342-8127)   (FAX 202-333-7417)

NAVAL COMMISSIONER & ATTACHE OFFICE
2141 WISCONSIN AVENUE, NW, SUITE J 20007
(OFFICE 202-337-6670)

PHILIPPINES

EMBASSY OF THE REPUBLIC OF THE PHILIPPINES
Chancery: 1600 MASSACHUSETTS AVENUE, NW 20036
(EMBASSY 202-467-9300)   (FAX 202-328-7614)

HIS EXCELLENCY JOSE JR LAMPE CUISIA
MRS. MARIA VICTORIA JOSE CUISIA
AMBASSADOR EXTRAORDINARY & PLENIPOTENTIARY

MRS. MARIA ANDRELITA S. AUSTRIA
MR. CARLITO EDUARDO AUSTRIA
MINISTER (DEPUTY CHIEF OF MISSION) & CONSUL

MR. ARIEL RODELAS PENARANDA
MRS. ROWENA DAYANGHIRANG PENARANDA
MINISTER & CONSUL

MRS. MARIA ROSENI MENDOZA ALVERO
COUNSELOR

MR. ELMER GOZUN CATO
MRS. MELANIE GLICERIA CATO
FIRST SECRETARY & CONSUL

MR. EMILIO TORRES FERNANDEZ
MRS. CRISTINA DE LEON FERNANDEZ
FIRST SECRETARY & CONSUL

MS. ARLENE TULLID MAGNO
MR. EDWIN LESTER QUIMPO MAGNO
FIRST SECRETARY & CONSUL

MRS. LILIBETH PAREDES ALMONTE
MR. MATHIAS CHARLES ARBEZ
SECOND SECRETARY

MR. ANGELITO AYONG NAYAN
MRS. MINERVA TAN NAYAN
SECOND SECRETARY & CONSUL

MRS. SHIENA RED ESCOTO TESORERO
MR. JOHN TERENCE JAVIER TESORERO
THIRD SECRETARY & VICE CONSUL

MRS. MA. CORINA APOSTOL REYES
MR. JERVIN JOHN CANDELARIA REYES
THIRD SECRETARY & VICE CONSUL

MR. GREGG APOLONIO ANGELES
MRS. YASMIN REYES ANGELES
ATTACHE

MR. FRANCISCO ESCOBEDO ENAJE
ATTACHE

MR. LYRIE FERNANDEZ FULGENCIO
ATTACHE

MR. MANUEL JR ALMEDA GASCON
ATTACHE (PROPERTY)

MRS. ARLOTA TAMBONGCO HALILI CASTANEDA
MR. ANTHONY MISO CASTANEDA
ATTACHE

MS. MA. CAROLINA M. INGLES CHRANS
ATTACHE

* U.S. Citizen

DR. JOSYLINE CHIO JAVELOSA
    MR. SEBASTIAN JOSE ORLINA JAVELOSA
ATTACHE (AGRICULTURE)

MRS. RENELL DALAWES MARTINEZ
    MR. JOSE TERESO REMOLLO MARTINEZ
ATTACHE (ASSISTANT FINANCE OFFICER)

MS. MA. LYRA ESCALANTE OCAMPO
ATTACHE (CONSULAR ASSISTANT)

MRS. LUZVIMINDA GUMATAY PADILLA
ATTACHE (LABOR)

MS. LAYDA OLPINDO PAGUITAL
ATTACHE

MRS. MARIA AURORA PALMA REAL
    MR. FERDINAND ARGENTE REAL
ATTACHE

MS. YOLANDA DUDAS RECANA
ATTACHE

MRS. MARIA LUISA LODRONIO REMULLA
    MR. LAURO JR IPAC REMULLA
ATTACHE

MR. EDGARDO FABULA RODRIGUEZ
    MRS. ELENITA TRINIDAD RODRIGUEZ
ATTACHE

MR. ALBERTO CRUZ ROGERO
    MRS. ELIZABETH VILLEGAS ROGERO
ATTACHE

MR. LAURENCE MANUEL SUMANDO
    MRS. ERLINDA MARQUEZ SUMANDO
ATTACHE

MRS. CYNTHIA DOROJA TAYAM
    MR. DOMINGO MANLANGIT TAYAM
ATTACHE (ADMINISTRATIVE)

MR. LAZARO RODOLFO VILLALOBOS
ATTACHE

MRS. MODESTA PARAGAS VILLALOBOS
    MR. LAZARO RODOLFO VILLALOBOS
ATTACHE

BRIGADIER GENERAL CESAR BADONG YANO
DEFENSE & MILITARY ATTACHE

CAPTAIN ELSON KHO AGUILAR
    MRS. BENILDA MEDINA AGUILAR
NAVAL ATTACHE

COLONEL ARNEL MERCADO DUCO
    MRS. VILMA NAVARRO DUCO
AIR ATTACHE

ARMED FORCES ATTACHE
    1600 MASSACHUSETTS AVENUE, NW 20036
        (OFFICE 202-467-9300)

COMMERCIAL COUNSELOR
    1600 MASSACHUSETTS AVENUE, NW 20036
        (OFFICE 202-467-9418)

CONSULAR OFFICE
    1600 MASSCHUSETTS AVENUE, NW 20036
        (OFFICE 202-467-9300)

POLAND

EMBASSY OF THE REPUBLIC OF POLAND
Chancery: 2640 16TH STREET, NW 20009
(EMBASSY 202-234-3800)   (FAX 202-328-6271)

HIS EXCELLENCY RYSZARD MARIAN SCHNEPF
AMBASSADOR EXTRAORDINARY & PLENIPOTENTIARY

MR. MACIEJ PISARSKI
    MRS. BEATA KUBOKOVA
MINISTER (DEPUTY CHIEF OF MISSION)

MR. MAREK KONARZEWSKI
MINISTER-COUNSELOR

MR. PIOTR KONOWROCKI
    MRS. JULIA EWA KONOWROCKA
MINISTER-COUNSELOR

MR. PAWEL LECHOWICZ
    MRS. DOROTA KRYSTYNA LECHOWICZ
MINISTER-COUNSELOR

MR. PAWEL PIETRASIENSKI
    MRS. EWA AGNIESZKA PIETRASIENSKA
MINISTER-COUNSELOR

MS. ELZBIETA CELINA GRYZIO
COUNSELOR

MR. MARCIN KNAPP
    MRS. HANNA KNAPP
COUNSELOR

MS. MONIKA ANNA LIPERT SOWA
COUNSELOR (POLITICAL)

MR. KONRAD PIOTR MAZIARZ
COUNSELOR

MS. MALGORZATA TERESA SZUM
COUNSELOR

MR. REMIGIUSZ URBANOWSKI
    MRS. AGNIESZKA ANNA URBANOWSKA
COUNSELOR

MS. BARBARA KATARZYNA WADACH
COUNSELOR

MS. BEATA AGNISZKA ADAMCZYK
FIRST SECRETARY

MRS. JUSTYNA M. BARTKIEWICZ GODLEWSKA
    MR. KRZYSZTOF S. GODLEWSKI
FIRST SECRETARY (POLITICAL)

MS. ANNA MALGORZATA IWANICKA-QUINN
    MR. JASON LEE QUINN*
FIRST SECRETARY

MR. RAFAL JAROSZ
    MRS. ANNA MATYLDA JAROSZ
FIRST SECRETARY

MR. ADAM GUSTAW NORMARK
    MRS. MARIETTA NORMARK
FIRST SECRETARY

MRS. ANNA AGNIESZKA PERL
    MR. RAFAL PAWEL PERL
FIRST SECRETARY

* U.S. Citizen

MR. RAFAL PAWEL PERL
    MRS. ANNA AGNIESZKA PERL
FIRST SECRETARY

MS. ANNA ANDRUSZKIEWICZ
SECOND SECRETARY

MR. ARTUR GRELA
    MRS. EWA ANNA KOSIARSKA GRELA
SECOND SECRETARY

MS. PATRYCJA EWA GROCHECKA
SECOND SECRETARY

MRS. EWA AGNIESZKA PIETRASIENSKA
SECOND SECRETARY

MR. KONRAD SKARPETOWSKI
    MS. AGATA SKARPETOWSKA
SECOND SECRETARY

MR. TOMASZ SOWA
SECOND SECRETARY

MR. ANDRZEJ DARIUSZ SOBIERAJ
    MRS. MIROSLAWA ANNA SOBIERAJ
ATTACHE

MR. MIROSLAW KOZIAREWICZ
    MRS. JOLANTA RENATA KOZIAREWICZ
ATTACHE (CIVIL)

MR. MARIAN BOLESLAW ZIOLKOWSKI
    MRS. HANNA KRYSTYNA ZIOLKOWSKA
ATTACHE (CIVIL) (ADMINISTRATION)

MAJOR GENERAL ANDRZEJ FALKOWSKI
    MRS. MARLENA ZOFIA FALKOWSKA
DEFENSE, MILITARY, NAVAL & AIR ATTACHE

MR. TOMASZ JANUSZ KISTER
    MRS. MARTA KISTER
ASST. DEFENSE & MILITARY ATTACHE

COLONEL MICHAL PRZEMYSLAW SPRENGEL
    MS. ANNA SPRENGEL
ASST. DEFENSE & MILITARY ATTACHE

COMMANDER DOROTA ROZA STACHURA
ASST. DEFENSE & NAVAL ATTACHE

CONSULAR DIVISION
    2224 WYOMING AVENUE, NW 20008
        (OFFICE 202-232-4517)   (FAX 202-328-2152)

DEFENSE ATTACHE OFFICE
    2224 WYOMING AVENUE, NW 20008
        (OFFICE 202-232-2303)   (FAX 202-328-2152)

ECONOMIC AND FINANCIAL COUNSELOR OFFICE
    1503 21ST STREET, NW 20036
        (OFFICE 202-467-6690)   (FAX 202-833-8343)

PORTUGAL

EMBASSY OF PORTUGAL
Chancery: 2012 MASSACHUSETTS AVENUE, NW 20036
(EMBASSY 202-328-8610)   (FAX 202-462-3726)

HIS EXCELLENCY NUNO F. ALVES SALVADOR E BRITO
    MRS. DE ATAIDE BATOREU SALVADOR BRITO
AMBASSADOR EXTRAORDINARY & PLENIPOTENTIARY

MRS. DE ATAIDE BATOREU SALVADOR BRITO
MINISTER (DEPUTY CHIEF OF MISSION)

MRS. LUISA MARQUES PAIS LOWE
    MR. GLYN EVAN LOWE
MINISTER-COUNSELOR

MS. ANA FILOMENA DA COSTA ROCHA
COUNSELOR (POLITICAL)

MR. ERNARDO FAUVELET RIBEIRO DA CUNHA
    MRS. FILIPA SILVA RIBEIRO DA CUNHA
COUNSELOR (POLITICAL)

MRS. JOANA MAYER CASTRO
COUNSELOR (TECHNICAL)

MR. LUIS MIGUEL LEANDRO DA SILVA
    MRS. NOEMIA ALICE PRADA FERNANDES
FIRST SECRETARY

COLONEL ANTONIO CARLOS DE AMORIN TEMPORAO
    MRS. ISABEL TEMPORAO
DEFENSE, MILITARY, NAVAL & AIR ATTACHE

CONSULAR SECTION
    2012 MASSACHUSETTS AVENUE, NW 20036
        (OFFICE 202-332-3007)   (FAX 202-387-2768)

DEFENSE, MILITARY, NAVAL AND AIR ATTACHE OFFICE
    2012 MASSACHUSETTS AVENUE, NW 20036
        (OFFICE 202-232-7632)   (FAX 202-328-6827)

QATAR

EMBASSY OF THE STATE OF QATAR
Chancery: 2555 M STREET, NW 20037
(EMBASSY 202-274-1600)   (FAX 202-237-0061)

HIS EXCELLENCY MOHAMED ABDULLA M AL RUMAIHI
    MS. MUNA FAHAD Q AL FAYHANI
AMBASSADOR EXTRAORDINARY & PLENIPOTENTIARY

MR. AHMED YOUSEF A.J. AL RUMAIHI
    MRS. JULIE LYNN LEESON*
FIRST SECRETARY (DEPUTY CHIEF OF MISSION)

MR. AHMED TURKI A. T. AL SOBAI
    MRS. KHOLOUD AHMMAD H. A. AL MANNAI
FIRST SECRETARY

MR. ALI SAAD M. H. ALHAJRI
    MRS. AISHA HAMAD J A AL KUWARI
FIRST SECRETARY

MR. ABDULLA SAAD R. A. AL MOHANNADI
THIRD SECRETARY

MR. MOHAMED ABDULAZIZ AL NASSR
ATTACHE (SECURITY)

MR. NASSER ALI NASSER AL SAADI
    MRS. FATMA HASSAN ABDULLA AL BANNA
ATTACHE (MEDICAL)

MR. SALAH MOHAMMED K. A. AL MALKI
ASST. ATTACHE (MEDICAL)

BRIGADIER GENERAL ABDULRAHMAN IBRAHIM AL HEMAIDI
    MRS. HEND MOHAMMED AHMED AL QATARI
DEFENSE, MILITARY, NAVAL & AIR ATTACHE

MEDICAL, CULTURAL & MILITARY ATTACHE OFFICES
2555 M STREET, NW 20037
(OFFICE 202-274-1600)   (FAX 202-237-0061)

ROMANIA

EMBASSY OF ROMANIA
Chancery: 1607 23RD STREET, NW 20008
(EMBASSY 202-332-4846)   (FAX 202-232-4748)

HIS EXCELLENCY ADRIAN COSMIN VIERITA
MRS. EUGENIA CODRINA VIERITA
AMBASSADOR EXTRAORDINARY & PLENIPOTENTIARY

MRS. STELUTA ARHIRE
MINISTER (DEPUTY CHIEF OF MISSION)

MR. VIOREL ONEL
MRS. MARIA MOGLAN ONEL
MINISTER-COUNSELOR

MRS. EUGENIA CODRINA VIERITA
MINISTER-COUNSELOR

MR. SILVIU GRADINARU
MRS. ROXANA GRADINARU
COUNSELOR

MR. CRISTINEL PETRESCU
MRS. CRISTINA PETRESCU
COUNSELOR

MR. GABRIEL CATALIN SOPANDA
COUNSELOR (POLITICAL)

MS. LAURA BIANCA MIHAI
FIRST SECRETARY

MR. ROBERT OCTAVIAN DUMITRESCU
MRS. AMELIA DUMITRESCU
SECOND SECRETARY

MS. LAVINIA OCHEA
SECOND SECRETARY

MISS ANDRA CATERINA POPESCU
SECOND SECRETARY

MS. DIANA TASE
SECOND SECRETARY

MRS. RODICA TOMESCU OLARIU
MR. DRAGOS TOMESCU OLARIU
SECOND SECRETARY (POLITICAL)

MR. OVIDIU ADRIAN TUDORACHE
MRS. CARMEN MIHAELA TUDORACHE
SECOND SECRETARY (POLITICAL)

MR. SERBAN BREBENEL
MS. OANA ADRIANA BREBENEL
THIRD SECRETARY

MRS. JANINA MARIA CISMARU
MR. ANDREI LAURENTIU CISMARU
THIRD SECRETARY

MR. BOGDAN GEORGE VADUVA
THIRD SECRETARY

MR. MIHAI ADRIAN DRAGOMIR
MRS. GABRIELA OANA DRAGOMIR
ATTACHE

* U.S. Citizen

MR. DANIEL IVANOIU
MRS. IOANA IVANOIU
ATTACHE (COMMUNICATIONS)

MR. ADRIAN CIPRIAN MIRON
ATTACHE (HOME AFFAIRS)

COLONEL LAURENTIU DRAGUSIN
MRS. MARIANA DRAGUSIN
DEFENSE, MILITARY, NAVAL & AIR ATTACHE

MAJOR ROBERT CALINOIU
MRS. GABRIELA CICI CALINOIU
ASST. DEFENSE, MILITARY, NAVAL & AIR ATTACHE

CAPTAIN CATALIN VALENTIN EREMIA
MRS. CORINA ELENA EREMIA
ASST. DEFENSE, MILITARY, NAVAL & AIR ATTACHE

LIEUTENANT COLONEL DORINEL IOAN MOLDOVAN
MRS. MARIANA MAGDALENA MOLDOVAN
ASST. DEFENSE, MILITARY, NAVAL & AIR ATTACHE

CONSULAR AFFAIRS
1607 23RD STREET, NW 20008
(OFFICE 202-232-4747)   (FAX 202-232-4748)

DEFENSE, MILITARY, NAVAL AND AIR ATTACHE
1607 23RD STREET, NW 20008
(OFFICE 202-234-6206)   (FAX 202-232-4748)

ECONOMIC COUNSELOR
1607 23RD STREET, NW 20008
(OFFICE 202-232-6593)   (FAX 202-332-4858)

RUSSIA

EMBASSY OF THE RUSSIAN FEDERATION
Chancery: 2650 WISCONSIN AVENUE, NW 20007
(EMBASSY 202-298-5700)   (FAX 202-298-5735)

HIS EXCELLENCY SERGEY IVANOVICH KISLYAK
MRS. NATALIA MIKHAYLOVNA KISLYAK
AMBASSADOR EXTRAORDINARY & PLENIPOTENTIARY

MR. OLEG NIKOLAYEVICH BURMISTROV
MRS. KAPITOLINA YEGOROVNA BURMISTROVA
MINISTER-COUNSELOR

MR. RINAT MINGALIYEVICH DOSMUKHAMEDOV
MRS. EKATERINA ALEKSANDRO BELYAEVSKAYA
MINISTER-COUNSELOR (TRADE REPRESENTATIVE)

MR. OLEG VLADIMIROVICH STEPANOV
MRS. YULIA ANATOLYEVNA STEPANOVA
MINISTER-COUNSELOR

MR. AYDAR RASHIDOVICH AGANIN
MRS. ALFIYA RIFATOVNA AGANINA
COUNSELOR

MR. ALEXANDER NIKOLAYEVICH BALAKIN
MRS. TATIANA ALEKSEYEVNA BALAKINA
COUNSELOR

MR. VASILY VLADIMIROVICH BORYAK
MRS. OLGA ALEKSANDROVNA BORYAK
COUNSELOR

MR. DMITRY DMITRIYEVICH CHERKASHIN
MRS. ANZHELIKA VLADISLAVOV CHERKASHINA
COUNSELOR

MR. VLADISLAV S. CHERNYSHOV
    MRS. SVETLANA SERGEYEVNA CHERNYSHOVA
COUNSELOR

MR. SERGEY LEONIDOVICH CHUMAREV
COUNSELOR

MR. ALEXEY YURYEVICH DROBININ
    MRS. NATALIA ALEKSANDROVNA DROBININA
COUNSELOR

MR. ANDREY VIKTOROVICH DROZDOV
    MRS. VALERIA ALEKSANDROVNA BELOUSOVA
COUNSELOR

MR. VALERY YEVGENYEVICH ETNYUKOV
    MRS. NATALIA IVANOVNA ETNYUKOVA
COUNSELOR

MR. DENIS VLADIMIROVICH GONCHAR
    MRS. ELENA NIKOLAYEVNA GONCHAR
COUNSELOR

MR. EVGENY VIKTOROVICH KHORISHKO
    MRS. OLGA V. KHORISHKO
COUNSELOR

MR. VALERY DMITRIYEVICH KHROMCHENKOV
    MRS. ELENA OLEGOVNA KHROMCHENKOVA
COUNSELOR

MR. ALEXEY ANATOLYEVICH KISELEV
    MRS. LIUDMILA IVANOVNA KISELEVA
COUNSELOR

MR. ALEXANDER LEONIDOVICH KOZLOV
    MRS. ELIZAVETA VALERYEVNA SOROKINA
COUNSELOR

MR. ANATOLY NIKOLAYEVICH KUTYAVIN
    MRS. NATALIA NIKOLAYEVNA KUTYAVINA
COUNSELOR

MR. NIKOLAY YURYEVICH LYASHCHENKO
COUNSELOR

MR. ALEXEY ANDREYEVICH NIKOLAEV
    MRS. OLGA YURYEVNA NIKOLAEVA
COUNSELOR (DEPUTY TRADE REPRESENTATIVE)

MR. NIKOLAY VITALYEVICH PUKALOV
    MRS. TATIANA PAVLOVNA PUKALOVA
COUNSELOR (HEAD OF CONSULAR DIV.)

MR. SERGEY YURYEVICH RESHCHIKOV
    MRS. IRINA ALEKSANDROVNA RESHCHIKOVA
COUNSELOR

MR. OLEG VLADIMIROVICH RYKOV
    MRS. ELENA VLADIMIROVNA RYKOVA
COUNSELOR

MR. EDUARD ANATOLYEVICH SINITSYN
    MRS. ANNA ALEKSEYEVNA SINITSYNA
COUNSELOR

MR. OLEG VENYAMINOVICH SLEPOV
    MRS. ALLA VASILYEVNA SLEPOVA
COUNSELOR (DEPUTY TRADE REP.)

MR. ANDREY VIKTOROVICH SOROKA
    MRS. ANZHELA GEORGIYEVNA SOROKA
COUNSELOR (DEPUTY TRADE REP.)

MR. IGOR VIKTOROVICH SUKHININ
    MRS. GALINA VLADIMIROVNA SUKHININA
COUNSELOR

MR. ALEXEY GENNADYEVICH TIMOFEEV
    MRS. NATALIA GEORGIYEVNA TIMOFEEVA
COUNSELOR

MR. OLEG VLADIMIROVICH VASILIEV
    MRS. OXANA MIKHAYLOVNA VASILIEVA
COUNSELOR

MR. ANTON VALERYEVICH VUSHKARNIK
    MRS. OLGA BORISOVNA BRYZGALOVA
COUNSELOR

MR. EVGENY ANDREYEVICH YASASHNYY
    MRS. ZOYA ALEKSANDROVNA YASASHNAYA
COUNSELOR

MR. YURY ALEKSANDROVICH ZAYTSEV
    MRS. GALINA ALEKSANDROVNA KOMISSAROVA
COUNSELOR

MR. DMITRY ALEKSANDROVICH ZHIRNOV
COUNSELOR

MR. ALEXANDER ANATOLYEVICH BOCHANOV
    MRS. IRINA VIKTOROVNA BOCHANOVA
FIRST SECRETARY

MR. ANDREY BORISOVICH BONDAREV
    MRS. DARIA VLADIMIROVNA BONDAREVA
FIRST SECRETARY

MR. OLEG GEORGIYEVICH DIVANOV
    MRS. EVGENIA ANATOLYEVNA SHARAPOVA
FIRST SECRETARY

MR. ALEXANDER PETROVICH EGOROV
    MRS. GALINA VIKTOROVNA EGOROVA
FIRST SECRETARY

MR. RUBEN EDUARDOVICH MALAYAN
    MRS. ELENA VLADIMIROVNA BAKHTIAROVA
FIRST SECRETARY

MRS. NATALIA SIDOROVNA MOROZ
    MR. MIKHAIL PROKOFYEVICH MOROZ
FIRST SECRETARY

MR. ANDREY YEVGENYEVICH NASTASIN
    MRS. ANASTASIA ANDREYEVNA NASTASINA
FIRST SECRETARY

MR. VASILY VIKTOROVICH SAVKIN
    MRS. MARIA VLADIMIROVNA SAVKINA
FIRST SECRETARY

MR. ANDREY YURYEVICH SAVUSHKIN
    MRS. EKATERINA A. SAVUSHKINA
FIRST SECRETARY

MR. PAVEL GENNADYEVICH SPITSYN
FIRST SECRETARY

MR. ALEXANDER VLADIMIROVICH TROFIMOV
    MRS. ELENA YURYEVNA KUDRYAVTSEVA
FIRST SECRETARY

MR. ALEXANDER FEDOROVICH BELYAEV
    MRS. MARINA VLADIMIROVNA BELYAEVA
SECOND SECRETARY

MR. YURY VLADIMIROVICH BORODAY
    MRS. OLESYA GENNADYEVNA BORODAY
SECOND SECRETARY

MR. MIKHAIL ALEKSANDROVICH KALUGIN
SECOND SECRETARY

* U.S. Citizen

MRS. MARIA YURYEVNA KALUGINA
SECOND SECRETARY

MR. DENIS VLADIMIROVICH KAREV
MRS. SVETLANA YEVGENYEVNA KAREVA
SECOND SECRETARY

MR. MAXIM PAVLOVICH KONVISAR
MRS. VALERIA ALEKSANDROVNA KONVISAR
SECOND SECRETARY

MRS. ELENA YURYEVNA KUDRYAVTSEVA
MR. ALEXANDER VLADIMIROVICH TROFIMOV
SECOND SECRETARY

MR. SERGEY IGOREVICH KUZNETSOV
MRS. EKATERINA PAVLOVNA KUZNETSOVA
SECOND SECRETARY

MR. YURY YURYEVICH MELNIK
MRS. ELENA ALEKSANDROVNA MELNIK
SECOND SECRETARY

MR. MIKHAIL VYACHESLAVOVICH SATUNKIN
SECOND SECRETARY & VICE CONSUL

MS. SVETLANA VIKTOROVNA SHATALOVA
SECOND SECRETARY

MR. ANDREY ANDREYEVICH TARELIN
MS. EVGENIA OLEGOVNA MIKHAYLOVA
SECOND SECRETARY

MR. MIKHAIL KONSTANTINOVICH TOLCHENOV
SECOND SECRETARY

MR. ALEXANDER ALEKSANDROVICH ZAKHAROV
MRS. SVETLANA VIKTOROVNA ZAKHAROVA
SECOND SECRETARY

MR. MAXIM DMITRIYEVICH ABRAMOV
MRS. ANNA IGOREVNA ABRAMOVA
THIRD SECRETARY

MR. ALEXANDER VALERYEVICH BELOUSOV
MRS. ALEXANDRA SERGEYEVNA BELOUSOVA
THIRD SECRETARY

MR. IGOR GENNADYEVICH BOLDYREV
MRS. LIDIA ALEKSANDROVNA BOLDYREVA
THIRD SECRETARY

MS. POLINA RUSLANOVNA CHEPINITSKAYA
THIRD SECRETARY

MS. NATALIA ALEKSEYEVNA DEMENTIEVA
THIRD SECRETARY

MR. ALEXEY VLADIMIROVICH GULYAEV
MRS. OLGA VALERIYEVNA GULYAEVA
THIRD SECRETARY

MR. DENIS NIKOLAYEVICH KOLESNIK
MRS. LIUDMILA SERGEYEVNA KOLESNIK
THIRD SECRETARY

MR. DENIS VALENTINOVICH KONOVALOV
MRS. YULIA FLAVIANOVNA KONOVALOVA
THIRD SECRETARY

MR. ILYA ALEKSANDROVICH KUZNETSOV
MRS. ANNA VLADIMIROVNA KUZNETSOVA
THIRD SECRETARY

MR. ANDREY SERGEYEVICH MEDYNSKIY
MRS. OXANA YURYEVNA MEDYNSKAYA
THIRD SECRETARY

MR. SERGEY VLADIMIROVICH PONAMAREV
MRS. ANASTASIA MIKHAYLOVNA PONAMAREVA
THIRD SECRETARY

MR. MIKHAIL ALEKSANDROVICH PROTSENKO
MRS. IRINA ANDREYEVNA PROTSENKO
THIRD SECRETARY

MR. PAVEL SERGEYEVICH SHAMRAY
MRS. TATIANA NIKOLAYEVNA SHAMRAY
THIRD SECRETARY

MR. ALEXANDER VASILYEVICH SHLIKHUNOV
MRS. ELENA VLADIMIROVNA SHLIKHUNOVA
THIRD SECRETARY

MR. VADIM ALEKSANDROVICH SOKOLOV
MS. ANNA VIKTOROVNA SOKOLOVA
THIRD SECRETARY

MR. EVGENY ANDREYEVICH TIKHONOV
MRS. MARIA VLADIMIROVNA TIKHONOVA
THIRD SECRETARY

MR. VLADIMIR IVANOVICH CHEPURNOV
MRS. IRINA VALENTINOVNA CHEPURNOVA
ATTACHE

MR. VLADIMIR YURYEVICH CHERNOV
MRS. SVETLANA IGOREVNA CHERNOVA
ATTACHE

MR. DMITRY ANDREYEVICH CHERNYSHEV
MRS. YULIA VLADIMIROVNA CHERNYSHEVA
ATTACHE

MR. SERGEY IVANOVICH FEDORENKOV
MRS. MARINA DAMIROVNA FEDORENKOVA
ATTACHE

MR. IVAN YURYEVICH FILATOV
MRS. ARINA KONSTANTINOVNA FILATOVA
ATTACHE

MR. ILYA ANATOLYEVICH KASTORNOV
MRS. NATALIA ALIYYULLOVNA KASTORNOVA
ATTACHE

MR. ANDREY YURYEVICH KISELEV
MRS. NATALIA NIKOLAYEVNA KISELEVA
ATTACHE

MR. YURY VIKTOROVICH KOROLEV
MRS. ALLA YEVGENYEVNA KOROLEVA
ATTACHE

MR. SERGEY BORISOVICH KORYAGIN
MRS. IRINA IVANOVNA KORYAGINA
ATTACHE

MR. DMITRY VLADIMIROVICH KRAMAREV
MRS. NINA ALEKSANDROVNA KRAMAREVA
ATTACHE

MR. MIKHAIL SERGEYEVICH KRUTIKOV
MRS. OXANA IGOREVNA KRUTIKOVA
ATTACHE & VICE CONSUL

MR. KIRILL NIKOLAYEVICH KUZOVENKO
MRS. ELENA VIKTOROVNA KUZOVENKO
ATTACHE

MR. MAXIM ALEKSANDROVICH LITVINOV
MRS. SVETLANA VALERYEVNA LITVINOVA
ATTACHE

* U.S. Citizen

MR. VLADIMIR YEVGENYEVICH MASTEROV
MRS. MARINA YURYEVNA MASTEROVA
ATTACHE

MR. PAVEL SERGEYEVICH MATVEEV
MRS. ANNA VIKTOROVNA MATVEEVA
ATTACHE

MR. VITALY VITALYEVICH MINCHENKO
MRS. NATALIA LEONIDOVNA MINCHENKO
ATTACHE

MR. SERGEY NIKOLAYEVICH MIRONOV
MRS. LIUDMILA NIKOLAYEVNA MIRONOVA
ATTACHE

MR. ALEXANDER SERGEYEVICH NOVIKOV
MRS. ANNA BORISOVNA NOVIKOVA
ATTACHE

MR. VICTOR DANILOVICH PASTUKHOV
MRS. NINA NIKOLAYEVNA PASTUKHOVA
ATTACHE

MR. IGOR ROSTISLAVOVICH PROKOPIEV
ATTACHE

MR. EVGENY NIKOLAYEVICH SHUMILOV
ATTACHE

MR. EVGENY YURYEVICH SLAVNOV
MRS. TATIANA ALEKSANDROVNA SLAVNOVA
ATTACHE

MR. VLADIMIR VASILYEVICH TROITSKIY
MRS. OLGA ALEKSANDROVNA TROITSKAYA
ATTACHE

MR. ALEXEY PAVLOVICH VASILCHENKO
MRS. LIANA NODAROVNA VASILCHENKO
ATTACHE

MR. ALEXANDER GENNADYEVICH VINOGRADOV
MRS. VALENTINA VIKTOROVNA VINOGRADOVA
ATTACHE

MR. OLEG VYACHESLAVOVICH VORONIN
MRS. YULIA VIKTOROVNA VORONINA
ATTACHE

MR. VLADISLAV DMITRIYEVICH ZAYTSEV
MRS. IRINA PAVLOVNA ZAYTSEVA
ATTACHE

MR. SERGEY VLADIMIROVICH ZHURAVLEV
MRS. IRINA EDUARDOVNA ZHURAVLEVA
ATTACHE

MR. VALERY NIKOLAYEVICH BARANOVSKIY
MRS. NATALIA NIKOLAYEVNA BARANOVSKAYA
DEFENSE ATTACHE

COLONEL EVGENY VIKTOROVICH BOBKIN
MRS. ELENA BORISOVNA BOBKINA
MILITARY ATTACHE

MR. ALEXEY VALERYEVICH DEREVYANKIN
MRS. ANNA VALERYEVNA DEREVYANKINA
NAVAL ATTACHE

LIEUTENANT COLONEL VLADIMIR GENNADYEVICH BAYMYSHEV
MRS. INNA VALERYEVNA BAYMYSHEVA
AIR ATTACHE

LIEUTENANT COLONEL VYACHESLAV OLEGOVICH SAFRONOV
MRS. ELIZAVETA VLADIMIROVNA SAFRONOVA
ASST. DEFENSE ATTACHE

LIEUTENANT COLONEL DMITRY VLADIMIROVICH TARANTSOV
MRS. VITALIYA ANATOLYEVNA TARANTSOVA
ASST. DEFENSE ATTACHE

MR. VALERY NIKOLAYEVICH ZUBAREV
MRS. ZHANNA PAVLOVNA ZUBAREVA
ASST. DEFENSE ATTACHE

LIEUTENANT COLONEL VLADIMIR SERGEYEVICH SKORIKOV
MRS. NATALIA SERGEYEVNA SKORIKOVA
ASST. MILITARY ATTACHE

MAJOR ROMAN VITALYEVICH SMIRNOV
MRS. MARIA ALEKSANDROVNA SMIRNOVA
ASST. MILITARY ATTACHE

LIEUTENANT COLONEL YURY YURYEVICH GLADKOV
MRS. ANASTASIA VIKTOROVNA GLADKOVA
ASST. NAVAL ATTACHE

MR. ANDREY VLADIMIROVICH GRECHIKHO
MRS. NATALIA VIKTOROVNA GRECHIKHO
ASST. NAVAL ATTACHE

MR. VLADIMIR NIKOLAYEVICH DUKMASOV
MRS. OLGA ALEKSANDROVNA DUKMASOVA
ASST. AIR ATTACHE

MR. ANDREY VASILYEVICH SBOEV
MRS. YULIA ALEKSANDROVNA SBOEVA
ASST. AIR ATTACHE

MR. ALEXEY ALEKSANDROVICH VORONOV
MRS. NATALIA ANATOLYEVNA VORONOVA
ASST. AIR ATTACHE

CONSULAR DIVISION
2641 TUNLAW ROAD, NW 20007
(OFFICE 202-939-8907)   (FAX 202-939-8917)

DEFENSE, MILITARY, NAVAL AND AIR ATTACHE OFFICE
2552 BELMONT ROAD, NW 20008
(OFFICE 202-965-1181)

FISHERIES ATTACHE OFFICE
1609 DECATUR STREET, NW 20011
(OFFICE 202-726-3838)

INFORMATION OFFICE
1706 18TH STREET, NW 20009
(OFFICE 202-232-6020)

RUSSIAN CULTURAL CENTRE
1825 PHELPS PLACE, NW 20008
(OFFICE 202-265-3840)   (FAX 202-265-6040)

TRADE REPRESENTATIVE OF THE RUSSIAN FEDERATION
2001 CONNECTICUT AVENUE, NW 20008
(OFFICE 202-234-7170)

RWANDA

EMBASSY OF THE REPUBLIC OF RWANDA
Chancery: 1714 NEW HAMPSHIRE AVENUE, NW 20009
(EMBASSY 202-232-2882)   (FAX 202-232-4544)

HIS EXCELLENCY JAMES KIMONYO
MRS. MARIE MUREKATETE
AMBASSADOR EXTRAORDINARY & PLENIPOTENTIARY

MRS. JUSTINE MBABAZI NIYIBIZI
MR. FIDELE MUTUYIMANA
COUNSELOR (DEPUTY CHIEF OF MISSION)

* U.S. Citizen

MR. PERE BONNY MUSEFANO
    MRS. FIONA UMUTESI
COUNSELOR (ECONOMICS)

MR. MICHAEL RUKATA
COUNSELOR (POLITICAL)

MR. ANDREW TUSABE
    MRS. LEONCIA MUKAMWIZA
COUNSELOR

MR. GUILLAUME KAVARUGANDA
FIRST SECRETARY

MR. EUGENE SEGORE KAYIHURA
    MRS. NADIA RUYUKI SHAZA
SECOND SECRETARY

BRIGADIER GENERAL INNOCENT KABANDANA
    MRS. MAGNIFIQUE SABINE UWIZEYIMANA
DEFENSE, MILITARY, NAVAL & AIR ATTACHE

COLONEL FERDINAND SAFARI
    MRS. CLAUDETTE UMULISA
DEFENSE, MILITARY, NAVAL & AIR ATTACHE

SAMOA

EMBASSY OF THE INDEPENDENT STATE OF SAMOA
Chancery: 800 2ND AVENUE, FLOOR 4TH
NEW YORK, NY 10017
(EMBASSY 212-599-6196)   (FAX 212-599-0797)

HIS EXCELLENCY ALI'IOAIGA FETURI ELISAIA
    MRS. MARIA LEI SAM-ELISAIA
AMBASSADOR EXTRAORDINARY & PLENIPOTENTIARY

SAN MARINO

EMBASSY OF REPUBLIC OF SAN MARINO
Chancery: 1711 N STREET, NW, FLOOR 2ND 20036
(EMBASSY 202-250-1535)

HIS EXCELLENCY PAOLO RONDELLI
AMBASSADOR EXTRAORDINARY & PLENIPOTENTIARY

SAUDI ARABIA

EMBASSY OF SAUDI ARABIA
Chancery: 601 NEW HAMPSHIRE AVENUE, NW 20037
(EMBASSY 202-342-3800)   (FAX 202-944-3113)

HIS EXCELLENCY ADEL A M AL JUBEIR
    MRS. FARAH MESHAL D ALFAYEZ
*AMBASSADOR EXTRAORDINARY & PLENIPOTENTIARY &
CONSUL GENERAL*

HIS ROYAL HIGHNESS MOHAMMED FAISAL TURKI AL-SAUD
MINISTER

DR. NAILA IBRAHIM AL-SOWAYEL
MINISTER

MR. MOHAMMED BIN MUSLIH B.H. ALHARBI
    MRS. SALWA S.S. AL SSAEDI
MINISTER

MR. NASIR AYIAD MOUATLAQ ALJOAID
    MRS. MARYAM DHAIFALLAH MATAR ALJOAID
MINISTER

DR. MOHAMMED R A ALHUSSAINI AL SHARIF
    MRS. IMAN M. A. ATALLAH
COUNSELOR (ARAB LEAGUE AFFAIRS)

MR. MOHAMMED MANSOUR DAKHEIL ALMALIK
    MRS. ABEER SALEM A. ALKERAIDIS
COUNSELOR

MR. SALEH AHMED MOHAMMED ALOMARI
    MRS. MUEDAH AHMED ABDULLAH ALSHEHRI
COUNSELOR

MR. SAMI M. A ALSADHAN
    MRS. MAHAT M.I. ALBAWARDI
COUNSELOR

MR. HASSAN YOUSEF MOHAMMED YASSIN
COUNSELOR

MR. KHALEEL YOUSEF A. AFFAN
FIRST SECRETARY

MR. HUSSAIN ALI S. AL DOSARIY
FIRST SECRETARY

MR. ABDULAZIZ MOHAMMED A. AL GHIFAILI
    MISS NADA ABDULLAH H. ALMUTAWA
FIRST SECRETARY

MR. NAIL AHMED AL JUBEIR
    MS. MAYSOON MAZYED ALMAZYED*
FIRST SECRETARY

MR. KHALED H. H. AL NABHANI
    MRS. NABIHA H.E. AL SUFYANI
FIRST SECRETARY

MR. MOHAMMED ABDULRAHMAN AL SHOGIRAN
FIRST SECRETARY

MR. FAISAL EBRAHEEM M. A. ALGHAMDI
    MRS. DALAL SALEH ALI ALGHAMDI
FIRST SECRETARY

MR. HAMAD M.M. ALRASHEED
    MRS. NOUF M.Z. ALAJMI
FIRST SECRETARY

MR. IBRAHIM M.Z. ZAINI
    MRS. HANAA S. S. ABU ALOLA
FIRST SECRETARY

MR. ABDULAZIZ SULAIMAN A. AL BADDAH
    MRS. NAJLA JARALLAH S. AL JARALLAH
SECOND SECRETARY

MR. KHALID HMAAD H. AL HARTHI
SECOND SECRETARY

MR. MOHAMMED SULAIMAN M. ALASIRI
SECOND SECRETARY

MR. ABDULHAMID MOHAMMED S. ALBADR
    MRS. FAHDAH FAHAD O. BIN SALMAH
SECOND SECRETARY

MR. ABDULLAH FAEZ J. ALHAQBANI
    MRS. ALANOUD MOHAMMED S. ALHAQBAN
SECOND SECRETARY

MR. ABDULLAH ALI M. ALSHERYAN
SECOND SECRETARY

* U.S. Citizen

MR. HAMZAH AHMAD EDREES
    MRS. KHADIJAH AHMAD AL SAWI
SECOND SECRETARY

MR. JAMAL SALEH A. ABU KHAYAL
    MRS. SEHAM ABDULMALIK A. JASTANIYYAH
THIRD SECRETARY

MR. MOHAMMED H.I. AL HANO
    MRS. FAUZYAH A. H. AL MALIKY
THIRD SECRETARY

MR. SULIMAN SAAD A. ALAKEEL
    MRS. ABEER HENDI H. ALKATHIRI
THIRD SECRETARY

MR. ABDULRAHMAN ARKAN I. ALDAWOOD
    MRS. REEM IBRAHIM A. BIN HUSAIN
THIRD SECRETARY

MR. ABDULLAH MOHAMMED ALMADI
THIRD SECRETARY

MR. MUTEB MUTLAQ KH ALMULIHI
    MRS. GHADA FAHAD F. ALFAISAL
THIRD SECRETARY

MR. ABDULLAH MOHAMMED A. ALOTHMAN
    MRS. DEEMA ABDULRAHMAN M. ALOTHMAN
THIRD SECRETARY

MS. WAFA MAHMOUD M. ALSOMALI
THIRD SECRETARY

MR. SHALAN AQEEL O. BIN IJL
THIRD SECRETARY

MR. FAWZI M.D. BUGIS
    MRS. ZAINEB SAUD A. SALEH
THIRD SECRETARY

MR. FUAD M.F.I. SHUKREY
    MRS. AMEERA A.H. KHALLAF
THIRD SECRETARY

DR. KHALID MOHAMMED A ALHAZMI
    MRS. FAWZIYAH A H ALSHAMMARI
ATTACHE (ADMINISTRATIVE)

MR. NASSIR KH. AL AJMI
    MRS. AL JOHARAH M. AL SUDAIRI
ATTACHE (ADMINISTRATIVE)

LIEUTENANT COLONEL HAMID HUZAM H. AL BAKHAT
    MRS. KHAYRIAH ALGORABI
ATTACHE (ADMINISTRATIVE)

CHIEF WARRANT OFFICER FAHAD GHURMULLAH S. AL GHAMDI
    MRS. GHALIAH ABDULLAH M. AL GHAMDI
ATTACHE (ADMINISTRATIVE)

MR. FAISAL MOHAMMED JAMMAN AL GHAMDI
    MRS. LINA YOUSUF SAEED AL DAAJANI
ATTACHE

LIEUTENANT COLONEL FAHAD S. AL HARBI
    MRS. MANAL I. MUHAYA
ATTACHE (ADMINISTRATIVE)

MAJOR FAHAD YAHY Y AL MALKI
    MRS. SAMIAH JABER M. AL MALKI
ATTACHE (ADMINISTRATIVE)

MR. MOHAMMAD NAHIES F. AL MOHAMMADI
    MRS. MAHA HAMED H. ALSORAIHI
ATTACHE (ADMINISTRATIVE)

MR. BADR AL MUAIQIL
ATTACHE (PROTOCOL)

MR. ADEL MUBARAK A. AL MUBARAK
    MRS. FAWZIAH SAAD M. AL MUBARAK
ATTACHE (COMMERCIAL)

MR. MANSOUR ABDULRAHMAN A. AL QAHTANI
    MRS. FATEMA ALI SAEED AL QAHTANI
ATTACHE (ADMINISTRATIVE)

HIS ROYAL HIGHNESS PRINCE NAWAF BIN NAIF BIN A AL SAUD
ATTACHE (CULTURAL)

DR. SULIMAN MANSOUR HAMED AL SHUAIBI
    MRS. FAWZEYAH ALMAHMOUD
ATTACHE (HEALTH)

MR. MOHAMMAD ABDULLAH B. ALABAISHI
    MRS. MODHI RASHEED M ALRASHEED
ATTACHE (ADMINISTRATIVE)

DR. SULAIMAN ALI I. ALARAINI
    MRS. ZAHRA SULAIMAN I. ALHUWAIRINI
ATTACHE (ADMINISTRATIVE)

CAPTAIN SULAIMAN ZAAL S. ALBALWI
    MRS. HADAB NAJI H ALBALAWI
ATTACHE (ADMINISTRATIVE)

CAPTAIN SAMI ALBARRAK
    MRS. WEJDAN ABDULAZIZ M. ALSEDAIS
ATTACHE (ADMINISTRATIVE)

LIEUTENANT COLONEL ABDULLAH MOHAMMED F. ALBISHI
    MRS. MONA MOHAMMED A. ALYAMI
ATTACHE (ADMINISTRATIVE)

MR. FAHAD ABDULRAHMAN IBRAHIM ALDAYEL
    MRS. AMAAL HAMAD MOHAMMED ALHUMAID
ATTACHE

MR. ADEL ALI A. ALDWISAN
    MRS. GWAHER MOHAMMED A. ALTHIYAB
ATTACHE (ADMINISTRATIVE)

MR. MOHAMMED ABDULLAH SAUD ALEISSA
    MRS. HUSSAH MOHAMMED IBRAHIM ALEISSA
ATTACHE (CULTURAL)

MR. MUSHARI ALI A. ALFAGIR
ATTACHE

MR. ZAID FAHAD Z. ALFARRAJ
ATTACHE

MR. ALI HILAL ALI ALGHAMDI
    MRS. LAYLA MOHAMMAD A. ALGHAMDI
ATTACHE

LIEUTENANT COLONEL GASSIM MOHAMMED H ALGHORIBI
ATTACHE (ADMINISTRATIVE)

DR. WAEL OMAR M ALHADHRAMI
ATTACHE (ADMINISTRATIVE)

LIEUTENANT COMMANDER HAMEED ALASSI K. ALHATHAL
    MRS. NUZHA TURKI M. ALHATHAL
ATTACHE (ADMINISTRATIVE)

MR. ABDULAZIZ E.A. ALJUAID
ATTACHE

MRS. HAYAT MOQBIL A ALKHALAF
    MR. ABDULMOHSEN ABDULRAZAQ ALKHALF
ATTACHE

* U.S. Citizen

DR. MODY ABDULLAH H. ALKHALAF
ATTACHE

MR. KHALID MOHAMMED H. ALKHALDI
MRS. HIND ABDULAZIZ S. ALLUHAIB
ATTACHE (ADMINISTRATIVE)

MR. MOHAMMED A. A. ALMUDAINI
ATTACHE

MR. SAUD SALEH ALMUHANNA
MRS. AMAL MOHAMMED AL-NEJAIDI
ATTACHE

FIRST LIEUTENANT ALI ABDULAZIZ I ALOMAR
MRS. FATIMAH ABDULLAH H. ALSULAIMAN
ATTACHE (ADMINISTRATIVE)

CHIEF WARRANT OFFICER KHALID KH N. ALOTAIBI
MRS. TURKIAH H. N. ALOTAIBI
ATTACHE (ADMINISTRATIVE)

MAJOR MOHAMMAD GHAZI K ALOTAIBI
ATTACHE (ADMINISTRATIVE)

SERGEANT TURKI MUNEER THAWAB ALOTAIBI
MRS. HAYA FARI TH. ALRUQI
ATTACHE (ADMINISTRATIVE)

LIEUTENANT COLONEL HADI BAKER M. ALQAHTANI
MRS. SHATHA ABDULRAHEEM GHAMDI*
ATTACHE (ADMINISTRATIVE)

LIEUTENANT COLONEL HAZZA MOHAMMED GHAZI ALQAHTANI
MRS. GHAZIL HUNAIF H. ALQAHTANI
ATTACHE (ADMINISTRATIVE)

MR. ABDULAZIZ S. I. ALROBAYAN
MRS. HUDA R. A. ALTOUIJRI
ATTACHE (ADMINISTRATIVE)

MAJOR KHALID ABDULRAHMAN E ALSHALAWI
MRS. SALEHEH NASAR M. ALSHAHRANI
ATTACHE (ADMINISTRATIVE)

MR. THAMER NAIF ALSHAREIF
MISS SAHAR SALEH NASSER*
ATTACHE (ADMINISTRATIVE)

MR. ADEL AHMED M. ALSHUBAIKI
MRS. SARAH IBRAHIM H. ALSALMAN
ATTACHE (COMMERCIAL)

MAJOR MOHAMMAD DKHEELALLA ALWAGDANI
MRS. NADA SAUD ALHOSHAN
ATTACHE (ADMINISTRATIVE)

MRS. RUQAYA ALI F. ALZAMIA
ATTACHE

MS. RANIA HASSAN MAHMOUD AREF
ATTACHE

MR. ABDULJABBAR MOHAMMED A. BAKHSH
MRS. HAJAR HUSSAIN ALHUSAYNI
ATTACHE

MR. WALEED KHALID A. BIN ALLAM
MRS. RANA ZYAD M. ARAFAT
ATTACHE (COMMERCIAL)

MR. MOHAMMED FAHD A. BIN MOAMMAR
MRS. NOUF MOHAMMED A. ALSHEIKH
ATTACHE

MR. HASSAN AHMAD SALEH EMAM
MRS. SAMIAH SALIH MAHMAD AL HAIDARI
ATTACHE

MR. BANDAR HASSAN M. GHAZWANI
MRS. HALEEMAH QASEM Y. GHAZWANI
ATTACHE

MR. MOHAMMED ALI SH HAKAMI
ATTACHE

MR. MOHAMMED I. A. MASHRAQI
MRS. ALIA M. A. MASHRAQI
ATTACHE

SERGEANT MOHAMMED HAMMAD M. MUSA
MRS. ALANOUD BANDAR S ALSHALAN
ATTACHE (ADMINISTRATIVE)

MR. SALEH MOHAMMAD OBAID
MRS. SAMIAH A. HAMDAN
ATTACHE (ADMINISTRATIVE)

DR. NASSER MUHAMMED B AL ABRY
MRS. KHADIJAH NASSER B. AL ABRY
ASST. ATTACHE (CULTURAL)

MR. FAHAD AL BAWARDY
MRS. SARAH AL SHOHAIB
ASST. ATTACHE (CULTURAL)

MR. FAHAD E. T. AL MALKI
ASST. ATTACHE (CULTURAL)

MR. IBRAHIM A. A. AL MOWIS
MRS. FOUZIA H. A. AL MOZINI
ASST. ATTACHE (CULTURAL)

MR. ABDULMOHSEN SAAD AL OTAIBI
MRS. HESSAH SULAIMAN A. ALFAIZ
ASST. ATTACHE (CULTURAL)

MR. MOHAMMED SALEH AL ROBAYAN
MRS. LOLWAH M. AL ROBAYAN
ASST. ATTACHE (CULTURAL)

MR. MUHAMMED A S AL TURBAK
MRS. NADA I. A. AL AMMAR
ASST. ATTACHE (CULTURAL)

MR. ABDULLAH J. AL-JAMMAZ
MRS. SALWA A. AL-SUWAILEM
ASST. ATTACHE (CULTURAL)

MS. NAHLAH AHMED AL-JUBEIR
ASST. ATTACHE (HEALTH)

MR. ABDULAZIZ HAMAD A. ALAJLAN
MRS. AMAL MOHAMMED A. ALAJLAN
ASST. ATTACHE (CULTURAL)

MR. MESHARI I. M. ALANGARI
MRS. DALAL MUTAIR R. ALLUHAYBI
ASST. ATTACHE (CULTURAL)

MR. SULTAN ZAID M. ALBAWARDI
MRS. KHULUD HAMAD A. ALOFAYSAN
ASST. ATTACHE (CULTURAL)

MR. BANDER ABDULLAH O. ALBUSAIRI
MRS. TAHANI MOHAMMED A. ALSAEID
ASST. ATTACHE (CULTURAL)

MR. MOHAMMED SALEH D. ALDEHAIMAN
MRS. EBTIHAJ ABDULLAH M. ALSULAIMAN
ASST. ATTACHE (CULTURAL)

MR. YASSER MOHAMMED S. ALEISSA
MRS. SOMAYAH SULTAN S BIN NASSER
ASST. ATTACHE (CULTURAL)

* U.S. Citizen

MRS. HESSAH SULAIMAN A. ALFAIZ
    MR. ABDULMOHSEN SAAD AL OTAIBI
ASST. ATTACHE (CULTURAL)

MR. ALI MOHAMMAD H. ALFERAEHY
    MRS. NORAH SALEH A. ALAZAAM
ASST. ATTACHE (CULTURAL)

DR. NASSER ABDULLAH H. ALMASARY
    MRS. HUDA ABDULLAH S. ALZAHRANI
ASST. ATTACHE (CULTURAL)

MR. MOHAMMAD SULAIMAN H ALMATRODI
    MRS. RANA ABDULLAH H. ALHABIB
ASST. ATTACHE (CULTURAL)

DR. MOHAMMED SALEH M. ALNAIF
    MRS. HESSA ABDULRAHMAN S. ALSHEBEL
ASST. ATTACHE

MRS. NOURAH SALEH S. ALNEFISAH
    MR. MATLAB SALEH ABDULAZIZ ALNEFISAH
ASST. ATTACHE (CULTURAL)

MR. SULTAN ABDULRAHMAN A. ALOBAIDAN
    MRS. BASMAH MAHER B. ALOTAIBI
ASST. ATTACHE (CULTURAL)

DR. MOHAMMED ABDUL RAHMAN ALOMAR
    MRS. LATTIFAH MOHAMMED ALAIBAN
ASST. ATTACHE (CULTURAL)

DR. ABDULRAHMAN MOHAMMED ALSEBAIL
    MRS. JAMILAH YOUSEF M. ALYOUSEF
ASST. ATTACHE (CULTURAL)

MR. NASSER MOHAMMAD A. ARFAJ
    MRS. SHAIKHAH KHALAF M. ALAJAIMI
ASST. ATTACHE (CULTURAL)

MR. MUSAID A. H. ASSAF
    MS. EMAN M M AL-ZAHRI
ASST. ATTACHE (CULTURAL)

MR. MOHAMAD SULAIMAN I ASSALEEM
    MRS. SEHAM A.A. AZZAMEL
ASST. ATTACHE (CULTURAL)

MR. ALI MOHAMMED A. BAMASHMOUS
    MRS. EBTESAM HASAN M. BAMASHMOUS
ASST. ATTACHE (CULTURAL)

MR. NASSER M. S. EL ZALLAL
    MRS. BADAHA A. S. AL KAHTANI
ASST. ATTACHE (CULTURAL)

MR. YAHYA HAMAD YAHYA MASHYAKHY
    MRS. AMENA ALI N. SHOGAIGI
ASST. ATTACHE (CULTURAL)

MR. MOHAMMED FAHAD A. SAKABI
ASST. ATTACHE (CULTURAL)

DR. AMAL YOUSEF M. SHARBATLY
ASST. ATTACHE (HEALTH)

COLONEL AHMED N. S. ALQAHTANI
    MRS. JAWHARAH A. S. ALQAHTANI
DEFENSE ATTACHE

LIEUTENANT COLONEL AHMED ALI MODHEI AL DABEIS
    MRS. HASIBA MOHAMMED ZEID AL NASSER
MILITARY ATTACHE

CAPTAIN KHALED HUSSEIN H. ALSOFIANI
    MRS. ZAKIAH HAMDAN S. ALTHOBAITI
NAVAL ATTACHE

COLONEL MOHAMMED IBRAHEM M. ALSOBAY
    MRS. HANAN ABDULLAH A. ALTAMIMI
AIR ATTACHE

COMMERCIAL OFFICE
    601 NEW HAMPSHIRE AVENUE, NW 20037
        (OFFICE 202-337-4088)

DEFENSE AND ARMED FORCES ATTACHE OFFICE
    1001 30TH STREET, NW 20007
        (OFFICE 202-857-0122)

SAUDI ARABIAN CULTURAL MISSION
    2600 VIRGINIA AVENUE, NW, SUITE 800 20037
        (OFFICE 202-337-9450)

SAUDI ARABIAN CULTURAL MISSION
    8500 HILLTOP ROAD
    FAIRFAX, VA 22031

                (FAX 703-573-2595)
SAUDI ARABIAN NATIONAL GUARD OFFICE
    601 NEW HAMPSHIRE AVENUE, NW 20037
        (OFFICE 202-944-3344)   (FAX 202-944-3340)

SAUDI HEALTH MISSION
    601 NEW HAMPSHIRE AVENUE, NW 20037
        (OFFICE 202-342-7393)   (FAX 202-337-9251)

SENEGAL

EMBASSY OF THE REPUBLIC OF SENEGAL
Chancery: 2112 WYOMING AVENUE, NW 20008
(EMBASSY 202-234-0540)   (FAX 202-332-6315)

HIS EXCELLENCY CHEIKH NIANG
    MRS. AISSATA SALL NIANG
AMBASSADOR EXTRAORDINARY & PLENIPOTENTIARY

MR. MAMADOU BA
    COUNSELOR (ECONOMIC)

MR. DIAMANE DIOME
    MRS. MARIE MICHELLE DIOUF DIOME
    COUNSELOR (POLITICS)

MRS. MAME DIARRA BOUSSO FALL
    COUNSELOR

MR. OUMAR KANE
    COUNSELOR

MR. MAMADOU MOUSTAPHA LOUM
    MRS. ASTOU CISSE LOUM
    COUNSELOR

MR. KHASSIM MBACKE
    COUNSELOR

MR. BABACAR SARR
    COUNSELOR (COMMUNICATION)

MR. BECAYE AMALAH TRAORE
    MRS. MAGNE DIOP TRAORE
    COUNSELOR (POLITICAL & SOCIAL)

MR. MOUSSA KHADY CISSE
    MRS. DIENABA DIALLO CISSE
    FIRST SECRETARY

MR. ALIOU DEME
    MRS. SOKHNA ASTOU DIOUM DEME
    FIRST SECRETARY (FINANCE)

* U.S. Citizen

MRS. GNAGNA DIAKHAM EPOUSE KONE
SECOND SECRETARY

MR. ISMAILA THIAM
MRS. OLY DIASSE THIAM
SECOND SECRETARY (ADMINISTRATIVE)

MR. AMADOU NDIAYE
MRS. FATOU DIONE NDIAYE
ATTACHE (ADMINISTRATIVE)

DEFENSE, AIR & MILITARY ATTACHE OFFICE
1825 I STREET, NW, SUITE 400 20006
(OFFICE 202-429-2098)   (FAX 202-332-6315)

SERBIA

EMBASSY OF THE REPUBLIC OF SERBIA
Chancery: 2134 KALORAMA ROAD, NW 20008
(EMBASSY 202-332-0333)   (FAX 202-332-3933)

HIS EXCELLENCY VLADIMIR PETROVIC
MS. ADELA PETROVIC*
AMBASSADOR EXTRAORDINARY & PLENIPOTENTIARY

MR. VLADIMIR JOVICIC
MRS. MARINA JOVICIC
MINISTER-COUNSELOR (DEPUTY CHIEF OF MISSION)

MR. DJERDJ MATKOVIC
MRS. VERA MARKOVIC MATKOVIC
COUNSELOR (POLITICAL)

MR. MILAN VARADINOVIC
MRS. MARIJANA KOCIC
COUNSELOR (CONSULAR)

DR. ALEKSANDAR VIDOJEVIC
COUNSELOR

MS. SANDRA PEJIC
FIRST SECRETARY

MS. MILENA JOKSIMOVIC
SECOND SECRETARY

MS. KATARINA MARTINOVIC
THIRD SECRETARY

MS. KATARINA ZIVANOVIC
THIRD SECRETARY

MR. SRDJAN SPASIC
MRS. JELENA SPASIC
ATTACHE (POLICE)

COMMANDER MILAN KONJIKOVAC
MRS. DRAGANA KONJIKOVAC
ASST. DEFENSE, MILITARY, NAVAL & AIR ATTACHE

LIEUTENANT COLONEL GORAN NESTOROVIC
MRS. BRANKA NESTOROVIC
ASST. DEFENSE, MILITARY, NAVAL & AIR ATTACHE

MAJOR NEBOJSA SVJETLICA
MRS. SLAVICA SVJETLICA
ASST. DEFENSE, MILITARY, NAVAL & AIR ATTACHE

SEYCHELLES

EMBASSY OF THE REPUBLIC OF SEYCHELLES
Chancery: 800 2ND AVENUE, SUITE 400C
NEW YORK, NY 10017
(EMBASSY 212-972-1785)   (FAX 212-972-1786)

HER EXCELLENCY MARIE LOUISE CECILE POTTER
MR. CLEMENT ALFRED HERMAN POTTER
AMBASSADOR EXTRAORDINARY & PLENIPOTENTIARY

SIERRA LEONE

EMBASSY OF SIERRA LEONE
Chancery: 1701 19TH STREET, NW 20009
(EMBASSY 202-939-9261)   (FAX 202-483-1793)

HIS EXCELLENCY BOCKARI KORTU STEVENS
MRS. MUSU HAFSATU STEVENS
AMBASSADOR EXTRAORDINARY & PLENIPOTENTIARY

MR. IBRAHIM SORIE CONTEH
MINISTER (DEPUTY CHIEF OF MISSION)

MRS. ISATU SEMA AISHA SILLAH
COUNSELOR

MR. EDWARD KAWA
MRS. KADIATU KAWA
SECOND SECRETARY

MS. FATMATTA DAO
THIRD SECRETARY

MS. ELIZABETH MESI SHIRLEY FORAY
ATTACHE (INFORMATION)

MR. PAUL MERLVIN EDWARD KAMARA
MRS. FATMATA BECKIATU FATIMA KAMARA
ATTACHE (FINANCIAL)

MR. PASCO GERALD.H. TEMPLE
MRS. JANNIE NOVELLA TEMPLE
ATTACHE (INFORMATION)

SINGAPORE

EMBASSY OF THE REPUBLIC OF SINGAPORE
Chancery: 3501 INTERNATIONAL PLACE, NW 20008
(EMBASSY 202-537-3100)   (FAX 202-537-0876)

HIS EXCELLENCY ASHOK KUMAR
MRS. GOURI UPPAL
AMBASSADOR EXTRAORDINARY & PLENIPOTENTIARY

MR. AIK YEOW HENG
COUNSELOR (DEPUTY CHIEF OF MISSION)

MS. LIAN SEE JUNIPER LIM
COUNSELOR (ADMIN. & CONSULAR)

MR. TEK YEAN DARYL SNG
MS. EVELYN TEE
COUNSELOR

MR. HENG TEM RAYMOND WONG
MRS. LORNA YOKE LIAN CHIA
COUNSELOR

* U.S. Citizen

DR. LEAN WENG YEOH
    MRS. JENNY SOH
COUNSELOR

MS. GERALDYN MAN YI CHEN
    MR. CHI HOWE ONG
FIRST SECRETARY

MR. GUAN WEE JEROME LEE
    MS. CHIEW TING NG
FIRST SECRETARY

MS. NEDYAM NITYA MENON
FIRST SECRETARY (POLITICAL)

MR. CHUAN YEAN TAN
    MRS. CHOI WAN NG
FIRST SECRETARY

MR. KWANG WEI IAN TAN
    MS. KAI XIN MICHELLE LOH
FIRST SECRETARY

MR. WEIMING TAN
    MS. PEIRU THERESA MARIA FAN
FIRST SECRETARY

MS. FRENJE TSU FEN WEE
FIRST SECRETARY (ECONOMICS)

MR. CHIN FU ERVIN YEO
FIRST SECRETARY

MS. NUR AMIRA BINTE ABDUL KARIM
SECOND SECRETARY

MISS ZHIJIA CLARA KOH
SECOND SECRETARY

MR. ZHIJIAN LIU
SECOND SECRETARY

MR. ZHONG HUI LIM
    MRS. SHI NI LIM
ATTACHE

BRIGADIER GENERAL CHEE WEE TAN
    MRS. YEN NING LAU
DEFENSE, MILITARY, NAVAL & AIR ATTACHE

LIEUTENANT COLONEL YEW HOCK LIM
    MRS. SOCK HUI WEE
ASST. DEFENSE, MILITARY, NAVAL & AIR ATTACHE

SLOVAK REPUBLIC

EMBASSY OF THE SLOVAK REPUBLIC
Chancery: 3523 INTERNATIONAL COURT, NW 20008
(EMBASSY 202-237-1054)   (FAX 202-237-6438)

HIS EXCELLENCY PETER KMEC
    MRS. MONIKA KMECOVA
AMBASSADOR EXTRAORDINARY & PLENIPOTENTIARY

MR. PETER ZELENAK
    MRS. KATARINA ZELENAKOVA
COUNSELOR (DEPUTY CHIEF OF MISSION)

MS. KATARINA KOVACOVA
COUNSELOR

MR. NORBERT BRADA
    MS. HELENA SARKANOVA
FIRST SECRETARY

* U.S. Citizen

COLONEL PETER KOVARIK
FIRST SECRETARY

MR. VIT KOZIAK
    MRS. JANKA KOZIAKOVA
FIRST SECRETARY

MRS. MIROSLAVA PISOVA
    MR. FEDOR PIS
FIRST SECRETARY

MR. DUSAN SATEK
    MRS. ALENA SATEKOVA
FIRST SECRETARY (POLITICAL)

MR. PETER KOCIS
ATTACHE (ADMINISTRATIVE)

MAJOR GENERAL JURAJ BARANEK
    MRS. JANA BARANKOVA
DEFENSE, MILITARY & AIR ATTACHE

LIEUTENANT COLONEL MILAN HAZLINGER
    MRS. KATARINA HAZLINGEROVA
ASST. DEFENSE, MILITARY & AIR ATTACHE

COMMERCIAL AND ECONOMIC SECTION
429 E. 52ND STREET, SUITE 12A
NEW YORK, NY 10022
    (OFFICE 212-679-7044)   (FAX 212-679-7045)

SLOVENIA

EMBASSY OF THE REPUBLIC OF SLOVENIA
Chancery: 2410 CALIFORNIA STREET, NW 20008
(EMBASSY 202-386-6610)   (FAX 202-386-6633)

HIS EXCELLENCY ROMAN KIRN
    MRS. JOVANA KIRN
AMBASSADOR EXTRAORDINARY & PLENIPOTENTIARY

MS. ONDINA BLOKAR DROBIC
    MR. BOSTJAN DROBIC
MINISTER (DEPUTY CHIEF OF MISSION)

MS. PETRA LANGERHOLC
MINISTER-COUNSELOR

MR. GORAZD RENCELJ
    MRS. ISABEL GEORGINA OLIZAR
COUNSELOR

MR. BORUT BLAJ
    MS. MATEJA BLAJ
FIRST SECRETARY

MRS. TJASA DELEJA BALJA
    MR. ALEN BALJA
FIRST SECRETARY

MRS. EVA PRSA SIMONOVIC
    MR. DRAGAN SIMONOVIC
ATTACHE (ADMINISTRATIVE)

COLONEL LADISLAV GRABER
    MRS. ANKICA GRABER
DEFENSE, MILITARY, NAVAL & AIR ATTACHE

2412 CALIFORNIA STREET, NW, APT 7C 20008

SOLOMON ISLANDS

EMBASSY OF THE SOLOMON ISLANDS
Chancery: 800 2ND AVENUE, SUITE 400L
NEW YORK, NY 10017
(EMBASSY 212-599-6192) (FAX 212-661-8925)

HIS EXCELLENCY COLLIN D. BECK
MRS. HELEN I. BECK
AMBASSADOR EXTRAORDINARY & PLENIPOTENTIARY

SOUTH AFRICA

EMBASSY OF THE REPUBLIC OF SOUTH AFRICA
Chancery: 3051 MASSACHUSETTS AVENUE, NW 20008
(EMBASSY 202-232-4400) (FAX 202-265-1607)

HIS EXCELLENCY EBRAHIM RASOOL
MRS. ROSIEDA SHABODIEN
AMBASSADOR EXTRAORDINARY & PLENIPOTENTIARY

MR. JOHNNY MOLOTO
MRS. PAMELA THANDO MOLOTO
MINISTER (DEPUTY CHIEF OF MISSION)

MRS. TANDIWE FLORENCE FADANE
MINISTER (ADMINISTRATION)

MR. LIVHUWANI LAWRENCE NEMUKULA
MRS. GUMANI HILDA NEMUKULA
MINISTER

MRS. VANGILE BRENDA TITI MSUMZA
MINISTER

MR. SANDILE SYDNEY TYINI
MRS. NOCAWA LIVINIA TYINI
MINISTER (ECONOMIC)

DR. NOMONDE XUNDU
MINISTER

MR. LUCKY JOSHUA MOLEFE
MRS. LINDIWE SIZAKELE MARVELLOU MOLEFE
MINISTER-COUNSELOR (REVENUE SERVICE)

MR. THEODORE ALBRECHT
MRS. REINETTE MYRA ALBRECHT
MRS. REINETTE MYRA ALBRETCH
COUNSELOR

MR. JOHANNES HERMANUS JACOBS
MRS. SUSANNA JOUBERT JACOBS
COUNSELOR

MS. NOKUZOLA SIGNORIA MGENGO
MR. MLUNGISI KEITH MGENGO
COUNSELOR

MS. KHAYAKAZI CHARITY MGOJO
COUNSELOR (POLITICAL)

MRS. MARTHA BEZUIDENHOUT
FIRST SECRETARY

MR. MONGEZI EDMUND MAHLULO
MRS. BRIDGET MONEGI
FIRST SECRETARY (POLITICAL)

MRS. FREDA GABOINEWE MKHIZE
FIRST SECRETARY

MR. ALUWANI PERCY MUSEISI
MRS. FULUFHELO IRENE MUSEISI
FIRST SECRETARY

MRS. BAFEDILE THABITHA F. RAKGOLELA
MR. TSHEPO PETER RAKGOLELA
FIRST SECRETARY

MRS. SELINA SHADI SKOSANA
FIRST SECRETARY

MS. SIBONGILE SOMYALO
FIRST SECRETARY

MRS. STELLA VUYELWA DHLOMO IMIEKA
MR. ISIBOR OSARODION IMIEKA
SECOND SECRETARY

MR. SAGARIA DANIAL JONKER
SECOND SECRETARY

MS. VUYOKAZI MASISI
MR. GODWILL OFENTSE MASISI
SECOND SECRETARY (POLITICAL)

MS. BOIPELO ONKEMETSE LEFATSHE
THIRD SECRETARY

MR. THIZWILONDI THOMAS MALELA
THIRD SECRETARY

MRS. MALEWASI ELIZABETH MBONGO
MR. ANDRIES MOLELEKI MOFOKENG
THIRD SECRETARY

MR. EAGERBOY THABO MOROENG
MRS. NEO THERESSA MOROENG
THIRD SECRETARY

MS. SHARON VIVIENNE SOLOMON
ATTACHE

COLONEL MAFHUNGO DUNCAN MMBI
MRS. MUVHULAWA DAPHNEY MMBI
MILITARY & NAVAL ATTACHE & ASST. DEFENSE ATTACHE

AGRICULTURAL OFFICE
4301 CONNECTICUT AVENUE, NW, SUITE 200 20008
(OFFICE 202-232-4400) (FAX 202-363-8620)

COMMUNICATION SECTION
3051 MASSACHUSETTS AVENUE, NW 20008
(OFFICE 202-232-4400) (FAX 202-232-5370)

CONSULAR OFFICE
4301 CONNECTICUT AVENUE, NW 20008
(OFFICE 202-232-4400) (FAX 202-244-9417)

DEPARTMENT OF TRADE AND INDUSTRY
4301 CONNECTICUT AVENUE, NW 20008
(OFFICE 202-232-4400) (FAX 202-966-5919)

EMBASSY OF THE REPUBLIC OF SOUTH AFRICA
3400 INTERNATIONAL DRIVE, NW 2,3,4 20008

TECHNICAL OFFICE
4301 CONNECTICUT AVENUE, NW, SUITE 200 20008

TRADE/INDUSTRY/AGRICULTURAL
4301 CONNECTICUT AVENUE, NW, SUITE 200 20008
(OFFICE 202-966-8910)

* U.S. Citizen

SOUTH SUDAN

EMBASSY OF THE REPUBLIC OF SOUTH SUDAN
Chancery: 1233 20TH STREET, NW, SUITE 602 20036
(EMBASSY 202-293-7940)   (FAX 202-293-7941)

HIS EXCELLENCY AKEC KHOC ACIEW KHOC
AMBASSADOR EXTRAORDINARY & PLENIPOTENTIARY

MR. DHANOJAK OBONGO
         MRS. NADIA IMAM ELIA MOGGA ELIA
MINISTER-COUNSELOR (DEPUTY CHIEF OF MISSION)

MR. MOUN DENG AJUET
MINISTER

MR. ABAN PAGAN OTHOW
         MRS. ALIZA OKUC YUKWAN DENG
COUNSELOR

MR. JAMES CHUOL PAL
COUNSELOR

MR. DOMBEK YAI KUOL
FIRST SECRETARY

MR. LINO DENG WEK
FIRST SECRETARY

MS. ANGONG DHOL ACUIL
SECOND SECRETARY

MR. ALISON FARUK ROBERT FARUK
         MRS. MARY NICHOLAS OTTO
SECOND SECRETARY

MR. RAYMOND OPI SILAS AWIYO
THIRD SECRETARY

SPAIN

EMBASSY OF SPAIN
Chancery: 2375 PENNSYLVANIA AVENUE, NW 20037
(EMBASSY 202-452-0100)   (FAX 202-833-5670)

HIS EXCELLENCY RAMON GIL CASARES SATRUSTEGUI
AMBASSADOR EXTRAORDINARY & PLENIPOTENTIARY

MR. JUAN MANUEL MOLINA LAMOTHE
MINISTER-COUNSELOR (DEPUTY CHIEF OF MISSION)

MR. GUILLERMO JAVIER CORRAL VAN DAMME
         MRS. NATALIA ORJALES VIDAL
MINISTER (CULTURAL AFFAIRS)

MR. JESUS M. RODRIGUEZ ANDIA PARADA
         MRS. ROCIO M ARROSPIDE LOPEZ DE LETONA
MINISTER & CONSUL GENERAL

AMBASSADOR JUAN M. ROMERO DE TERREROS
         MRS. CARMEN FUENTE SALVADOR
MINISTER (CULTURAL)

MR. FRANCISCO JAVIER APARICIO ALVAREZ
         MRS. MARIA ASELA TORICES RASINES
COUNSELOR

MRS. ISABEL ARTIME GARCIA
         MR. JOSE I. FERNANDEZ ARAGONCILLO
COUNSELOR

MR. FELIPE DIAZ SUERO
         MRS. INES PEREZ MOURIN
COUNSELOR (ECON.& ADMIN. AFFAIRS)

MR. GONZALO GARCIA ANDRES
         MRS. ANA MARIA FRUTOS CAMARA
COUNSELOR (ECONOMIC & COMMERCIAL)

MR. JOSE GARCIA MOLINA
         MS. ROSA MARIA PEREZ LEGIDO
COUNSELOR (HOME AFFAIRS)

MR. GONZALO GIMENEZ COLOMA
         MRS. MARIA DE LAS NIEVES LOPEZ MANCEBO
COUNSELOR (LABOR & IMMIGRATION)

MR. FRANCISCO XAVIER GISBERT DA CRUZ
         MRS. VIRGINIA CAROLINA VINUESA BENITEZ
COUNSELOR (EDUCATION)

MRS. MARIA L. HUIDOBRO MARTIN LABORDA
         MR. JORGE ROMEU GONZALEZ BARROS
COUNSELOR

MR. GREGORIO LASO MOSTOLES
         MS. ELENA CRUZ CASADO
COUNSELOR (INFORMATION)

MR. LEONARDO MARCOS GONZALEZ
         MRS. MARIA PILAR FERNANDEZ GOMEZ
COUNSELOR (INFORMATION)

MR. FERNANDO MERRY DEL VAL
         MRS. MARIA CARMEN BETES DE TORO
COUNSELOR (ECONOMIC & COMMERCIAL)

MR. JORGE ROMEU GONZALEZ BARROS
         MRS. MARIA L. HUIDOBRO MARTIN LABORDA
COUNSELOR

MRS. ELENA SANCHEZ BLANCO
         MR. SANTIAGO RODRIGUEZ BUSTABAD
COUNSELOR

MRS. ALICIA SANCHEZ MUNOZ
         MR. FRANCISCO JAVIER SALAS PATINO
COUNSELOR (COMMERCIAL)

MR. MIGUEL SANDOMINGO NUNEZ
         MRS. SALUD LEON LOPEZ
COUNSELOR (FINANCIAL)

MR. CAMILO VILLARINO MARZO
         MRS. SUSANA JULIA DE FUNES CASELLAS
COUNSELOR

MR. ALVARO ORTEGA BARON
         MRS. ANA ELORZA MORENO
FIRST SECRETARY

MRS. LETICIA DE GUINDOS TALAVERA
ATTACHE (AGRICULTURAL)

MRS. CANDIDA LOZANO CARMONA
         MR. JUAN SEBASTIAN SANCHEZ CORVILLO
ATTACHE

MR. FRANCISCO MARTINEZ SANTANA
         MRS. EVA MARIA BUENO PEREZ
ATTACHE (CONSULAR)

MAJOR JOSE ANTONIO MELLADO VALVERDE
         MS. BELEN ENCARNACION LORENZO GILSANZ
ATTACHE (INTERIOR)

MR. JUAN ANTONIO PANDO NAVARRO
         MS. MARIA TERESA VILLEGAS MORENO
ATTACHE

* U.S. Citizen

REAR ADMIRAL JAVIER ROMERO
     MRS. MARIA DEL DE SOBRINO FERNANDEZ
DEFENSE ATTACHE

COLONEL MIGUEL ANGEL CONDE LOPEZ
     MRS. MARIA TERESA MENENDEZ MORO
MILITARY ATTACHE

CAPTAIN FRANCISCO JAVIER NIETO MANSO
     MRS. ANA MARIA BARBADILLO
NAVAL ATTACHE

COLONEL FULGENCIO SAURA CEGARRA
     MRS. ANA CRISTINA DEL PASO GALLEGO
AIR ATTACHE

COMMANDER JAIME MONTERO FERNANDEZ DE B.
     MRS. MILAGR RODRIGUEZ LOPEZ DE MEDRANO
ASST. DEFENSE & DEFENSE COOPERATION ATTACHE

MAJOR JESUS REVALIENTE LOPEZ
     MRS. MARIA PILAR ALFARO LOPEZ
ASST. DEFENSE & DEFENSE COOPERATION ATTACHE

COLONEL JOSE MANUEL NOVAL TOIMIL
     MRS. D. FERNANDEZ PINEYRO HERNANDEZ
DEFENSE COOPERATION ATTACHE

MAJOR DAVID BRAVO AYALA
     MRS. ESTHER MARTINEZ JIMENEZ
ASST. DEFENSE COOPERATION ATTACHE

AGRICULTURAL OFFICE
     2375 PENNSYLVANIA AVENUE, NW 20037
        (OFFICE 202-728-2339)　(FAX 202-728-2320)

AIR ATTACHE OFFICE
     4801 WISCONSIN AVENUE, NW, FLOOR 3RD 20016
        (OFFICE 202-244-2166)

CONSULAR OFFICE
     2375 PENNSYVANIA AVENUE, NW 20037

CULTURAL OFFICE
     2375 PENNSYLVANIA AVENUE, NW 20037
        (OFFICE 202-728-2334)　(FAX 202-728-2312)

DEFENSE ATTACHE OFFICE
     4801 WISCONSIN AVENUE, NW, FLOOR 4 20016
        (OFFICE 202-244-0093)　(FAX 202-362-3993)

DEFENSE COOPERATION ATTACHE OFFICE
     4801 WISCONSIN AVENUE, FLOOR 4TH 20016
        (OFFICE 202-244-0093)

ECONOMIC & COMMERCIAL OFFICE
     2375 PENNSYLVANIA AVENUE, NW 20037
        (OFFICE 202-728-2368)　(FAX 202-466-7385)

EDUCATION OFFICE
     2375 PENNSYLVANIA AVENUE, NW 20037
        (OFFICE 202-728-2335)　(FAX 202-728-2312)

EMPLOYMENT AND SOCIAL SECURITY OFFICE
     2375 PENNSYLVANIA AVENUE, NW 20037
        (OFFICE 202-728-2331)　(FAX 202-728-2304)

FINANCIAL OFFICE
     2375 PENNSYLVANNIA AVENUE, NW 20037
        (OFFICE 202-728-2338)　(FAX 202-728-2318)

INFORMATION OFFICE
     2375 PENNSYLVANIA AVENUE, NW 20037
        (OFFICE 202-728-2332)　(FAX 202-728-2308)

* U.S. Citizen

MILITARY ATTACHE OFFICE
     4801 WISCONSIN AVENUE, NW, FLOOR 3RD 20016
        (OFFICE 202-244-6161)　(FAX 202-362-3993)

NAVAL ATTACHE OFFICE
     4801 WISCONSIN AVENUE, NW, FLOOR 3 20016
        (OFFICE 202-244-2166)

SRI LANKA

EMBASSY OF THE DEMOCRATIC SOCIALIST REPUBLIC OF
SRI LANKA
Chancery: 2148 WYOMING AVENUE, NW 20008
(EMBASSY 202-483-4025)　(FAX 202-232-7181)

HIS EXCELLENCY JALIYA CHITRAN WICKRAMASURIYA
     MRS. PRIYANGA WICKRAMASURIYA
AMBASSADOR EXTRAORDINARY & PLENIPOTENTIARY

MR. ESALA RUWAN WEERAKOON
     MS. KRISHANTI MENAKA WEERAKOON
MINISTER (DEPUTY CHIEF OF MISSION)

MR. DON RANJITH KALUTHANTHIRIGE
     MRS. PADMA LALANI KALUTHANTHIRI
MINISTER

MR. BANDULA SOMAS PATABENDI MADDUMAGE
     MRS. INDRANI S PATHIRANA DISSANAYAKEGE
MINISTER (COMMERCIAL)

MRS. WASANTHA PERERA
     MR. ANURA MOHAN PERERA
MINISTER

MR. THANUJA GEETHENDRA USLIYANAGE
     MRS. HELANGA HESHANI USLIYANAGE
MINISTER

BRIGADIER DUDLEY SARANATH WEERAMAN
     MRS. TAKSHILA DHARSHANEE WEERAMAN
DEFENSE, MILITARY, NAVAL & AIR ATTACHE

ST. KITTS AND NEVIS

EMBASSY OF ST. KITTS AND NEVIS
Chancery: 3216 NEW MEXICO AVENUE, NW 20016
(EMBASSY 202-686-2636)　(FAX 202-686-5740)

HER EXCELLENCY JACINTH LORNA HENRY MARTIN
     MR. MICHAEL MC DONALD MARTIN
AMBASSADOR EXTRAORDINARY & PLENIPOTENTIARY

ST. LUCIA

EMBASSY OF SAINT LUCIA
Chancery: 3216 NEW MEXICO AVENUE, NW 20016
(EMBASSY 202-364-6792)　(FAX 202-364-6723)

HER EXCELLENCY SONIA MERLYN JOHNNY
     DR. LLOYD JACKSON*
AMBASSADOR EXTRAORDINARY & PLENIPOTENTIARY

MS. ELIZABETH DARIUS CLARKE
MINISTER-COUNSELOR

MISS KIMARI AMANDA SHENELLE STOREY
FIRST SECRETARY

MRS. JEVI ANNE DANIELLE MARCELLIN
    MR. DWIGHT AUDWIN MARCELLIN*
ATTACHE

ST. VINCENT AND THE GRENADINES

EMBASSY OF SAINT VINCENT AND THE GRENADINES
Chancery: 3216 NEW MEXICO AVENUE, NW 20016
(EMBASSY 202-364-6730)   (FAX 202-364-6736)

HER EXCELLENCY LA CELIA ARITHA PRINCE
AMBASSADOR EXTRAORDINARY & PLENIPOTENTIARY

MR. OMARI SEITU WILLIAMS
MINISTER-COUNSELOR (DEPUTY CHIEF OF MISSION)

MR. ASRAM YAHIR SANTINO SOLEYN
COUNSELOR

MS. SHAREN MERIL WYNNE
ATTACHE

SUDAN

EMBASSY OF THE REPUBLIC OF THE SUDAN
Chancery: 2210 MASSACHUSETTS AVENUE, NW 20008
(EMBASSY 202-338-8565)   (FAX 202-667-2406)

MR. EMAD MIRGHANI ABDELHAMID ALTOHAMY
    MRS. MAHA ABDELMONIM ABDO IBRAHIM
MINISTER (CHARGE D'AFFAIRES AD INTERIM)

MR. GAMAL MALIK AHMED GORAISH
    MRS. MONA MOHAMED ELFATIH AWAD ELKARIM
COUNSELOR (DEPUTY CHIEF OF MISSION)

MR. ELHAFIZ EISA ABDALLA ADAM
    MRS. DURRIA ADAM MOHAMMADAIN ADAM
MINISTER

MR. BUKHARI GHANIM MOHAMED AFANDI
    MRS. SARA IZELDIN ELSAID ABDELSALAM
MINISTER

MR. MOHAMED SOLIMAN ABDALLA
    MRS. AMAL ELTAYEB ABDALLA
COUNSELOR

MR. ALI ABDELAZIEM MOHAMED HUSSAIN
    MRS. HANADI HAMZA Z. SEED AHMED
COUNSELOR

MR. ASAAD ABD ELMUTALEB HAMAD AHMAD
    MISS BRAA SIDEEG HAMAD AHMAD
SECOND SECRETARY

MR. NASRELDIN ABDALLA MOHAMED AHMED
    MRS. HIND ELTAYEB HASSAN OSMAN
SECOND SECRETARY

MR. ABDELDAYEM SEED AHMED ABDELDAYEM
    MRS. RUGHAYA ALI ABDALLA ELKHATEEB
ATTACHE (ADMINISTRATIVE)

MS. AMANI ABDELGADIR MAHJOUB AHMED
ATTACHE (FINANCIAL)

MR. HAMZA IESAA MOHAMED AHMED
ATTACHE (ADMINISTRATIVE)

MR. MUBARAK HASHIM A. IBRAHIM
    MRS. SIHAM MOHAMED SALIH ABDELMAGID
ATTACHE (FINANCE)

MR. SALIH ABDALLA MOHAMED MAKKI
    MRS. SALHA MOHAMED ELIAS MOHAMED
ATTACHE (ADMINISTRATIVE)

MR. ABDELFATAH HAMZA AHMED MOHAMED
    MRS. AFAF ABBAS KHALIL MOHAMED
ATTACHE (ADMINISTRATIVE)

INFORMATION ATTACHE OFFICE
2210 MASSACHUSETTS AVENUE, NW 20008
    (OFFICE 202-797-8863)   (FAX 202-745-2615)

OFFICE OF THE CULTURAL COUNSELOR
2612 WOODLEY PLACE 20008
    (OFFICE 202-387-8001)

SURINAME

EMBASSY OF THE REPUBLIC OF SURINAME
Chancery: 4301 CONNECTICUT AVENUE, NW, SUITE 460
20008
(EMBASSY 202-244-7488)   (FAX 202-244-5878)

HIS EXCELLENCY SUBHAS CHANDRA MUNGRA
    MRS. DHARMKOEMARIE MUNGRA
AMBASSADOR EXTRAORDINARY & PLENIPOTENTIARY

MR. KENNETH JOHAN AMOKSI
    MRS. REINA BIANCA AMOKSI
COUNSELOR

MR. MICHIEL GLENN RAAFENBERG
    MRS. LYDIA RAAFENBERG
COUNSELOR (ALTERNATE REPRESENTATIVE)

MISS CHANTAL MERRYL MARIA ELSENHOUT
FIRST SECRETARY (ALTERNATE REPRESENTATIVE)

MS. HARGWATIE MAIKOE
FIRST SECRETARY

MS. FLORENCE MAVIS ELTENBERG
ATTACHE (ALTERNATE REPRESENTATIVE)

MS. FLORENCE MAVIS ELTENBERG
ATTACHE (FINANCIAL)

MRS. ODESSA MELISSA PLET CARROT
ATTACHE (ADMINISTRATIVE)

SWAZILAND

EMBASSY OF THE KINGDOM OF SWAZILAND
Chancery: 1712 NEW HAMPSHIRE AVENUE, NW 20009
(EMBASSY 202-234-5002)   (FAX 202-234-8254)

HIS EXCELLENCY REVEREND ABEDNEGO MANDLA NTSHANGASE
    MRS. PHINDILE FUTHI NTSHANGASE
AMBASSADOR EXTRAORDINARY & PLENIPOTENTIARY

MRS. NONHLANHLA DLAMINI
    MR. SIPHO SIHLE DLAMINI
FIRST SECRETARY (ADMINISTRATIVE)

* U.S. Citizen

MS. LINDIWE CYNTHIA TRIZAH KUNENE
FIRST SECRETARY (TRADE & INVESTMENT)

MS. PHINDILE GOODNESS NXUMALO
THIRD SECRETARY

PRINCE GCINA SAMUEL DLAMINI
MRS. BONISILE TEBO MAZIYA
ATTACHE (EDUCATION)

MRS. SIPHIWE P. MLANGENI MAHLANGU
ATTACHE (ADMINISTRATIVE)

PRINCESS BONISIWE LOSIMILO DLAMINI
ASST. ATTACHE (EDUCATION)

SWEDEN

EMBASSY OF SWEDEN
Chancery: 2900 K STREET, NW 20007
(EMBASSY 202-467-2600)   (FAX 202-467-2699)

HIS EXCELLENCY SVEN JONAS HAFSTROEM
MRS. EVA ERNA TORNERHJELM HAFSTROEM
AMBASSADOR EXTRAORDINARY & PLENIPOTENTIARY

MS. KARIN MARIA HOEGLUND
MINISTER-COUNSELOR (DEPUTY CHIEF OF MISSION)

MR. JOHAN PONTUS MELANDER
MS. EVA MARGARETA SCHYBERG MELANDER
MINISTER

MR. MAGNUS OLOF RYDEN
MS. MALIN ANNE MARIE RYDEN
MINISTER

MS. SONJA GABRIELLA AUGUSTSSON
MR. PER ARNE AUGUSTSSON
COUNSELOR (PUBLIC AFFAIRS)

DR. PER JOACHIM BERGSTROM
COUNSELOR

MS. DITTE KATARINA HEDLUND EGNELL
MR. CLAES ROBERT CLAESSON EGNELL
COUNSELOR

MR. ROLF OLA GOERANSSON
COUNSELOR

MR. PETER UNO VALDEMAR HAELLKVIST
MRS. ANNA LOUISE NELLSJOE HAELLKVIST
COUNSELOR

MR. KURT PERCY OEIWIND HARTOFT
MS. ERIKA EVA HARTOFT
COUNSELOR

MR. ROLF HOEIJER
MS. ANNA SOFIA BJOERNSDOTTER HOEIJER
COUNSELOR

MR. HANS INGE MAGNUS INGESSON
COUNSELOR

MR. LENNART ERIC KILLANDER LARSSON
MRS. HELENA KILLANDER
COUNSELOR

MS. ELSA MARIA KRISTINA MARTIGNIER
COUNSELOR & CONSUL GENERAL

MS. EVA KRISTINA RENNERSTEDT
COUNSELOR

MR. ANDERS ROBERT WAHLBERG
MS. BRITA KRISTINA BOERJESON
COUNSELOR

MRS. ANNA KRISTINA LAMBERT
MR. GEORGE GAVIN LAMBERT*
FIRST SECRETARY & CONSUL

MRS. ANN KRISTIN LUND
MR. KARL DAVID IAGNEMMA*
FIRST SECRETARY

MS. SANNA KATARINA M. ZANDEN KJELLEN
FIRST SECRETARY

MISS PERNILLA ELISABETH ALMEN
THIRD SECRETARY

MS. ANITA GUNHILD ENGVALL
MR. KARL JESPER ENGVALL
THIRD SECRETARY

MS. RITVA LENA WAHLGREN
MR. JAN MIKAEL WAHLGREN
THIRD SECRETARY

DR. GRETA SOFIE CHARLOTTE BJOERLING
ATTACHE

REAR ADMIRAL JOERGEN FREDRIK ERICSSON
MRS. MALIN EVA ERICSSON LENNMOR
DEFENSE ATTACHE

COLONEL DAG OLAV AMBJOERN LIDEN
MRS. CARINA MARGARETHA LIDEN
MILITARY ATTACHE & ASST. DEFENSE ATTACHE

COLONEL JOHAN ERIK SVETOFT
MS. MARGARETA ELISABETH SVETOFT
AIR ATTACHE & ASST. DEFENSE ATTACHE

COLONEL HANS MIKAEL GRANLUND
MS. ANNICA ELISABETH GRANLUND
NAVAL ATTACHE & ASST. DEFENSE ATTACHE

SCIENCE AND TECHNOLOGY OFFICE
2900 K STREET, NW 20007
(OFFICE 202-467-2600)   (FAX 202-467-2678)

SWITZERLAND

EMBASSY OF SWITZERLAND
Chancery: 2900 CATHEDRAL AVENUE, NW 20008
(EMBASSY 202-745-7900)   (FAX 202-387-2564)

HIS EXCELLENCY MANUEL SAGER
MRS. CHRISTINE ANNE SAGER*
AMBASSADOR EXTRAORDINARY & PLENIPOTENTIARY

MR. GUILLAUME BERTRAND SCHEURER
MS. FARIN SCHEURER
MINISTER (DEPUTY CHIEF OF MISSION)

MR. JOSEF PHILIPP RENGGLI
MRS. CINZIA SEBASTIANI RENGGLI
MINISTER (ECONOMIC AFFAIRS)

MR. NORBERT DANIEL BAERLOCHER
MRS. VALERIA ALBER CAFLISCH BAERLOCHER
COUNSELOR (COMMUNICATIONS & CULTURAL AFFAIRS)

MR. JOHANN CHRISTOPH EBELL
    MRS. JACQUELINE YVONNE EBELL HAENNI
COUNSELOR (SCIENCE & TECHNOLOGY)

MS. SABINE GABRIELLE G JENKINS
    MR. NICOLAS JON JENKINS
COUNSELOR

MR. EDUARD KRALL
    MRS. HEIDI KRALL ROTHENBUEHLER
COUNSELOR & CONSUL GENERAL

MR. MARCO MOSCA
    MRS. PAOLA DE LUME MOSCA
COUNSELOR

MR. FRANCOIS ANDRE SCHMIDT
COUNSELOR (TRADE)

MR. MARTIN ANDREAS BAUMGARTNER
FIRST SECRETARY

MRS. VERONIQUE REGULA IDA HALLER
    MR. PIERRE LIENHARD
FIRST SECRETARY

MS. RICCARDA TORRIANI
FIRST SECRETARY

MS. ANNE LISE CATTIN HENNIN
    MR. CEDRIC HENNIN
SECOND SECRETARY

MRS. MARIE NOELLE CHAPPATTE
THIRD SECRETARY & VICE CONSUL

MS. LUZIA CLAUDIA FURRER
THIRD SECRETARY

MRS. MONIQUE ANNE MARIE SERRA GRELLE
    MR. FEDERICO CARLOS GRELLE
THIRD SECRETARY

MR. KURT ROBERT BLEUER
ATTACHE

MR. PHILIPPE ALEXANDRE DAYER
    MRS. ROSANGELA VIEIRA BENTO DAYER
ATTACHE

MR. LEO ROMAN KARRER
    MRS. MAGALI HERRMANN KARRER
ATTACHE

MR. HUBERT FRANZ STEINHAUSER
    MRS. JOHANNA ELISABETH STEINHAUSER
ATTACHE (DEFENSE ENGINEERING)

MAJOR GENERAL PETER FRIEDRICH EGGER
    MRS. FRANZISKA EGGER ZAHNO
DEFENSE, MILITARY, NAVAL & AIR ATTACHE

MR. DANIEL ANDRE ROUSSELOT
    MRS. BIANCA REBECCA ELLINOR ROUSSELOT
ASST. DEFENSE, MILITARY, NAVAL & AIR ATTACHE

2900 CATHEDRAL AVENUE, NW 20008

SYRIA

EMBASSY OF THE SYRIAN ARAB REPUBLIC
Chancery: 2215 WYOMING AVENUE, NW 20008
(EMBASSY 202-232-6313)   (FAX 202-234-9548)

MR. MOUNIR KOUDMANI
    MRS. ABIR FAHEL
MINISTER-COUNSELOR (CHARGE D'AFFAIRES AD INTERIM)

MR. BASSAM BARABANDI
    MRS. RIHAM ARYAN
FIRST SECRETARY

MRS. ROUA SHURBAJI
    MR. ANAS DEEB
THIRD SECRETARY

MR. HASHEM YAZIJI
    MRS. WAFAA SHEHAB
ATTACHE

TAJIKISTAN

EMBASSY REPUBLIC OF TAJIKISTAN
Chancery: 1005 NEW HAMPSHIRE AVENUE, NW 20037
(EMBASSY 202-223-6090)   (FAX 202-223-6091)

HIS EXCELLENCY NURIDDIN SHAMSOV
    MS. NIGINA RAJAB
AMBASSADOR EXTRAORDINARY & PLENIPOTENTIARY

MR. FARHOD SALIM
    MRS. MARHABO BILOLOVA
COUNSELOR (DEPUTY CHIEF OF MISSION)

MR. ZOKIRJON ZARIFOV
THIRD SECRETARY

TANZANIA

EMBASSY OF THE UNITED REPUBLIC OF TANZANIA
Chancery: 1232 22ND STREET, NW 20037
(EMBASSY 202-939-6125)   (FAX 202-797-7408)

MRS. LILY LETAWO MUNANKA
MINISTER-COUNSELOR (CHARGE D'AFFAIRES AD INTERIM)

MR. ABBAS ABEID MISSANA
    MRS. MANSURA ABDUL MUTUNGI
MINISTER (CONSULAR)

MR. PAUL AMBINDWILE MWAFONGO
    MRS. BERTHA NDARO BWIMBO MWAFONGO
MINISTER (ECONOMIC)

MISS MINDI HELLEN PAMELA KASIGA
MINISTER-COUNSELOR

MS. ASIA ATHUMANI DACHI
COUNSELOR (ADMINISTRATION)

DR. SWITBERT ZACHARIA MKAMA
    MRS. MATRIDA PIUS MASASI
COUNSELOR (SOCIAL AFFAIRS)

MS. JUSTA MATARI NYANGE
　　MR. HERBERT HERME NYANGE
　　COUNSELOR (POLITICAL)

MR. SULEIMAN AHMED SALEH
　　MRS. FARIDA SULEIMAN SALEH
　　SECOND SECRETARY (POLITICAL AFFAIRS)

MRS. CATHERINE DEODATH LUBUVA KIJUU
　　MR. VINCENT YUST KIJUU
　　ATTACHE (ADMINISTRATIVE)

MRS. AGNES KATANGA LUSINDE
　　ATTACHE (ADMINISTRATIVE)

MR. EDWARD DAVID MASANJA
　　MRS. PENDO ANDERSON MWANG'AMBA
　　ATTACHE (FINANCIAL)

BRIGADIER GENERAL EMMANUEL EDWARD MAGANGA
　　MRS. LOVE EPHRAIMY MAGANGA
　　DEFENSE, MILITARY, NAVAL & AIR ATTACHE

STORAGE
　　2139 R STREET, NW 20008

　　1232 22ND STREET, NW 20037

THAILAND

EMBASSY OF THAILAND
Chancery: 1024 WISCONSIN AVENUE, NW 20007
(EMBASSY 202-944-3600)　(FAX 202-944-3611)

HIS EXCELLENCY CHAIYONG SATJIPANON
　　AMBASSADOR EXTRAORDINARY & PLENIPOTENTIARY

MR. SAROJ THANASUNTI
　　MRS. GANISTA THANASUNTI
　　MINISTER (DEPUTY CHIEF OF MISSION)

MRS. SASIPHAND BHANARAI
　　LIEUTENANT SUTTI BHANARAI
　　MINISTER (ECONOMIC)

MR. ADISORN PROMTHEP
　　MRS. JARINYA PROMTHEP
　　MINISTER

MS. WACHIRA TIRAKORNVISESPHUKDI
　　MINISTER

MISS BENCHAWAN UKRID
　　MINISTER (COMMERCIAL)

MR. ANUGOON CHERMMONGKOL
　　MISS NUCHANART NGAMJUMRAT
　　MINISTER-COUNSELOR

MR. ALONGKORN LAOWNGAM
　　MRS. AMPAIPORN LAOWNGAM
　　MINISTER-COUNSELOR

MISS NANTAWAN SANGTONG
　　MINISTER-COUNSELOR

MISS ARJAREE SRIRATANABAN
　　MINISTER-COUNSELOR

MR. SIRA SWANGSILPA
　　MRS. JITSUKON PAISANAUTPHONG
　　MINISTER-COUNSELOR

MR. PERAPAT UTHAISRI
　　MRS. CHATCHAYA UTHAISRI
　　MINISTER-COUNSELOR

MRS. NUNNADDA PHATTIYAKUL
　　MR. SAKOLTEE PHATTIYAKUL
　　COUNSELOR (COMMERCIAL)

MS. WANLADA RATANAPANICH
　　COUNSELOR

MISS SIRINDARA ATTHAKOR
　　FIRST SECRETARY

MISS CHAKSUDA CHAKKAPHAK
　　FIRST SECRETARY

MS. PANALEE CHOOSRI
　　FIRST SECRETARY

MISS BANARASI KOANANTAKUL
　　FIRST SECRETARY

MISS SUCHADA MAKTARA
　　FIRST SECRETARY

MISS BENJARAT PHARELAI
　　FIRST SECRETARY

MISS NILOBOL PIMDEE
　　MR. TANAPOL MANGSA
　　FIRST SECRETARY

MR. SOMPHOB UNNAHA
　　MRS. SUPAPORN UNNAHA
　　FIRST SECRETARY

MR. PRASIT VISETKAEW
　　FIRST SECRETARY

MR. KAJTITI WIWATWANONT
　　MRS. HIROKO WIWATWNONT
　　FIRST SECRETARY

MRS. ATCHARA JONGJITPISAMAI
　　SECOND SECRETARY

COMMANDER CHAITHAT MALASAI
　　MRS. KEERATIYA MALASAI
　　ATTACHE (PROCUREMENT OFFICER)

COLONEL SARANYU VIRIYAVEJAKUL
　　MRS. JARUVARINTRA OSATHANUKUROH
　　DEFENSE & MILITARY ATTACHE

CAPTAIN TANASAK METANANTA
　　MRS. MONRUEDEE METANANTA
　　AIR ATTACHE & ASST. DEFENSE ATTACHE

COLONEL KRITTIJAK CHANAGATE
　　ASST. DEFENSE & MILITARY ATTACHE

COLONEL CHANAGATE KRITTIJAK
　　MRS. SUPATTRA CHANAGATE
　　ASST. DEFENSE & MILITARY ATTACHE

CAPTAIN GRAISRI GESORN
　　MRS. VENA GESORN
　　ASST. DEFENSE & NAVAL ATTACHE

CAPTAIN YUTTANAPONG NOPPAKULSATIT
　　MRS. PATRANUCH NOPPAKULSATIT
　　ASST. NAVAL ATTACHE

AGRICULTURAL AFFAIRS OFFICE
　　1024 WISCONSIN AVENUE, NW 20007

* U.S. Citizen

AIR ATTACHE
1024 WISCONSIN AVENUE, NW 20007
(OFFICE 202-338-9700)

COMMERCIAL AFFAIRS
1024 WISCONSIN AVENUE, NW 20007
(OFFICE 202-944-2111)

ECONOMIC AND FINANCIAL AFFAIRS
1024 WISCONSIN AVENUE, NW 20007
(OFFICE 202-467-6790)

EDUCATION AFFAIRS
1906 23RD STREET, NW 20008
(OFFICE 202-667-9111)

EMBASSY OF THAILAND
1024 WISCONSIN AVENUE, NW 20007

MILITARY ATTACHE
1024 WISCONSIN AVENUE, NW 20007
(OFFICE 202-338-9381)

NAVAL ATTACHE
1024 WISCONSIN AVENUE, NW 20007
(OFFICE 202-944-3629)

SCIENCE AND TECHNOLOGY
1024 WISCONSIN AVENUE, NW 20007
(OFFICE 202-944-5203)

TIMOR LESTE

EMBASSY OF THE DEMOCRATIC REPUBLIC OF TIMOR
LESTE
Chancery: 4201 CONNECTICUT AVENUE, NW, SUITE 504
20008
(EMBASSY 202-966-3202)   (FAX 202-966-3205)

HIS EXCELLENCY CONSTANCIO DA CONCEICAO PINTO
MRS. GABRIELA LOPES DA CRUZ PINTO
AMBASSADOR EXTRAORDINARY & PLENIPOTENTIARY

MRS. ADELINA SOARES MARTINS
MR. FERNANDO BAPTISTA ANUNO
FIRST SECRETARY

MRS. SONIA MARIA DA SILVA MAIA
MR. RUI A. BORROMEU DA COSTA PACHECO
SECOND SECRETARY

TOGO

EMBASSY OF THE REPUBLIC OF TOGO
Chancery: 2208 MASSACHUSETTS AVENUE, NW 20008
(EMBASSY 202-234-4212)   (FAX 202-232-3190)

HIS EXCELLENCY EDAWE LIMBIYE KADANGHA BARIKI
MRS. ESSOZIMANA KADANGHA BARIKI
AMBASSADOR EXTRAORDINARY & PLENIPOTENTIARY

MR. BRUNO FINEL
COUNSELOR (PRESS & COMMUNICATION)

MR. MBALEMBOU HODABALO PATO
MRS. PANABAYI AWATE SPOUSE PATO
COUNSELOR

MR. OHINI KWASSIVI AQUEREBURU
SECOND SECRETARY

* U.S. Citizen

MRS. ADJOKE ADEYEMI ISSIFOU
MR. ZAKARI TCHATCHIBARA ISSIFOU
ATTACHE

MR. ADE BASSO ANOUNKOU
MRS. GMANI OUPERE N SEWA EPSE ANOUNKOU
ATTACHE (FINANCIAL)

MS. BEHEZA GNASSINGBE
ATTACHE (CULTURAL)

MR. MOUZA TCHALIM
MRS. ESSOBOUYOU HALSASSIBA TCHALIM
ATTACHE (CONSULAR)

TONGA

EMBASSY OF THE KINGDOM OF TONGA
Chancery: 250 E. 51ST STREET
NEW YORK, NY 10022
(EMBASSY 917-369-1025)   (FAX 917-369-1024)

HIS EXCELLENCY SONATANE TUA TAUMOEPEAU TUPOU
AMBASSADOR EXTRAORDINARY & PLENIPOTENTIARY

TRINIDAD AND TOBAGO

EMBASSY OF THE REPUBLIC OF TRINIDAD AND TOBAGO
Chancery: 1708 MASSACHUSETTS AVENUE, NW 20036
(EMBASSY 202-467-6490)   (FAX 202-785-3130)

HIS EXCELLENCY DR. NEIL NADESH PARSAN
MRS. LUCIA DIANE MAYERS PARSAN
AMBASSADOR EXTRAORDINARY & PLENIPOTENTIARY

MISS DONNA HENRY
COUNSELOR

MS. KATHLEEN SEENARINE
COUNSELOR

MS. AVIANNE CONYETTE BONEY
FIRST SECRETARY

MS. KAANITA FARHAANA SHAH
SECOND SECRETARY

MS. DANA AVION WALLACE
SECOND SECRETARY

MS. DIANNE PATRICE COWIE
ATTACHE (IMMIGRATION)

MRS. SANDRA MCSHINE
ATTACHE (ADMINISTRATIVE)

MRS. YASMIN INDRA ROUFF BOBAN
ATTACHE

MS. SUSAN NICOLE SIRJOO
ATTACHE

MS. ADANNA KALIFA TAYLOR
ATTACHE

COLONEL COLIN LINDSAY RUSSEL MITCHELL
MRS. DAWN CHRYSTAL C. FRITZ MITCHELL
DEFENSE & MILITARY ATTACHE (ALT.REP(OAS))

TUNISIA

EMBASSY OF TUNISIA
Chancery: 1515 MASSACHUSETTS AVENUE, NW 20005
(EMBASSY 202-862-1850)   (FAX 202-862-1858)

MR. TAREK AMRI
    MRS. RADHIA GHARBI AMRI
    COUNSELOR (CHARGE D'AFFAIRES AD INTERIM)

MR. MUSTAPHA BELGACEM
    MS. ASMA GDIRI BELGACEM
    COUNSELOR (ADMINISTRATIVE)

MR. KAIS DARRAGI
    MRS. WIDED BELHAJ DARRAGI
    COUNSELOR (CONGRESSIONAL AFFAIRS)

MR. BOUZEKRI RMILI
    MRS. INES YOUSSEF RMILI
    COUNSELOR (ECONOMIC AFFAIRS)

MS. FATEN BAHRI
    FIRST SECRETARY (CULTURAL)

MRS. CHAHRAZED LAMARI REZGUI
    MR. SLAHEDDINE REZGUI
    FIRST SECRETARY (PRESS)

MR. YASSINE SALAH
    FIRST SECRETARY (CONSULAR)

MR. MOHAMED HICHEM SAHRAOUI
    MRS. SAMIA MAAOUI SAHRAOUI
    SECOND SECRETARY

MR. SALAH ARFAOUI
    ATTACHE

MR. ADEL DABOUSSI
    ATTACHE (ADMINISTRATIVE)

WARRANT OFFICER SADOK GHANDOUSSI
    ATTACHE

MR. TAREK HAMAD
    ATTACHE (ADMINISTRATIVE)

MR. ALI NEILI
    ATTACHE

COLONEL MAJOR NEJIB EL GHALI
    MRS. WAHIBA BEN ABDELLATIF EL GHALI
    DEFENSE, MILITARY, NAVAL & AIR ATTACHE

COLONEL MONCEF BEN RHOUMA
    ASST. DEFENSE, MILITARY, NAVAL & AIR ATTACHE

DEFENSE ARMED FORCES ATTACHE
    1515 MASSACHUSETTS AVENUE, NW 20005
    (OFFICE 202-862-1850)

TUNISIAN INFORMATION
    1515 MASSACHUSETTS AVENUE, NW 20005
    (OFFICE 202-446-2546)

TURKEY

EMBASSY OF THE REPUBLIC OF TURKEY
Chancery: 2525 MASSACHUSETTS AVENUE, NW 20008
(EMBASSY 202-612-6700)   (FAX 202-612-6744)

HIS EXCELLENCY NAMIK TAN
    MRS. TALIA FUGEN TAN
    AMBASSADOR EXTRAORDINARY & PLENIPOTENTIARY

MR. TAHSIN TIMUR SOYLEMEZ
    MRS. CARLA JONES SOYLEMEZ*
    MINISTER-COUNSELOR (DEPUTY CHIEF OF MISSION)

MRS. KIRAZ GULSUN BOR GUNER
    MR. NIYAZI SELCUK GUNER
    COUNSELOR (ECONOMIC)

MR. ONUR BULBUL
    MRS. GONCA ISTANBULLUOGLU BULBUL
    COUNSELOR (DEPUTY COMMERCIAL)

DR. YASAR COLAK
    MRS. NAZIRE COLAK
    COUNSELOR

MR. RAUF ALP DENKTAS
    COUNSELOR

MR. YUKSEL ERDOGAN
    MRS. ZEYNEP ERDOGAN
    COUNSELOR (LEGAL)

MS. BURCU KERIMAN ERDOGDU
    COUNSELOR

MR. BEHIC HATIPOGLU
    MS. TUBA HATIPOGLU
    COUNSELOR

MS. TUBA HATIPOGLU
    COUNSELOR

MR. MEHMET AKIF INAM
    MRS. KRISTI INAM
    COUNSELOR

MR. RIZA MEHMET KORKMAZ
    MRS. DERYA KORKMAZ
    COUNSELOR

MR. ABDULLAH KOTEN
    MRS. HACER KOTEN
    COUNSELOR (COMMERCIAL)

MR. OMER MURAT
    MRS. MERYEM MURAT
    COUNSELOR

MR. CAN OGUZ
    MRS. HUMEYRA OGUZ
    COUNSELOR

MR. MESUT OZBEK
    MRS. BELGIZAR OZBEK
    COUNSELOR

MS. GUL SARIGUL WEN
    MR. HAN WEN*
    COUNSELOR

MR. ENES SUNEL
    MRS. SEVIM BETUL SUNEL
    COUNSELOR (ECONOMIC)

* U.S. Citizen

MR. MUSTAFA KEMAL SUNGUR
    MRS. FATMA SUNGUR
COUNSELOR (PRESS)

MR. GORKEM BARIS TANTEKIN
    MRS. OMUR DAMLA TANTEKIN
COUNSELOR

MR. HALIL YILMAZ
    MRS. TULAY YILMAZ
COUNSELOR (SECURITY)

MR. EMIRHAN YORULMAZLAR
    MRS. AYSEGUL YORULMAZLAR
COUNSELOR

MR. ARIF HAKAN YETER
    MRS. ESRA ELIF YETER
FIRST SECRETARY

MR. HASAN AKIN
    MRS. SEBAHAT AKIN
SECOND SECRETARY

MR. NAMIK GEBELEK
    MRS. YONCA AYSE GEBELEK
SECOND SECRETARY

MR. ONCU KECELI
    MRS. SANEM ALTAYLI KECELI
SECOND SECRETARY

MR. UTKU KUNDAKCI
    MRS. GORKEM AYDEMIR KUNDAKCI
SECOND SECRETARY

MS. MINE OZGUL
SECOND SECRETARY

MR. RESIT TOGAN TURGUT
    MRS. FUNDA TURGUT
SECOND SECRETARY

MR. YUNUS EMRE ACIKGONUL
THIRD SECRETARY

MS. OZLEM TURKMEN
THIRD SECRETARY

MR. FAHRETTIN ACIKGOZ
    MRS. ZEYCAN ACIKGOZ
ATTACHE

MR. RAMAZAN AKTAS
    MS. AYGUL AKTAS
ATTACHE

MR. SELAHATTIN AYDIN
    MS. YELIZ AYDIN
ATTACHE

CHIEF PETTY OFFICER CIHAN AYGUNES
ATTACHE (ADMINISTRATIVE)

MR. ORHAN CAM
    MRS. FATMA CAM
ATTACHE

MR. ALPER CETINKAYA
    MRS. FATMA CETINKAYA
ATTACHE

MR. ERGUN DEMIRCIOGLU
    MRS. SEVINC DEMIRCIOGLU
ATTACHE

MS. SEVTAP EYYUBI
ATTACHE

* U.S. Citizen

MR. TAHIR CUMHUR KAHRAMAN
    MRS. SIBEL KAHRAMAN
ATTACHE (ADMINISTRATIVE)

MR. NURI KALENDER
    MRS. AYSE KALENDER
ATTACHE

MAJOR SERDAR KAYA
    MRS. HATICE KAYA
ATTACHE (MEDICAL)

MASTER SERGEANT ZAFER KEDIKLI
ATTACHE (AIR SUPPLY)

MR. ERHAN KOLBASI
    MRS. FATMA KOLBASI
ATTACHE

MR. MERVE OZSOY
    MRS. PINAR DENIZARSLANI OZSOY
ATTACHE

MASTER SERGEANT MURAT POLAT
    MRS. FATMA NURAY POLAT
ATTACHE (ADMINISTRATIVE)

MR. GOKHAN YUCEL
    MS. TUGBA YUCEL
ATTACHE

MR. UFUK CANOZ
    MRS. RESIDE SERAP CANOZ
ASST. ATTACHE

MR. FETHI ALPAY
    MRS. ADILE ALPAY
DEFENSE & AIR ATTACHE

MR. MEHMET ALI TUNA
    MRS. GONCA LEYLA TUNA
MILITARY ATTACHE

LIEUTENANT COMMANDER MAHMUT ARDUC
    MRS. AYSE ARDUC
NAVAL ATTACHE

MAJOR AHMET DURGUT
    MRS. VILDAN DURGUT
ASST. MILITARY ATTACHE

MR. NUMAN YONER
    MRS. BIRGUL YONER
ASST. MILITARY ATTACHE

LIEUTENANT COMMANDER CEM GULHAN
    MRS. ELVAN GULHAN
ASST. NAVAL ATTACHE

LIEUTENANT COLONEL ATTILA SERT
    MRS. BURCU SERT
ASST. AIR ATTACHE

AGRICULTURAL COUNSELOR
    2525 MASSACHUSETTS AVENUE, NW 20008
        (OFFICE 202-612-6700)

COMMERCIAL COUNSELOR
    2525 MASSACHUSETTS AVENUE, NW 20008
        (OFFICE 202-612-6780)

DEFENSE ATTACHE OFFICE
    2202 MASSACHUSETTS AVENUE, NW 20008
        (OFFICE 202-939-1860)

DEFENSE, AIR, MILITARY & NAVAL ATTACHE OFFICE
2525 MASSACHUSETTS AVENUE, NW 20008
(OFFICE 202-612-6770)

ECONOMIC COUNSELOR
2525 MASSACHUSETTS AVENUE, NW 20008
(OFFICE 202-612-6790)

EDUCATIONAL COUNSELOR
2525 MASSACHUSETTS AVENUE, NW 20008
(OFFICE 202-612-6810)

FINANCIAL AND CUSTOMS COUNSELOR
2525 MASSACHUSETTS AVENUE, NW 20008
(OFFICE 202-612-6812)

PLANNING OFFICE
2525 MASSACHUSETTS AVENUE, NW 20008
(OFFICE 202-612-6814)

PRESS COUNSELOR
2525 MASSACHUSETTS AVENUE, NW 20008
(OFFICE 202-612-6807)

SOCIAL AFFAIRS
2525 MASSACHUSETTS AVENUE, NW 20008
(OFFICE 202-612-6816)

TOURISM COUNSELOR
2525 MASSACHUSETTS AVENUE, NW 20008
(OFFICE 202-612-6800)

1526 18TH ST STREET, NW 20036

TURKMENISTAN

EMBASSY OF TURKMENISTAN
Chancery: 2207 MASSACHUSETTS AVENUE, NW 20008
(EMBASSY 202-588-1500)   (FAX 202-588-0697)

HIS EXCELLENCY MERET BAIRAMOVICH ORAZOV
MRS. IRINA BORISOVNA ORAZOVA
AMBASSADOR EXTRAORDINARY & PLENIPOTENTIARY

MR. GUYCHMYRAT AKMAMMEDOV
MRS. OGULKEYIK AKMAMMEDOVA
FIRST SECRETARY

MAJOR GURBANMYRAT PATYSHOV
MRS. MARAL MATIYEVA
DEFENSE & MILITARY ATTACHE

TUVALU

EMBASSY OF TUVALU
Chancery: 800 SECOND AVENUE, SUITE 400D
NEW YORK, NY 10017
(EMBASSY 212-490-0534)

HIS EXCELLENCY AUNESE MAKOI SIMATI
MRS. SUNEMA PIE SIMATI
AMBASSADOR EXTRAORDINARY & PLENIPOTENTIARY

UGANDA

EMBASSY OF THE REPUBLIC OF UGANDA
Chancery: 5911 16TH STREET, NW 20011
(EMBASSY 202-726-0416)   (FAX 202-726-1727)

MR. ALFRED NNAM
MS. GUEDIA ROSE TAMEZE
MINISTER (CHARGE D'AFFAIRES AD INTERIM)

MR. DICKSON OGWANG
MINISTER-COUNSELOR

MR. GUMA PATRICK MUGANDA
MRS. BEATRICE AJALO GUMA
COUNSELOR

MR. BHOI SAM OMARA
MRS. JOSEPHINE LILIAN B. NANTIBA OMARA
FIRST SECRETARY

MISS ROSEBELL KIRUNGI
THIRD SECRETARY

COLONEL LEOPOLD ERIC KYANDA
MRS. JUDY RUGASIRA
DEFENSE, MILITARY, NAVAL & AIR ATTACHE

CHANCERY ANNEX
5909 16TH STREET 20011
(OFFICE 202-726-7100)   (FAX 202-726-1727)

UKRAINE

EMBASSY OF UKRAINE
Chancery: 3350 M STREET, NW 20007
(EMBASSY 202-349-2920)   (FAX 202-333-0817)

HIS EXCELLENCY OLEXANDER MOTSYK
MRS. NATALIIA TERLETSKA
AMBASSADOR EXTRAORDINARY & PLENIPOTENTIARY

MR. YAROSLAV BRISIUCK
MRS. MARIIA CHUCHVARA
MINISTER-COUNSELOR (DEPUTY CHIEF OF MISSION)

MRS. VLADYSLAVA BONDARENKO
MR. VITALII POPOV
COUNSELOR

MR. VALENTYN KARVAN
MRS. NATALIYA KARVAN
COUNSELOR

MR. ANDRIY NIKITOV
MRS. MARIIA NIKITOVA
COUNSELOR

MR. VITALII POPOV
MRS. VLADYSLAVA BONDARENKO
COUNSELOR (CONSULAR)

MR. STANISLAV YEZHOV
MRS. YULIA MIROSHNIKOVA
COUNSELOR

MR. IHOR BARANETSKYI
MRS. KATERYNA BARANETSKA
FIRST SECRETARY

* U.S. Citizen

MR. KOSTIANTYN BOIKO
MRS. TAMARA BOIKO
FIRST SECRETARY

MR. OLEKSANDR GIRENKO
MRS. TETYANA GIRENKO
FIRST SECRETARY

MRS. NADIYA KOSTENKO
MR. DMYTRO MOSHUN
FIRST SECRETARY

MR. MAKSYM KRAVCHUK
MRS. TETIANA KRAVCHUK
FIRST SECRETARY

MR. YURII KUCHERIAVYI
MRS. TETIANA KUCHERIAVA
FIRST SECRETARY

MR. ARTEM NOSKO
MRS. OLENA NOSKO
FIRST SECRETARY

MR. ALBERT RIABTSEV
MRS. IRYNA RIABTSEVA
FIRST SECRETARY

MR. VOLODYMYR SHALKIVSKYI
FIRST SECRETARY

MRS. ORESTA STARAK
MR. TARAS STARAK
FIRST SECRETARY

MRS. TETIANA SHALKIVSKA
MR. VOLODYMYR SHALKIVSKYI
SECOND SECRETARY

MR. ANDRIY BAZIV
THIRD SECRETARY

MR. OLEKSANDR BEREZHNYI
MRS. LIUBOV BEREZHNA
THIRD SECRETARY

MRS. RITA CHUBAROVA
MR. DENYS VORONOVYCH
THIRD SECRETARY

MR. IHOR HRYBAN
MRS. IRYNA HRYBAN
THIRD SECRETARY

MS. NATALIIA MUSIIENKO
THIRD SECRETARY & VICE CONSUL

MS. OLEKSANDRA NESTERCHUK
THIRD SECRETARY

MR. IVAN PELESCHAK
MRS. LIUDMYLA PELESCHAK
THIRD SECRETARY

MS. OLENA SHEPETIUK
THIRD SECRETARY

MS. YAROSLAVA ZAYETS
MR. PETRO BOIEPRAV
THIRD SECRETARY & VICE CONSUL

VICE ADMIRAL IHOR KNIAZ
MRS. LARYSA KNIAZ
DEFENSE ATTACHE

COLONEL ANDRIY YAKOVLIEV
MRS. MARYNA YAKOVLIEVA
MILITARY ATTACHE & ASST. DEFENSE ATTACHE

* U.S. Citizen

CAPTAIN YURIY CHERNYKH
MRS. OLENA CHERNYKH
NAVAL ATTACHE

MR. OLEKSANDR BAZHORA
MRS. MARIIA BAZHORA
AIR ATTACHE & ASST. DEFENSE ATTACHE

LIEUTENANT COLONEL DMYTRO KRYLOV
MRS. VIKTORIA KRYLOVA
ASST. DEFENSE ATTACHE

UNITED ARAB EMIRATES

EMBASSY OF THE UNITED ARAB EMIRATES
Chancery: 3522 INTERNATIONAL COURT, NW 20008
(EMBASSY 202-243-2400)   (FAX 202-243-2432)

HIS EXCELLENCY YOUSIF MANA SAEED ALOTAIBA
MRS. ABEER MOHAMED MOUSTAFA SHOKRY
AMBASSADOR EXTRAORDINARY & PLENIPOTENTIARY

MR. OMAR OBAID MOHD ALHESAN ALSHAMSI
MRS. MOZA HINDI ALSHAMSI
MINISTER (DEPUTY CHIEF OF MISSION)

MR. SAUD HASSAN MOHAMED ALI ALNOWAIS
COUNSELOR (TRADE)

MR. SALEM ALI KHAMIS O. ALSHAMSI
MRS. MUNA O. ALDHABBAH
FIRST SECRETARY

MR. ABDULRAHMAN AHMED SULTAN ALJABER
MRS. MOZA GHANIM ALMAZRUI
SECOND SECRETARY

MR. ABDULAZIZ ALSHAREEF
MRS. AYESHA A ALMARZOOQI
SECOND SECRETARY

MR. ABDULLA OMAR ALAHMED
THIRD SECRETARY

MS. AL SAGHIRA WABRAN HAMAD AL AHBABI
MR. MOHAMED HUSSAIN MOHAMED MOHAMED
ATTACHE (ADMINISTRATIVE)

LIEUTENANT SUROUR SHAWAN SUROUR ALDHAHERI
ATTACHE (FINANCE)

WARRANT OFFICER JASEM MOHAMED ALMAS ALDHANHANI
MRS. HAIFAA SAEED ALMESMARI
ATTACHE (FINANCE)

MISS SHAMMA EISSA HUSAIN E. ALHOSANI
ATTACHE

WARRANT OFFICER ABDULLA SAEED SAIF ALJADIDI
MRS. NADIA RASHED
ATTACHE (ADMINISTRATIVE)

MR. MAKTOUM ABDULLA ALKAABI
ATTACHE (ADMINISTRATIVE)

DR. ASMA MOHAMED JASEM M. A. ALKETBI
ATTACHE (CULTURAL)

FIRST LIEUTENANT RUBAYA SAEED SALEM ALMARRI
MRS. SARA IBRAHIM ALMEHAIRBI
ATTACHE

SERGEANT EISSA SALEM OBAID ALMAZROUEI
MRS. NAJAT ALI ALMUTAWWA
ATTACHE (ADMINISTRATIVE)

WARRANT OFFICER SALEM SAEED ALI SAEED ALMAZROUEI
MRS. SHAIKHA SAEED OBAID A ALQAYDI
ATTACHE (ADMINISTRATIVE)

MAJOR IBRAHIM SALMIN SALEM ALNAIMI
MRS. MARYAM SAEED ALNAIMI
ATTACHE (ADMINISTRATIVE)

FIRST SERGEANT WAYEL ALI HAMAD ALI ALNAQBI
MRS. JULIA TRAHE
ATTACHE (ADMINISTRATIVE)

SHEIKH KHALED MOHD BIN ZAYED ALNEHAYAN
ATTACHE (ADMINISTRATIVE)

WARRANT OFFICER MOHAMED SALMEEN ALNUAIMI
MRS. ZAHEYA K. ALMARRI ALNUAIMI
ATTACHE

MR. ABDULAZIZ SALEM M R ALREMEITHI
ATTACHE (ADMINISTRATIVE)

DR. HESSAM MOHD JALIL SULTAN ALULAMA
MRS. KHAIRUNNISA AHMAD
ATTACHE (CULTURAL)

MISS ASMAA ALI SAEED ALI ALYAMMAHI
ATTACHE

SERGEANT ALI AHMED QADOUR
MRS. FATMAH SAEED QADOUR
ATTACHE (ADMINISTRATIVE)

SECOND LIEUTENANT MATAR HASSAN ALI ALKHZAIMI
ASST. ATTACHE (ADMINISTRATIVE)

WARRANT OFFICER SULTAN RASHED SAEED ALSHEHHI
ASST. ATTACHE (ADMINISTRATIVE)

COLONEL ABDELRAHMAN IBRAHIM ABDEL ALMAZMI
MRS. MUNA ALI
DEFENSE, MILITARY, NAVAL & AIR ATTACHE

LIEUTENANT COLONEL OBAID ALI OBAID RASHED ALMANSOORI
MRS. MARYAM ALI AL MEHRZI AL MEHRZI
ASST. DEFENSE, MILITARY, NAVAL & AIR ATTACHE

CHIEF WARRANT OFFICER MOHAMED SAIF KHALAF A ALKAABI
ASST. MILITARY ATTACHE (CHIEF OF SECURITY)

FIRST LIEUTENANT KHALFAN AWAD KHALFAN B ALNUAIMI
MRS. AYSHA MOHAMMED ALKTEBI
ASST. MILITARY ATTACHE (ADMINISTRATIVE)

WARRANT OFFICER AHMED NASER AHMED BIN J ALZAABI
MRS. NEHAYA KHALFAN ALZAABI
ASST. MILITARY ATTACHE (ADMINISTRATIVE)

CULTURAL OFFICE
1010 WISCONSIN AVENUE, NW, SUITE 700 20007
(OFFICE 202-672-1050)   (FAX 202-672-1082)

DEFENSE, MILITARY, NAVAL AND AIR ATTACHE OFFICE
3522 INTERNATIONAL COURT, NW, ROOM 300 20008
(OFFICE 202-243-4300)   (FAX 202-243-4305)

MEDICAL OFFICE
3522 INTERNATIONAL COURT, NW, ROOM 200 20008
(OFFICE 202-243-4200)   (FAX 202-243-2475)

UNITED KINGDOM

BRITISH EMBASSY
Chancery: 3100 MASSACHUSETTS AVENUE, NW 20008
(EMBASSY 202-588-6500)   (FAX 202-588-7870)

HIS EXCELLENCY SIR PETER JOHN WESTMACOTT
LADY SUSAN NEMAZEE*
AMBASSADOR EXTRAORDINARY & PLENIPOTENTIARY

MR. PHILIP ROBERT BARTON
MRS. AMANDA JOY BARTON
MINISTER (DEPUTY CHIEF OF MISSION)

MR. STEPHEN ALAN FRENCH
MRS. SUSAN AILSA FRENCH
MINISTER (DEFENSE MATERIAL)

MR. ALEXANDER GIBBS
MRS. SONJA GIBBS*
MINISTER (ECONOMIC)

MS. SHUNA T. LINDSAY
MR. DAVID R. WAGGOTT
MINISTER (DEFENSE MATERIAL)

MR. WILLIAM MARK JESSETT
MRS. SARAH JANE JESSETT
MINISTER-COUNSELOR (DEFENSE MATERIAL)

MS. KAREN ELIZABETH BETTS
MR. CHRISTOPHER GLYN HUGHES
COUNSELOR

MS. ROSALIND LUCY ELIZABETH CAMPION
COUNSELOR

MR. DAVID DEARDEN
MRS. GLORIA JEAN DEARDEN
COUNSELOR (DEFENSE)

MR. ALEXANDER SINCLAIR DEWDNEY
MRS. LORRAINE JULIET DEWDNEY
COUNSELOR

MR. ROBERT DAVID EASON
MRS. DEBBIE SARA EASON
COUNSELOR

MR. PETER CHARLES WILLIAM GODWIN
MRS. CAROL GODWIN
COUNSELOR

MS. ALEXANDRA HALL HALL
MR. DANIEL TWINING*
COUNSELOR

MR. ERIC DOUGLAS HEPBURN
MRS. DEBORA LOUISE HEPBURN
COUNSELOR

MR. NORMAN JAMES HOUSTON
COUNSELOR

MR. JAMES KENYANJUI KARIUKI
MS. PASCALE ANNE FRANCE PUTHOD
COUNSELOR

MR. NICHOLAS JOHN LEWIS
MRS. MICHAELA JANE LEWIS
COUNSELOR (NARCOTICS)

MR. CHRISTOPHER JOHN MARTIN
COUNSELOR

* U.S. Citizen

MR. PETER MATHESON
COUNSELOR (ECONOMICS)

MR. ROBIN SHAND NAYSMITH
MRS. ELIZABETH KELLY
COUNSELOR (SCOTTISH AFFAIRS)

MR. JOHN PHILIP NOBLE
DR. ALISON ELIZABETH NOBLE
COUNSELOR

DR. LYNSEY PINFIELD
MR. JAMIE PINFIELD
COUNSELOR (DEFENSE)

MR. ANDREW CHRISTOPHER PRESTON
MS. SONAL BHATT
COUNSELOR

MR. JOHN V. SILCOCK
MRS. ELIZABETH A. SILCOCK
COUNSELOR

MR. PAUL JONATHAN SMITH
MRS. FNU VIVEKA KUMARI
COUNSELOR

DR. PETER DAVID SMYTH
MRS. YVONNE JULIA SMYTH
COUNSELOR

MR. RICHARD SPEARMAN
MRS. CAROLINE JILL SPEARMAN
COUNSELOR

MS. EMMA LESLEY WADE
COUNSELOR

DR. IAIN STUART WILLIAMS
MRS. LOUISE VALERIE WILLIAMS
COUNSELOR

MR. GARY LEN BALCH
MRS. IRENE SOPHIA BALCH
FIRST SECRETARY (LIAISON PROSECUTOR)

MS. SARAH ANN BAMBER
MR. RICHARD NEVILLE EDE
FIRST SECRETARY

MR. JAMES ANDREW BARBOUR
MS. CAROLYN LESLIE
FIRST SECRETARY (PRESS & PUBLIC AFFAIRS)

MR. THEODORE BARRY
MRS. JANE BARRY
FIRST SECRETARY

MRS. SUSANNA GISELA BERRY
MR. PAUL MICHAEL ADAMS
FIRST SECRETARY (REGIONAL AFFAIRS)

MS. BRIDGET DIANA BRIND
FIRST SECRETARY

MR. BARRY JOHN BRISTOW
FIRST SECRETARY

MR. OMAR TALAL ALI DAAIR
FIRST SECRETARY

MR. ANDREW J. DAWSON
MRS. SARAH F. DAWSON
FIRST SECRETARY (ECONOMIC)

MR. JAMES OMAR DEAN
MRS. PATRICIA DEAN
FIRST SECRETARY

MR. STEPHEN JOHNS ELSBY
MRS. SARAH JANE ELSBY
FIRST SECRETARY

MR. RICHARD BOSWELL EVERITT
MRS. JANINE EMMA EVERITT
FIRST SECRETARY

MRS. JULIA SUSAN FILER
MR. JOHN EDWIN FILER
FIRST SECRETARY

MR. STUART RUSSELL FORRESTER
MRS. RACHEL EMMA LOUISE FORRESTER
FIRST SECRETARY

MR. DUNCAN GILBERT FULTON
MRS. LOUISE PATRICIA FULTON
FIRST SECRETARY

MR. SCOTT LEONARD FURSSEDONN
MRS. ELIZABETH JANE FURSSEDONN WOOD
FIRST SECRETARY

MR. DANIEL WILLIAM GALLAGHER
MRS. CAROLINE ANNE SPENCER
FIRST SECRETARY

MR. ST JOHN B. E. GOULD
MRS. SIAN E. E. GOULD
FIRST SECRETARY

MS. HELEN KIRSTY GUEDALLA
FIRST SECRETARY

MRS. PATRICIA HAYES
MR. ANDREW HAYES
FIRST SECRETARY (TRANSPORT)

MR. NEIL RIDGWAY HOLLAND
MRS. SARAH HOLLAND
FIRST SECRETARY

MR. MICHAEL ROBERT HOWELLS
MRS. COURTNEY MARISSA B. BUDD HOWELLS
FIRST SECRETARY

MR. CHRISTOPHER IAN KEAY
MRS. GRETCHEN BECKER KEAY*
FIRST SECRETARY (DEFENSE POLICY)

MR. MARK TERRENCE KELLY
FIRST SECRETARY

MRS. ELEANOR ANNE KILOH
MR. MARK JAMES PORTER
FIRST SECRETARY

MR. LEE JEREMY LITMAN
MS. STACY GAIL KANGISSER*
FIRST SECRETARY

MR. NIALL ANDREW MACGINNIS
MRS. LUCINDA MACGINNIS
FIRST SECRETARY

MR. SPENCER DOUGLAS MAHONY
MRS. NATASHA ISLA CROWE
FIRST SECRETARY

MR. STEWART TREVOR MATTHEWS
DR. SUZANNE ELIZABETH MATTHEWS
FIRST SECRETARY

MS. FIONA MAY JOAN MCILWHAM
FIRST SECRETARY

* U.S. Citizen

MR. ALAN MCKERRON
MRS. SUSAN CATHERINE MCKERRON
FIRST SECRETARY

MRS. SUSAN CATHERINE MCKERRON
MR. ALAN MCKERRON
FIRST SECRETARY & CONSUL

MS. SARA MOONEY
FIRST SECRETARY

MR. CARL EDWIN FRANCIS NEWNS
MRS. CHRISTINA NEWNS
FIRST SECRETARY

MR. ANDREW ARTHUR PARHAM
MRS. TRACIE ANGELA PARHAM
FIRST SECRETARY (TRADE)

MR. IAN ROBERT PATERSON
MRS. DIANE PATERSON
FIRST SECRETARY

MR. IAN DONALD PURVIS
MRS. VALERIE PURVIS
FIRST SECRETARY

MISS JUDITH HELEN RITCHIE
FIRST SECRETARY

MR. MATTHEW JOHN RYCROFT
MRS. ALISON EMMA VICTORIA RYCROFT
FIRST SECRETARY

MR. MARTIN WILLIAM SKINNER
FIRST SECRETARY (DEFENSE TRADE)

MR. JOHN LAWRENCE SMITH
FIRST SECRETARY

MR. DAVID JOHN SMITHERS
MRS. MICHELLE ANN SMITHERS
FIRST SECRETARY

MR. JOHN LEONARD STEERS
MRS. CLAIRE MARGARET STEERS
FIRST SECRETARY

MRS. CLARE SWIFT
MR. HANS SWIFT
FIRST SECRETARY

MR. SIMON TOWLER
MRS. LOUISE TOWLER
FIRST SECRETARY (TRADE)

MR. ANDREW STUART WHITE
MRS. MAUREEN ELIZABETH WHITE
FIRST SECRETARY

MR. IAN DAVID WIGGINS
MRS. KATIE JANE WIGGINS
FIRST SECRETARY

MS. SOPHIA MADELEINE T. WILLITTS KING
MR. PETER BARNABY WILLITTS KING
FIRST SECRETARY

MR. ORLANDO WILLIAM AMES LEWIS
MRS. CLAUDIA ROCIETA BARDOUILLE LEWIS
SECOND SECRETARY

MISS JANE ANSELL
SECOND SECRETARY

MS. SUZANNE ELIZABETH AUSTIN
MR. MARK STEPHEN BOYLIN
SECOND SECRETARY

MR. GIDEON SAMUEL BRESLER
SECOND SECRETARY (POLITICAL)

MR. DARREN GRAHAM BURGESS
SECOND SECRETARY

MR. MATTHEW NEIL CHALMERS
MRS. KATHARINE CHALMERS
SECOND SECRETARY

MR. ROGER COLIN CLARKE
MRS. MARIA LOUISE WESSTROM CLARKE
SECOND SECRETARY

MR. PAUL CALDWELL CRAWFORD
SECOND SECRETARY

MR. ANDREW JOHN DEAN
MRS. PAULINE LESLEY DEAN
SECOND SECRETARY

MISS LAURA ELIZABETH DUNBAR
SECOND SECRETARY

MR. JAMES ROBERT EKE
SECOND SECRETARY

MR. RICHARD JAMES LEE SMITH
SECOND SECRETARY

MR. EDWARD GEORGE MATTACOLA
SECOND SECRETARY

MR. STEVEN ANDREW MOYNHAM
SECOND SECRETARY

MRS. CAROL ANN PRIESTLEY
MR. LAWRENCE PRIESTLEY
SECOND SECRETARY (MANAGEMENT)

MR. CHRISTOPHER BARRY SUTTON
MRS. ELAINE SUTTON
SECOND SECRETARY

MR. MERVYN HOY CHUN JOSEPH TANG
SECOND SECRETARY

MR. RICHARD MATTHEW WARNER
SECOND SECRETARY

MR. CHRISTOPHER DAVID WRIGHT
SECOND SECRETARY

MR. IAN ALLAN
MRS. JANE ALLAN
THIRD SECRETARY

MISS SARAH ELIZABETH FEETAM
THIRD SECRETARY

MS. ELAINE MARSH
THIRD SECRETARY (PASSPORTS)

MR. CRAIG KEITH MARTIN
MRS. NATALIE JAYNE MARTIN
THIRD SECRETARY (TECHNICAL)

MR. MATTHEW JOHN ORMOND
THIRD SECRETARY (TECHNICAL)

MR. ADAM RADCLIFFE
MRS. JULIE ANNE RADCLIFFE
THIRD SECRETARY

MR. ROBERT JOHN BAYLISS
MRS. MICHELLE JAYNE BAYLISS
ATTACHE (DEFENSE EQUIPMENT)

* U.S. Citizen

MR. RICHARD ANDREW JONES
MRS. DENISE BRIDGET VAN MOL
ATTACHE (DEFENSE EQUIPMENT, POLICY & TRADE)

MR. NICHOLAS ALEXANDER T MATHESON
DR. KATHERINE MATHESON
ATTACHE (DEFENSE AQUISITION)

MR. STEWART ALAN MOFFATT
MRS. ELIZABETH ANNE MOFFATT
ATTACHE (DEFENSE EQUIPMENT/PROJECTS)

MR. JAMES BRENDAN PEDDELL
MRS. ANNA JANE PEDDELL
ATTACHE

MAJOR GENERAL FRANCIS HEDLEY ROBERTON HOWES
MRS. JENNIFER CATHERINE QUINTON
DEFENSE ATTACHE

BRIGADIER TIMOTHY JOHN LAI
MRS. JENNIFER MORAG LAI
MILITARY ATTACHE

COMMODORE ERIC FRASER
MRS. AGNES DICKIE FRASER
NAVAL ATTACHE

AIR COMMODORE KENNETH BRUCE MCCANN
MRS. SHEILA NORTON MCCANN
AIR ATTACHE

COLONEL DAVID CHRISTOPHER BORLEY ADAMS
MRS. REBECCA ANNE ADAMS
ASST. DEFENSE ATTACHE

COLONEL RICHARD MICHAEL SMITH
MRS. JOANNE LOUISE SMITH
ASST. MILITARY ATTACHE

COMMANDER IAN ATKINS
MRS. AMANDA POLLY MARSH ATKINS
ASST. NAVAL ATTACHE

GROUP CAPTAIN WILLIAM RICHMOND GIBSON
MRS. DIANNE FRANCES GIBSON
ASST. AIR ATTACHE

COLONEL NIGEL PETER BROWN
MRS. BEVERLEY ANN BROWN
ASST. DEFENSE & ASST. NAVAL ATTACHE

BRITISH NAVAL STAFF OFFICE
2221 JEFFERSON DAVIS HIGHWAY, SUITE 708
ARLINGTON, VA 22202

CIVIL AVIATION AND MISSION TO THE FAA OFFICE
1730 RHODE ISLAND AVENUE, NW, SUITE 419 20036
(OFFICE 202-463-7529)

NORTHERN IRELAND BUREAU
601 13TH STREET, NW, SUITE 570 SOUTH 20005
(OFFICE 202-367-0464)   (FAX 202-367-0468)

URUGUAY

EMBASSY OF URUGUAY
Chancery: 1913 I STREET, NW 20006
(EMBASSY 202-331-1313)   (FAX 202-331-8142)

HIS EXCELLENCY JUAN CARLOS PITA ALVARIZA
MRS. MARIELLA MORA BECERRA
AMBASSADOR EXTRAORDINARY & PLENIPOTENTIARY

* U.S. Citizen

MS. MARIA DEL L. BARCELO DEBENEDETTI
MR. RODOLFO JOSE PASCUAL TORRENS
COUNSELOR & CONSUL GENERAL

MR. MANUEL ETCHEVARREN AGUERRE
MRS. ANA SOLIVELLAS FERNANDEZ
COUNSELOR

MRS. MARIA RAMONA FRANCO OXLEY
MR. CARLOS RAUL SAGRERA IBARRA
COUNSELOR

MR. MARCELO CLOVIS MAGNOU PEREZ
MRS. HAOWEI ZHO
FIRST SECRETARY (CULTURAL)

MRS. BEATRIZ ANA SILVA PRESTINARI
MR. DIEGO ROGER SIGNORELLI PROTO
FIRST SECRETARY

MRS. PAOLA MARIA REPETTO AMESTOY
MR. FERNANDO DANIEL BLANCO ALONSO
THIRD SECRETARY

CAPTAIN FRANCISCO E. CAAMANO CERNADAS
MRS. ROSA MARIA SUAREZ POMMERENCK
NAVAL ATTACHE

COLONEL RUBEN ARIEL FROS LUZARDO
MRS. SILVANA GARRONE MISA
AIR ATTACHE & ASST. DEFENSE ATTACHE

FINANCIAL AFFAIRS OFFICE
1025 CONNECTICUT AVENUE, NW, SUITE 902 20036
(OFFICE 202-223-9833)   (FAX 202-223-2119)

MILITARY, NAVAL AND AIR ATTACHE OFFICE
1913 I STREET, NW, FLOOR 3RD 20006
(OFFICE 202-466-3167)

TRADE BUREAU
1030 15TH STREET, NW, SUITE 760 20005
(OFFICE 202-789-8225)

UZBEKISTAN

EMBASSY OF THE REPUBLIC OF UZBEKISTAN
Chancery: 1746 MASSACHUSETTS AVENUE, NW 20036
(EMBASSY 202-293-6803)   (FAX 202-293-6804)

HIS EXCELLENCY ILHOMJON TUYCHIEVICH NEMATOV
MRS. GYUL ASAL KURBANOVNA NEMATOVA
AMBASSADOR EXTRAORDINARY & PLENIPOTENTIARY

MR. MUZAFFARBEK MADRAKHIMOV
MRS. MUKARRAM MADRAKHIMOVA
COUNSELOR (DEPUTY CHIEF OF MISSION)

MR. SHERZOD ABDULLAEV
MRS. MUBORAKKHON ABDULLAEVA
COUNSELOR

MR. LAZIZ KUDRATOV
MRS. LOLA BAKHTIYAROVNA KUDRATOVA
COUNSELOR (ECONOMIC)

MR. MAMAN KALLIBEKOVICH ISMAILOV
MRS. GULSHAD MAKSETOVNA ISMAILOVA
FIRST SECRETARY & CONSUL

MR. FURKAT AKHMEDOVICH SIDIKOV
   MRS. GULCHEKHRA SAYFUTDINOVNA SIDIKOVA
FIRST SECRETARY

MR. NURILLA NIGMATILLAEVIC ABDULLAYEV
   MRS. DINARA ABROROVNA ABDULLAYEVA
SECOND SECRETARY

MR. BEKHRUZ ABDUVALIEV
   MRS. GOVKHAR ABDUVALIEVA
ATTACHE (ASSISTANT TO AMBASSADOR)

MR. FARKHOD GAIBNAZAROVICH FAYZILLAEV
   MRS. DILBAND NURITDINOVNA FAYZILLAEVA
ATTACHE

MR. NODIRJON KIRGIZBAEV
   MRS. MOKHIGUL S. KIRGIZBAEV
ATTACHE & CONSUL

MR. SOBIRJON MAMADAMINOV
ATTACHE

MR. UMID RUSTAMOVICH SHADIEV
   MRS. NARGIZA DJAMILOVNA SHADIEVA
ATTACHE

MAJOR SADULLO SHUKURBOEVICH RASULOV
   MRS. NARGIZA KHOLBOEVNA RASULOVA
DEFENSE, MILITARY & AIR ATTACHE

VENEZUELA

EMBASSY OF THE BOLIVARIAN REPUBLIC OF VENEZUELA
Chancery: 1099 30TH STREET, NW 20007
(EMBASSY 202-342-2214)   (FAX 202-342-6820)

MR. ANGELO AGUSTIN RIVERO SANTOS
DR. CHANDAN JAYANT VAIDYA*
MINISTER-COUNSELOR (CHARGE D'AFFAIRES AD INTERIM)

MRS. NANCY JOSEFINA LIRA OCHOA
MR. JOSE GREGORIO FRANQUIS
COUNSELOR (CULTURAL AFFAIRS)

MR. IGNACIO LUIS CAJAL AVALOS
   MRS. LUISA FERNANDA MEZA PAREDES
FIRST SECRETARY (CONSULAR)

MRS. DEISI CAROLINA PEREIRA FAGUNDEZ
MR. SOCRATES A. CALDERON OVALLES
FIRST SECRETARY (ECONOMIC AND POLITICAL AFFAIRS)

MRS. MARIELBA ALVAREZ SALAZAR
SECOND SECRETARY (PRESS)

MRS. VALENTINA FIGUERA MARTINEZ
SECOND SECRETARY (PRESS)

MR. MARCOS JOSE GARCIA FIGUEREDO
   MRS. IVELISSE DEL SOCORRO DIAZ PAEZ
SECOND SECRETARY (LABOR AFFAIRS)

MRS. CAROLINA CLARETH GONZALEZ LOPEZ
SECOND SECRETARY

MR. MARCO JULIO MARIN GONZALEZ
   MRS. ALEXANDRA NANEZ ARACIL
SECOND SECRETARY

MRS. LUISA FERNANDA MEZA PAREDES
SECOND SECRETARY

MR. ORLANDO JOSE MONTANEZ OLIVARES
   MRS. ERIKA FLORES HERRERA
SECOND SECRETARY

MR. BORYS EDUARDO ORTEGA RODRIGUEZ
SECOND SECRETARY (POLITICAL)

MRS. CLARA SARAI RODRIGUEZ ARIAS
SECOND SECRETARY (ENVIRONMENTAL AFFAIRS)

MRS. MONICA ALEJANDRA SANCHEZ MORLES
   MR. DAVID ANTONIO LOPEZ SANCHEZ
SECOND SECRETARY (PRESS)

MS. MARINA ALEJANDRA ULECIA SANZ
SECOND SECRETARY

MRS. MARIA ANTONIA YSAYA FLORES
ATTACHE (CONSULAR)

COLONEL JOSE ALIRIO JAIMES
   MRS. MARIA ANGELICA LOPEZ DE JAIMES
ASST. DEFENSE ATTACHE

LIEUTENANT COLONEL JOSE LUIS SILVA SILVA
ASST. AIR ATTACHE

DEFENSE AND NAVAL ATTACHE OFFICES
2437 CALIFORNIA STREET, NW 20008
(OFFICE 202-265-7323)

INFORMATION SERVICE OFFICE
1099 30TH STREET, NW 20007

MILITARY AND AIR ATTACHE OFFICES
2409 CALIFORNIA STREET, NW 20008
(OFFICE 202-234-3436)

VIETNAM

EMBASSY OF VIETNAM
Chancery: 1233 20TH STREET, NW, SUITE 400 20036
(EMBASSY 202-861-0737)   (FAX 202-861-0917)

HIS EXCELLENCY CUONG QUOC NGUYEN
   MRS. HA THI MINH HOANG
AMBASSADOR EXTRAORDINARY & PLENIPOTENTIARY

MR. TUNG VU NGUYEN
   MRS. LAN TU TRINH
MINISTER-COUNSELOR (DEPUTY CHIEF OF MISSION)

MRS. BICH NGOC TRAN
MINISTER-COUNSELOR

MR. MANH CHI BUI
   MRS. CHAU KIM DUONG
COUNSELOR

MR. NHAN TRAN DAO
   MRS. LOAN THI KIM NGUYEN
COUNSELOR

MR. DUNG CHI LE
   MRS. HA THI THANH LE
COUNSELOR (ECONOMIC)

MR. ANH TUAN LE
   MRS. HANH THI MY LE
COUNSELOR

MR. BINH THANH LE
   MRS. NGUYET THU PHAM
COUNSELOR (SCIENCE & TECHNOLOGY)

* U.S. Citizen

MRS. DUONG THUY LUAN
    MR. TRI VAN NGUYEN
    COUNSELOR

MR. THANG TOAN NGO
    MRS. LINH PHUONG NGUYEN
    COUNSELOR

MR. AN HA NGUYEN
    MRS. YEN THI HAI HOANG
    COUNSELOR

MR. HA HONG NGUYEN
    MRS. HUONG THU NGUYEN
    COUNSELOR

MR. HAI THANH NGUYEN
    MRS. LAN MAI DO
    COUNSELOR (POLITICAL)

MR. DIEN DUY TRAN
    MRS. LE THI ANH TRUONG
    COUNSELOR

MR. DUNG ANH TRAN
    MRS. YEN THI NGOC NGUYEN
    COUNSELOR

MRS. DIEU NGOC DO
    MR. PHUC HONG LE
    FIRST SECRETARY

MR. GIANG HOANG NGUYEN
    FIRST SECRETARY (PRESS)

MR. THANH CHI THAI
    MRS. HOA THI NGUYEN
    FIRST SECRETARY

MR. TUNG THANH TRAN
    MRS. TAM THANH THI LE
    FIRST SECRETARY

MRS. THI THU HA TRINH
    FIRST SECRETARY

MR. TRUONG XUAN DO
    MRS. THAO THU TANG
    SECOND SECRETARY

MR. NGUYEN HOANG NGUYEN
    MRS. PHUONG HOAI THI NGUYEN
    SECOND SECRETARY

MR. QUANG HONG NGUYEN
    MRS. PHUONG THU NGUYEN
    SECOND SECRETARY

MR. TUAN ANH PHAM
    SECOND SECRETARY

MR. BANG HUU PHAM
    MRS. THAO THANH HAN
    SECOND SECRETARY

MRS. BINH THI THANH PHAM
    MR. NGOC CHIEN BACH
    SECOND SECRETARY

MR. TRUNG NAM TRAN
    MRS. HA NGOC NGUYEN
    SECOND SECRETARY (SCIENCE AND TECHNOLOGY)

MR. TUNG HOANG DO
    MRS. ANH THI LAN PHAM
    THIRD SECRETARY

MR. HIEU MINH LE
    THIRD SECRETARY

MR. SON NGOC NGUYEN
    MRS. XUYEN THI DUONG
    THIRD SECRETARY

MRS. THU THI MINH NGUYEN
    MR. LICH TO NGUYEN
    THIRD SECRETARY

MR. NINH VAN DAO
    MRS. HA THANH NGUYEN
    ATTACHE (COMMERCIAL)

MRS. GIANG HUONG NGUYEN
    ATTACHE (COMMERCIAL)

MR. VUONG THANG NGUYEN
    MRS. HIEN THI THU NGUYEN
    ATTACHE (COMMERCIAL)

MR. VIET TRAN
    MRS. YEN THI NGOC HA
    ATTACHE (COMMERCIAL)

COLONEL TIEU HUU NGUYEN
    MRS. ANH TRAN HONG PHAM
    DEFENSE, MILITARY, NAVAL & AIR ATTACHE

MAJOR DUC NHU NGUYEN
    MRS. HIEN THUY NGUYEN
    ASST. DEFENSE, MILITARY, NAVAL & AIR ATTACHE

DEFENSE ATTACHE OFFICE OF VIETNAM
    1233 20TH STREET, NW, SUITE 201 20036
    (OFFICE 202-293-1822)

TRADE OFFICE OF VIETNAM
    1730 M STREET, NW, SUITE 501 20036
    (OFFICE 202-463-9419)

    1233 20TH STREET, NW, SUITE 401 20036

YEMEN

EMBASSY OF THE REPUBLIC OF YEMEN
Chancery: 2319 WYOMING AVENUE 20008
(EMBASSY 202-965-4760)   (FAX 202-337-2017)

MR. ADEL ALI AHMED ALSUNAINI
    MRS. ANTESAR ALI ABODINYA
    COUNSELOR (CHARGE D'AFFAIRES AD INTERIM)

MR. YAHYA ALI MOHAMED AL ERYANI
    MINISTER

MR. IBRAHIM M. A. ALKIBSI
    MRS. ILHAM ALI ALSSIRAJI
    MINISTER

MR. ALI AL SALAHI
    MRS. MUSSADH MUFFRAH MOHAMMED BUHIBH
    THIRD SECRETARY

MS. EMAN ABDULLAH ABDULLAH AL-SANFI
    THIRD SECRETARY

MR. WAEL NOORALDEEN ALI AL-SHEHARY
    MRS. ROQIAH MOHAMMED AHMED AL-SHAMY
    THIRD SECRETARY

* U.S. Citizen

MISS ASMAA LUTF AHMED KATAH
THIRD SECRETARY

MR. AKRAM ALI SALEH ABDULLAH
ATTACHE

MR. ABDULRAHMAN MOHAMMED A. AL ERYANI
MRS. HADIL ABDULKALEK SALEH ALKADI
ATTACHE

DR. FAHD MOHAMMED ABDULLAH AL SHAEBI
MRS. SALMA SHAIF ABOBAKR AL SHAEBI
ATTACHE (CULTURAL)

MR. MAEEN MOHAMMED SALEH ALAHMAR
ATTACHE (ECONOMIC)

MR. KANAN YAHIA MOHAMED SALEH
MRS. AISHA HUSSEIN ALI AL HAMDANI
ATTACHE

MR. KHALED ALI ABDULLAH SALEH
ATTACHE

MR. SALAH ALI ABDULLAH SALEH
MRS. AMENA MABKHOUT YAHYA ALMASHRAQI
ATTACHE (SECURITY)

BRIGADIER GENERAL MOHAMMED ZEID MAHMOOD IBRAHEM
DEFENSE, MILITARY, NAVAL & AIR ATTACHE

ZAMBIA

EMBASSY OF THE REPUBLIC OF ZAMBIA
Chancery: 2419 MASSACHUSETTS AVENUE, NW 20008
(EMBASSY 202-265-9717)   (FAX 202-332-0826)

HIS EXCELLENCY PALAN MULONDA
MRS. MUTINTA VALERIE MULULUMA MULONDA
AMBASSADOR EXTRAORDINARY & PLENIPOTENTIARY

MR. BERNARD KANGWA
MRS. JAYNE DOROTHY AWONGO KANGWA
MINISTER-COUNSELOR

MR. JAMES CHISENGA
MRS. RIBBER LONGWANI CHISENGA
COUNSELOR (ECONOMIC)

MR. BRIAN MULENGA
MRS. JANET JERE MULENGA
COUNSELOR (POLITICAL)

MS. INONGE LIMBAMBALA
MR. MUSA MWENYA
FIRST SECRETARY (TRADE)

MS. PATRICIA MWALYE LITTIYA
FIRST SECRETARY (PRESS)

MR. MUTALE MBALAMWESHI
MS. MAUREEN MUTALE MULENGA
FIRST SECRETARY (ACCOUNTS)

MR. CHEMBO FELIX MBULA
MRS. KAPEMBA MUTEBA MBULA
FIRST SECRETARY

MS. BEATRICE KAMPAMBA MWENDELA
FIRST SECRETARY (IMMIGRATION)

MS. FLORENCE CHEEMBO
MR. LEONARD CHILAI
SECOND SECRETARY (ADMINISTRATION)

* U.S. Citizen

COLONEL HENRY CHISANGA SHADDIE MUKUKA
MRS. LUCY CHANSA MUKUKA
DEFENSE, MILITARY & AIR ATTACHE

ZIMBABWE

EMBASSY OF REPUBLIC OF ZIMBABWE
Chancery: 1608 NEW HAMPSHIRE AVENUE, NW 20009
(EMBASSY 202-332-7100)   (FAX 202-483-9326)

HIS EXCELLENCY DR. MACHIVENYIKA T. MAPURANGA
MRS. SHUPIKAYI V. D. MAPURANGA
AMBASSADOR EXTRAORDINARY & PLENIPOTENTIARY

MR. RICHARD CHIBUWE
MRS. EUGENIA PASSMORE CHIBUWE
MINISTER-COUNSELOR

MR. WHATMORE GOORA
MS. DOREEN GOORA
COUNSELOR (POLITICAL)

MR. RWATIRISA MATSIKA
MRS. MEMORY MATSIKA
COUNSELOR (POLITICAL & CONSULAR)

MR. LUKE MUKUPE
MRS. ENGELINE MUKUPE
SECOND SECRETARY (CONSULAR & ADMINISTRATIVE)

MS. ABIGAL NYAMAPFENI
SECOND SECRETARY (ADMIN)

MRS. PRISCA GURUMANI
MR. PETER GURUMANI
THIRD SECRETARY

LIEUTENANT COLONEL GEORGE CHINOINGIRA
MRS. MIRIAM CHINOINGIRA
DEFENSE, MILITARY & AIR ATTACHE

INTEREST SECTIONS

CUBA

EMBASSY OF SWITZERLAND, CUBAN INTERESTS SECTION
Chancery: 2630 16TH STREET, NW 20009
(202-797-8518)

MR. JOSE RAMON CABANAS RODRIGUEZ
    MRS. EDILIA GONZALEZ DENCAUSE
COUNSELOR (CHIEF OF INTERESTS SECTION)

MR. AGUSTIN MISAEL BATISTA LICEA
    MRS. DEBORAH NIDIA MESA ANGULO
FIRST SECRETARY

MR. ARMANDO BENCOMO ZAMORA
    MRS. TERESA MARTINEZ GARCIA
FIRST SECRETARY

MRS. KARIN DIEZ B. HAMEL
    MR. DANIEL AQUILES RODRIGUEZ SANSO
FIRST SECRETARY

MR. LLANIO GONZALEZ PEREZ
FIRST SECRETARY

MR. HECTOR HERRERA DOMINGUEZ
    MRS. LEANNIS FONT FONT
FIRST SECRETARY

MR. JUAN MARIO LAMIGUEIRO LEON
    MRS. IVETTE ISABEL CANEDO TAPANES
FIRST SECRETARY (DEPUTY CHIEF)

MR. WARNEL LORES MORA
    MRS. AYLIN PEREZ VALIENTE
FIRST SECRETARY

MS. PATRICIA LAZARA PEGO GUERRA
FIRST SECRETARY

MR. YANIEL PEREZ FLORES
    MRS. MELBA DAYAMI BRAVO RODRIGUEZ
FIRST SECRETARY

MR. JESUS DIOSDADO PERZ CALDERON
    MRS. MARIA MAGDALENA VALDES NORIEGA
FIRST SECRETARY

MR. RAUL SANCHEZ CORDOVI
    MRS. NIURKA AMARO MENESES
FIRST SECRETARY

MR. SERGIO JAVIER VAZQUEZ DEL RIO
FIRST SECRETARY

MR. MANUEL ANTONIO ARGUELLES SANCHEZ
    MRS. LOURDES DE LA MONTESINOS GONZALEZ
SECOND SECRETARY

MR. ARIEL HERNANDEZ HERNANDEZ
    MRS. NINA ALMEIDA PARAMONOVA
SECOND SECRETARY

MR. JUAN JACOMINO CASTELLANO
    MRS. MADELYN HUICI LUGO
SECOND SECRETARY

MR. RODNEY AMAURY GONZALEZ MAESTREY
THIRD SECRETARY

MR. DANIEL ALVAREZ PREVAL
    MRS. AMBAR ROSA GUZMAN MORALES
ATTACHE

MRS. YAIMA BRINIS PROVEYER
    MR. MEYDEL PEREZ OLIVER
ATTACHE

MRS. GRETEL GARCIA GOMEZ
    MR. ODIN CASTANEDA CAO
ATTACHE

MS. ANAYANSY GONZALEZ ALONSO
ATTACHE

MRS. LILIA DE LA CARIDAD JUNCO PEREZ
    MR. RAUL PALACIO MORA
ATTACHE

MRS. DAYLIN MENES DE LA FE
    MR. OMAR GALEGO FLOREZ
ATTACHE

MR. RAUL RODRIGUEZ MORA
    MRS. DAISY PEREZ ESTRADA
ATTACHE

IRAN

EMBASSY OF PAKISTAN, IRANIAN INTERESTS SECTION
Chancery: 2209 WISCONSIN AVENUE, NW 20007
(202-965-4990)   (FAX 202-965-1073)

* U.S. Citizen